Also by Doan Van Toai and David Chanoff

A Vietcong Memoir
(with Truong Nhu Tang)

THE VIETNAMESE GULAG

BASED UPON THE ENGLISH
TRANSLATION FROM
THE FRENCH BY
SYLVIE ROMANOWSKI AND
FRANÇOISE SIMON-MILLER

DOAN VAN TOAI
DAVID CHANOFF

Simon and Schuster · New York

The photograph on page 335 is reprinted courtesy of Bernard Charlon, *L'Express.*
The rest of the photographs are either the property of the author or have previously
appeared in periodicals now defunct.

COPYRIGHT © 1986 BY DOAN VAN TOAI AND DAVID CHANOFF
ALL RIGHTS RESERVED
INCLUDING THE RIGHT OF REPRODUCTION
IN WHOLE OR IN PART IN ANY FORM
PUBLISHED BY SIMON AND SCHUSTER
A DIVISION OF SIMON & SCHUSTER, INC.
SIMON & SCHUSTER BUILDING
ROCKEFELLER CENTER
1230 AVENUE OF THE AMERICAS
NEW YORK, NEW YORK 10020
SIMON AND SCHUSTER AND COLOPHON ARE REGISTERED TRADE-
MARKS OF SIMON & SCHUSTER, INC.
ORIGINALLY PUBLISHED IN FRANCE AS LE GOULAG VIETNAMIEN
BY EDITIONS ROBERT LAFFONT-OPERA MUNDI. COPYRIGHT © 1979
BY OPERA MUNDI, PARIS. PART OF CHAPTER 20, "GOING TO 'THE
COUNTRY,'" PREVIOUSLY APPEARED IN THE NATIONAL REVIEW AND
IS PUBLISHED HERE BY PERMISSION.
DESIGNED BY LEVAVI & LEVAVI
MANUFACTURED IN THE UNITED STATES OF AMERICA
10 9 8 7 6 5 4 3 2 1
LIBRARY OF CONGRESS CATALOGING-IN-PUBLICATION DATA

DOAN, VAN TOAI, DATE–
    THE VIETNAMESE GULAG.

    TRANSLATION OF: LE GOULAG VIETNAMIEN.
    1. DOAN, VAN TOAI, DATE–   . 2. VIETNAM—POLITICS
AND GOVERNMENT—1975–   . 3. REFUGEES, POLITICAL—
VIETNAM—BIOGRAPHY.   I. CHANOFF, DAVID.   II. TITLE.
DS559.912.D6313   1986   959.704   85–27671
ISBN: 0-671-60350-7

Acknowledgments

I wish to express my deepest gratitude to Joan Baez for her efforts to better the condition of the Vietnamese people, who continue to suffer daily the violation of their most basic human rights. My thanks go also to Carl Gershman, president of the National Endowment for Democracy, and to John Roche, academic dean of the Fletcher School of Law and Diplomacy. Mr. Gershman was instrumental in bringing me to the United States, and Dean Roche provided me with my first academic home in this country. I am grateful as well to the Institute for Educational Affairs, which generously funded the translation of *Le Goulag Vietnamien* into English.

This book is dedicated to the memory of my father and mother, and to all of the Vietnamese fathers and mothers who have died while waiting for an impossible return.

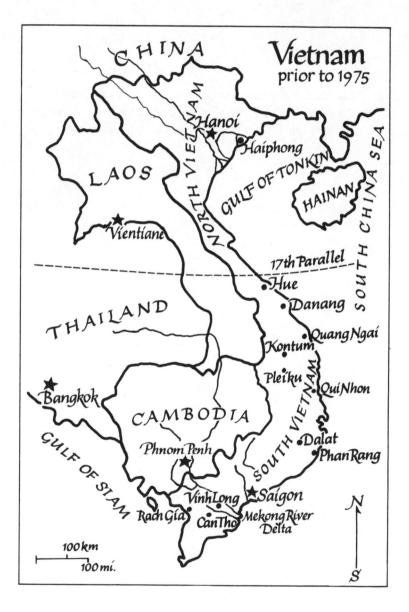

CHINA

Hanoi ★

Haiphong

NORTH VIETNAM

GULF OF TONKIN

SOUTH CHINA SEA

HAINAN

LAOS

Vientiane ★

17th Parallel

Hue

Danang

THAILAND

Quang Ngai

Kontum

Pleiku

QuiNhon

Bangkok ★

CAMBODIA

SOUTH VIETNAM

Dalat

Phnom Penh ★

PhanRang

GULF OF SIAM

Saigon ★

VinhLong

Rach Gia

CanTho

Mekong River
Delta

100 km

100 mi.

Vietnam
prior to 1975

N

S

Contents

1

Is Your Name Toai?

On the evening of June 22, 1975, less than two months after the fall of South Vietnam, there is a concert in Ho Chi Minh City, formerly known as Saigon.

Vietnam's National Orchestra has come here from Hanoi. At 8:00 P.M. it will perform at the Grand Theater—formerly the home of South Vietnam's parliament. For the past week it's been impossible to get tickets. Ages have passed since the southern capital has heard a classical concert played by a real symphony orchestra. I'm thirty years old, and I've never heard anything but third-rate bands featuring electric guitars and syrupy songs with the most astonishingly affected lyrics. American ersatz. As for traditional Vietnamese music, it's been killed off by the war.

But that evening I'm at the Grand Theater, thanks to some Communist party friends who are repaying a favor. The Vietnamese National Orchestra isn't the Berlin Philharmonic. But for the first time I am enjoying a true professional orchestra,

11

over a hundred musicians, live. I'm amazed. So this is one of
the luxuries peace has to offer, this peace I have never known.

The orchestra has just finished a Beethoven concerto. I am
in heaven. The master of ceremonies now announces that a
ballet performance will follow. That's when I notice the four
bo dois (soldiers) in their green uniforms at the end of my row.

One by one they are taking away the people sitting between
me and the aisle, and talking to them. The *bo dois* are obviously looking for someone. When my turn comes, one of the
soldiers leads me to the lobby. I'm curious about what they
want, but calm. In the lobby there are maybe ten more soldiers, all from the North, to judge by their accents. One of
them, very young, eighteen at the most, shouts at me, clipping
his words, "Is your name Toai?"

"Yes," I say. I'm about to add "why?" but before I can, he
takes a step forward and slaps me. Then one of the others
holds him back, and I'm quickly surrounded and hustled up
the stairs toward the manager's office on the second floor. As
I'm being rushed along, struggling to keep my balance, I remember when I raced up these same stairs five years ago at the
head of several hundred university students—members of the
Saigon Student Union. We were about to take over the National Assembly building, to demand that a number of our imprisoned comrades be freed. That episode had earned me a
stay in President Thieu's jails.

The Communist party and the NLF* certainly know all
about my antiwar activities as a student leader. They know that
even though I had never formally joined either one of them, I
was always their ally. What could they possibly want with me
now?

In the manager's office I'm forced to stand in front of a
North Vietnamese Army lieutenant. While *bo dois* on both
sides pin my arms, the lieutenant stares at me and asks, "Are
you Ngo Vuong Toai?"

* The National Liberation Front (NLF) was a political umbrella organization
founded in 1960 to direct the insurgency in South Vietnam.

I suddenly understand. Now I know what's wrong. About ten years ago, Ngo Vuong Toai was president of a small anti-Communist student organization that was a front for the Thieu government, and probably the Americans as well. It was commonly known that the NLF had condemned him to death, and in 1966 they tried to assassinate him. Toai had been wounded in the stomach and had barely survived. Afterward he left his little group and went to work directly for the government, in the well-guarded offices of the Ministry of Information.

Obviously there's been a misunderstanding; I'm being mistaken for this other Toai.* "No," I tell the lieutenant. "I'm not Ngo Vuong Toai. I don't have anything to do with him. I'm Doan Van Toai. I was vice-president of the student union. I fought against the puppets. I worked for the Front. I've been in jail for it. Now I'm working with the PRG Finance Committee.† You can verify everything with Colonel Nguyen Ngoc Hien and with the Association of Patriotic Intellectuals."

I take a certain pride in listing my titles and credentials. I watch for the effect, waiting for the apology I so richly deserve. The lieutenant is obviously embarrassed. He's been told to arrest a certain Toai, who was supposed to be at the concert. Apparently he has the wrong man.

But while I watch him trying to decide what to do, something else occurs to me. How did I happen to be in the very row he was told to search? Is this really just a simple misunderstanding? Somebody who knew I was at the concert has to be involved. What are the chances that the *bo dois* would know exactly where to find me, yet mistake me for Ngo Vuong Toai? Not so good, I think.

---

* In Vietnamese the family name comes first and the given name last. But there are relatively few family names, and so the given name is most often used for identification. Nguyen Van Thieu (given name, Thieu), South Vietnam's political strongman from the mid-sixties until 1975, was known as President Thieu. North Vietnam's defense minister, Vo Nguyen Giap, was General Giap.
† The Provisional Revolutionary Government (PRG) was founded by the insurgency in 1969 to challenge the Saigon regime for recognition in international forums as South Vietnam's true representative government.

Meanwhile, as far as the lieutenant is concerned, my person matches all too well the individual described in his orders. Or at least I'm not so bad a fit as to be dismissed out of hand. So he reacts as any policeman would. "Not the right Toai? Maybe so, maybe not. Take him in and we'll check it out."

Outside the theater, I'm ordered to climb on the back of a Honda motorcycle, and accompanied by two other Hondas, we speed off to the police headquarters on Tran Hung Dao Boulevard. I haven't given them a bit of trouble. Although I'm beginning to have some doubts about what's really happening, I'm still convinced it's a misunderstanding that I'll be able to clear up quickly. Several years earlier I had read the first volume of Alexander Solzhenitsyn's *Gulag Archipelago*. I vividly remember chapter 2, entitled "Arrest." Even in the Vietnamese translation, the writing was dazzling, memorable—though I had dismissed the substance of the book as propaganda. But now the words come back to me, the thoughts of someone who's just been arrested. "Who, me? What for?" "It's a mistake, they'll clear it up." But that was in Russia. Who knows whether things like that really go on there? Anyway, this is Vietnam, the new Vietnam.

At police headquarters I wait in the hallway, guarded by three *bo dois*. I listen as the lieutenant discusses my case with the duty officer. The lieutenant is trying to unload this potential embarrassment on the officer. This may not be the Toai he was told to arrest, but he's not sure. "We'd better keep him." But the duty officer doesn't want any trouble, doesn't want to be saddled with the responsibility of arresting the wrong person—someone who might be able to cause problems. But the lieutenant says, "Look, you'll have even more problems if you don't lock him up and he turns out to be the right guy."

The discussion goes on forever, until both men suddenly realize it's already eleven o'clock. That puts an end to it. At this hour there's no way anybody can disturb a higher-ranking officer to resolve the matter. Better to lock up the prisoner until tomorrow, when they can ask someone what to do.

So I'm pushed up to the desk.

"You are Doan Van Toai?"

"Yes, Doan Van Toai! Not Ngo Vuong Toai, the one you were supposed to arrest. I protest this treatment. I demand. . . ."

The duty officer cuts me off with a wave of his hand and says loudly, "We'll clear it all up in the morning. Right now, you're under arrest."

"Under arrest!" Now I'm beginning to get excited, raising my voice. "That doesn't make any sense. I'm not Ngo Vuong Toai. I never collaborated with the puppets. I was a student opposition leader. I spent time in jail. Can't you understand that? This treatment is unacceptable!" By now I'm shouting. "How can you arrest me? What am I supposed to have done?"

The officer has been drumming his fingers on the desk, not looking at me. Now he raises his eyes and says in a formal tone, "You are accused of suspicious acts."

"Me? Suspicious acts? What suspicious acts? Who has denounced me? I demand to see the liar who denounced me!"

Already I know I don't have a chance. Any more discussion with this low-level nonentity is useless. It doesn't make any difference to him that he might be jailing an innocent man. I'll have to explain myself to somebody else, somebody in charge. Meanwhile, this individual is reciting a catechism to me.

"If the revolution decides to arrest someone, it has its reasons. If a mistake is made, that will be acknowledged. Be patient and wait for the revolution's judgment. While you wait, you'd better keep your voice down."

I start to protest again, but my heart's not in it. This representative of the revolution has decided I should be locked up. So I'll be locked up. If I keep shouting, they'll beat me. That's pretty clear.

A *bo doi* removes my belt and searches my pockets, taking my wallet. It's ten minutes before midnight, according to my watch, which I glance at as the *bo doi* pulls it over my wrist. Then two of them push me down a hallway with doors on each side, cell doors. The air is heavy, stale with the smell of unwashed bodies. Snoring comes from behind the doors. I have the feeling that the place is full.

That's my first surprise about prison. During the war the NLF often declared it would eliminate prisons. After victory, Le Duan, the Communist party general secretary, personally visited Thieu's famous tiger cage cells in the Con Son Island jail. Looking at the symbols of the southern regime's repressiveness, Le Duan declared: "We will transform the jails into schools!" Yet this place seems full. The prisoners here must be some of the thieves and traffickers who operated so blatantly during the last weeks before the old regime died—the dregs of a Vietnamese society corrupted by war. I feel humiliated at being here with such people, ashamed to be associated with them in any way. I'm relieved when the *bo dois* shove me into an individual cell that boasts a bare cement bench to sleep on, a toilet hole, and a faucet.

I lie down and try to stay calm, to control the feelings that are boiling up inside me. Above me, behind a vent in the ceiling, a light bulb throws off a weak glare. The prison's nocturnal sounds come alive, just as I remember them from my previous stays in Thieu's jails: the sighs of the sleeping prisoners, the padded footfalls of the guards, who watch you through the peepholes while they remain unseen. I tell myself, "Tomorrow I'll clear everything up. Then they'll let me out." I fall asleep repeating that.

Morning wake-up is an insistent, raspy voice coming through the cell door's eye-level peephole. "What the hell do you think you're doing? Sleeping? What's your name? Don't you know you have to be up at six and straighten your bed?" (I'm using my rolled-up pants as a pillow and my shirt as a half sheet.)

With a free man's logic I try to answer the voice, this prison system that already possesses me as a spider possesses a fly caught in its web. "But I don't even know why I'm here."

"You don't, huh?" rasps the voice through the peephole.

"No, I don't. I was mistaken for . . ."

I'm interrupted by a humorless laugh. "Ha, ha! If there weren't any reason, ha, ha, why have they brought you here? Listen, you weren't up on time, you don't eat."

And the peephole shutter closes. No breakfast. I lie on the cement bench staring at the ceiling, until a few minutes later the voice is back, louder this time. "Prisoner, didn't I tell you to get up? You think you're going to sleep all day? Lying down is forbidden! You sit, or you stand."

I sit up. What can I do? I look at my hands and listen to the noises. I begin pacing the cell, three steps one way, three the other. The prisoner's domain is quickly measured. Prisoner! Several times before I was a prisoner. But not exactly like this. Being a prisoner under Thieu was like being a celebrity. Outside, my family and friends were doing everything they could for me; politicians were challenging the government; newspapers were denouncing the repression of the students. Dozens of foreign correspondents were covering the whole affair for papers all over the world.

Suddenly I feel chilled. My isolation comes home to me and begins to settle in. Nobody knows I'm here. Even when they find out, what can they do? Hire a lawyer? There are no more lawyers; there haven't been any since liberation. Nor are there any political parties. The newspapers are gone too, and the foreign correspondents. Vietnam is cut off from the world. Before, the demonstrations and protests had an international audience. But now there's only the party. The party runs the new Vietnam. Maybe that's not so bad, for the job of reconstruction. But for a prisoner. . . . I can feel the walls around me getting thicker, heavier. I am alone here.

Not quite. There are certainly others. Signals are coming at me from neighboring cells. "Psst, newcomer." "You . . . in cell five." "Hey, newcomer." I ignore them. Why should I talk to thieves and profiteers? I'll wait. The duty officer had to submit my case to someone in charge. Soon enough they'll realize there's been a misunderstanding.

Meanwhile, I wait, in this cell where one has no way to measure time. The only light is from the weak bulb set into a vent in the ceiling. Under the bulb a fan turns, one of those old-style colonial fans left behind by the French.

Finally, the shutter opens. I rush to it. A woman's hand

sticks in a large bowl of "red rice," as we call it, a coarse rice that's usually fed to the pigs. "Wait a minute," I shout. "I want to see someone in charge!"

On the other side of the shutter a girl's face stares at me—she can't be more than eighteen. She looks at me apologetically and whispers, "I can't do anything for you." Then loudly: "Talking is forbidden, prisoner." Later I learn that she too is a prisoner, being used as a servant. Her boyfriend had been arrested with a gun in his possession. Unaware that he was in trouble, she had gone to his house and was taken herself.

Ravenous, I begin to shovel the rice into my mouth with the plastic spoon they've given me, but there's sand in it, or some kind of grit. This rice meant for pigs seems to have been picked up from the ground.

Later in the day a second bowl appears at the shutter, the same red rice with lots of sand and a little salt. This time I discover a trick. If I run some water into the bowl and stir, the sand collects on the bottom. It's disgusting, but at least now I can swallow it. A few days later a guard tells me the sand is there for a purpose, mixed in "so prisoners will think of their mistakes while they eat."

Night comes—I can tell from the coolness in the air circulating through the ceiling vent. I'm beginning to worry. No one has tried to talk to me all day, except for the raspy-voiced *bo doi* and the girl servant. And the prisoners in the nearby cells whom I'm still ignoring, though they're very persistent. "Hey, you, newcomer! Young man! You in number five!"

How do they know I'm a young man? With my ear pressed up against the shutter crack I can hear their stage whispers clearly, calling me, telling me who they are, talking to each other. If I lie flat I can hear even better through the wide space under the ill-fitting metal door. I can even see a little through it, and through the crack between the door and the frame on the hinge side. "He's a young man . . . looks like he's educated . . . maybe an official." Little by little I realize that these voices don't belong to criminals. Most of them seem to be Saigon army officers.

Still I keep quiet. I don't want to do anything that might jeopardize my imminent release. But what are all these army people doing here? As far as I know, there have been very few arrests since liberation. Another night goes by, then day. The conversations go on, though now the voices have stopped trying to draw me out. I am beginning to understand that I was wrong. There obviously have been arrests, lots of them. But it's all been done so quietly, without disturbing the general public feeling of relief that the war is over.

During the day two bowls of red rice appear at the shutter. While I eat, I read the inscriptions on the cell wall, most of them dating back to the former regime: "Down with Thieu!" "Down with the Americans!" But others are more recent. One says, "I am Nguyen Tu, a reporter for *Chinh Luan*.* I was arrested on May 2d. I am seventy years old. Better to die than to stop writing."

May 2d! Nguyen Tu was arrested two days after liberation. What happened to him after he left this cell? Another message has no date. It says, "Nothing is more precious than independence and liberty"—Ho Chi Minh's most famous saying. Is it the defiant statement of some prisoner of the Saigon regime, or the bitter irony of a more recent guest? In any case, during the fifty-two days since Saigon's fall, at least several people have occupied this cell. One of them has written in large letters, "Down with communism"—a sentiment that wouldn't have made any sense two months ago.

I too scratch a message on the wall with a sliver of stone I've found on the floor: "Doan Van Toai, thirty years old. Former vice-president of the student union. Previously arrested by Thieu as pro-Communist. Arrested again June 22, 1975, 9:00 P.M. Don't know why. Am not against communism. Am against those who misapply it." Mine is the longest statement on the wall, even longer than Nguyen Tu's.

That night I am overwhelmed by the injustice I'm suffering. I can imagine the anxiety my mother and father are feeling,

---

* *Chinh Luan* was a right-wing newspaper, one of the thirty or so Saigon dailies the Thieu government allowed to exist. After liberation the number dropped to two.

and my wife and three little boys, the oldest of whom is four. Luckily, I'm in good health. I begin to do a little yoga. A few stretches, then some relaxation exercises to help me fall asleep.

On the third day I manage to attract the attention of a *bo doi* walking past in the hallway. I've been listening for an opportunity for hours. "Hey," I shout, "in here." The shutter opens. "I've been here for three days. I don't know why. I want to see someone in charge."

A solemn young face looks back at me. All the *bo dois* seem so young. "You're not the only one here, you know. The officials are very busy. You're a prisoner, right? So you'll wait until they're ready to talk to you."

My hopes evaporate. Even if it is a misunderstanding, now I know I'm not going anywhere, at least not soon. But in a way I'm relieved. I make a conscious decision to stop worrying about my misfortune. It's impossible to live in the constant expectation of release. Expectations merely turn the long, empty hours into an eternity on the rack. Instead I begin to organize my time.

Daytimes in Tran Hung Dao Prison, inmates may neither read nor write, talk nor sleep. The famous "walks" described in all the well-knows prisoners' memoirs don't exist. Thrown back on my own resources, I begin to practice yoga as I've never practiced it before, the "prison yoga" that's become traditional in Vietnamese jails and that I learned during my previous arrests. I stand up straight, my feet pointed directly forward, pressing the ground with my toes and the ridge of my palate with my tongue. Then I raise my arms in front of my body and force them back in an energetic swing, letting them rise up again naturally. A thousand repetitions. To prevent hemorrhoids and high blood pressure.

Afterward I do a little real yoga: shoulder stands to reverse the blood flow, the "preserver of youth" to concentrate blood in the pelvis. (They say it enhances sexual performance. I wonder when I'll get a chance to find out.) Then a few breathing exercises. Breathe in, two, three, four, five; out, two, three, four, five. In through the nose, out through the mouth. Finish up with whole body relaxation. See if I can induce a state of well-being, put myself beyond the present, beyond this cell.

Yoga for the body, memory exercises for the mind. I remember that the great Vietnamese philosopher Ho Huu Tuong had written of his imprisonment on Con Son Island that the greatest danger is memory loss. To prevent that, I begin thinking back on my life, back to my earliest memories, reliving each period, each day if I can, in as much detail as possible. As the days pass I also start to compose books in my head, the books I'll write when I get out of here. I'm damned if the time I spend in this place is going to be wasted, lost to me entirely.

The only distractions from this routine, and from the tedium, are the conversations one can have with fellow prisoners, under the door or through the shutter cracks. By the third day I'm ready to talk. "Hey, you, sir. You in cell five. Will you tell us who you are?" So I tell them, getting down on my hands and knees, putting my head on the floor and whispering hoarsely through the space at the bottom. From door to door the information moves quickly down the hallway. Ten cells in all, numbered like houses on a street: even on one side, odd on the other.

To the inevitable, "What are you in for?" I can only whisper, "I don't know." Grunts of skepticism sound along the floor. My answer cuts off more detailed questions. Later, after I'm moved to a collective cell, I'm told that the others have taken me for an old hand, on guard against *cho san*—"hunting dogs" (stool pigeons). They think that maybe I'm a leader of opposition to the new regime. Now my new friends become more prudent in their questions. But they show their sympathy by sending down some cigarettes, pushing them along from one door crack to the next with long pieces of straw from the mats that enhance the cells of a few lucky ones.

These "conversations," if you can call them that, don't last long. There's a limited amount you can say, keeping an ear out for guards and unsure about whom you are talking to. But in this desert of time, talk is like a glass of fresh, cool water. For the rest, you're on your own. In order to survive, you must create an inner life.

Some can't manage the strain and crack. Then the hallway resounds with fits of hysterics. Especially at night. Somebody will start to shriek "Death to communism!" "Death to the Communists!" They yell furiously, insanely, until the *bo dois* come to carry them away to some unknown place. They never come back. The prisoners say that they've been "eliminated." I don't know. Nobody knows. But they're never seen again.

From day to day new prisoners arrive, sometimes women with little children, sometimes peasants from far-off provinces. Squinting through the crack, I catch glimpses of them as they walk by. (Later on my food port was left open occasionally, as it was for most of the longtime prisoners.) Some have their hands tied, and bloody feet. Some are blindfolded. The next morning they ask, "Where am I?"

On my "street" in Tran Hung Dao Prison I see two Buddhist monks and a Catholic priest led by, chained hand and foot. I see Thai, Chinese, and Cambodians. I also see four white prisoners dressed in black Vietnamese pajamas. I hear that one of them is the French owner of the Brodard Café on rue Catinat, the gathering place of intelligentsia and reporters. The others are said to be Americans on their way north.

Day merges into night and night into day. Asleep one night, about a month after my arrival, I am startled awake by the sound of my door slamming shut. A guard has pushed someone into the cell. He's sitting on the floor near my bench. He speaks to me in a low voice. "Where are we? Which jail? Is there any water?"

I point to the faucet. "You'll have to use your hands, I don't have a glass."

"Can you help me?" he says. "My hands . . ."

I look at his hands and see that his left wrist is handcuffed to his right ankle and his right wrist to his left ankle. The poor man can't stand up, or get himself out of his awkward, knees-drawn-up position. I help him to sit on the bench, then bring him water in my cupped hands. He drinks thirstily, then thanks me. I'm dying to ask him questions, but I have to be cautious. Why have they put him here?

He looks to be about fifty. He speaks with the sharp sibilants of a northern accent, and his refined speech contrasts with his miserable physical condition. He looks emaciated. He hasn't shaved in a while, and he certainly hasn't bathed. His body gives off a pungent smell. He asks when I was arrested.

"A month ago. How about you?"

"Two months ago." Until now he's been in jail in Saigon's Third District.

"What did you do before?" I ask.

"Dean of the law school," he says. I can't believe it. Flabbergasted, I look at him more closely: "Are you Professor Thong?" I blurt out.

"Yes. Do you know me?"

"I was one of your students."

Of course I know him. This filthy, emaciated man, grotesquely hunched up on the bench, is the brilliant Professor Thong. The way he looks, it's no wonder I didn't recognize him at first. But he is indeed my former professor, one of Vietnam's best-known lawyers. I introduce myself, adding, "I was sure you left before the fall."

"I wanted to," he says. "But I couldn't desert my old mother. Besides, I thought they wouldn't go after a law professor. You can see that I was wrong. They accused me of being a CIA spy. They tortured me. But I don't have anything to confess."

Professor Thong tells me that almost all the law school faculty was arrested, and the school itself shut down. "It's like the French Revolution," he says. "They used to say that the republic doesn't need learned men. Now our revolutionaries are saying that Vietnam doesn't need any lawyers. And no judges either. What do we need any of them for when the party decides what's legal and what's not?"

We talk for hours.

Early in the morning a *bo doi* takes Professor Thong away. Where, I don't know. That evening another one comes in with handcuffs and trusses me up like the professor. "Asshole [*lo dich*]," he growls. "You can't be trusted, can you!"

I can see it coming. They're letting me know that Professor Thong has told them what I've said to him, that it's because of his tattling that I'm chained up like this. They want to make me angry at him, so that I'll tell them myself what he has said to me. It's a standard technique.

Sure enough, two days later I'm taken out of the cell to an interrogation room. Apparently, Professor Thong has made some accusations against me, based on what I told him. I play dumb. "I don't understand. I only gave him some water. We talked a little, then I fell asleep. What can he have said?"

The *can bo* (official) is disappointed. But he doesn't give up hope that I'll tell him something interesting about the professor. I'm kept chained for the next two weeks. Twice a day my handcuffs are unlocked, for five minutes at a time. Sometimes a little more if the guard's in a good mood. My ration of sandy rice is cut in half. I can't get to the faucet. Instead I'm given two cans of water a day, about a liter and a half—for drinking, washing the rice, and washing myself. My body begins to itch all over. It's agonizing. I didn't have any idea how well off I was before.

After they remove the cuffs I'm kept in cell five for another month and a half. Eating the sandy rice, doing yoga, exercising my memory. Once they decide I won't say anything about Professor Thong, there are no more interrogations. I am left alone. My only connection with life outside cell five is the guarded whispering under the door, and the occasional glimpse of prisoners arriving or departing. The universe consists of six square yards of cell and a handful of people locked up near me, whose faces I do not know. That and a hallway where *bo dois* and sometimes prisoners pass quietly. Night and day are the same. I develop the impression I am living underground, among ghosts. In spite of the discipline I impose on myself, I feel that I am drifting away, as if a gauzy veil is settling over my mind.

2

Growing Up
in the Delta

One morning the veil is pierced by the voice of a guard calling the inhabitant of cell eight, diagonally across the hall.

"You, prisoner! You are Nguyen Van Hien? Known as Hai Huong?* You have a letter from Hanoi, from your wife."

I'm dumbfounded. Who is this prisoner who can receive mail? Who is this wife who can get mail to him?

Even the *bo doi* seems a bit confused. At first he calls the prisoner *bo* (an informal address, like the French *tu*), then decides to change it to *anh*, indicating a degree of respect. He's as curious as the rest of us listening behind our doors. "Excuse me," he says in more deferential tones, "could you tell me

---

* *Hai Huong* (literally, Number Two Perfume). In Vietnam nicknames are universal and almost always reflect place in the family. A first son or daughter would be called *Hai* (Number Two), that is, second to the father. Second children are *Ba* (Number Three), and so on. In order to differentiate all the number twos, threes, etc., an identifying characteristic is commonly added to the nickname. A protruding nose, for example, might tag someone for life as Number Four Beak. Communist party members and other revolutionaries complicated this system by concealing their identities under one or more noms de guerre.

what you've done, why you're here?" The answer comes shooting back, electrifying the listening prisoners.

"I betrayed the party."

The *bo doi* is a northerner, too young or too simple to catch the bitter irony in the prisoner's voice. He can hardly believe what he's just heard.

"What?"

"I betrayed the party." This time it's loud enough for the most distant cells to hear.

Amazed at such a monstrous confession, the *bo doi* stammers, "But what have you done?"

"That's none of your business," came the reply.

The *bo doi* is impressed, but also anxious to assert himself. His voice assumes an air of authority.

"You lived in Hanoi? What neighborhood? *I* lived on Kham Thien." (Kham Thien is Hanoi's best-known thoroughfare.)

"I've lived in many places in Hanoi," says Hien. "But none of them can match cell number eight."

I stifle a laugh. I can sense the hilarity of the other listeners in their cells.

"And your wife?" says the *bo doi*. "She's from Hanoi too. What does she do?"

Hien, quietly now, "She teaches at the Nguyen Ai Quoc Institute."

This is too much for the poor *bo doi*. How could the wife of a prisoner be a teacher at the party's most prestigious political school? Or rather, how could a prisoner be the husband of a. . . . It doesn't make any sense. His whole value system has just been upended.

"That's impossible! How could you be here?"

"I've already told you, that's none of your business."

By now the *bo doi* understands he's being toyed with. He's angry. "You're awfully smart for someone who's locked up!" The shutter slams, and I can hear him walking quickly down the hall, fleeing from this upsetting encounter. Even though the *bo doi* managed to get in the last word, he's been caught off guard. He feels humiliated that he's shown his confusion, and that the prisoner demonstrated his superiority. Hien has just won a moral victory that's shared by all the prisoners. The peephole confrontation has also confirmed my feeling that there are indeed political prisoners here. Even some authentic Communists.

I replay the interchange in my mind, relishing the mixture of arrogance and ironic politeness with which Hien treated the *bo doi.* I have discovered among my fellow inmates a true revolutionary, like those I have admired from my childhood, admired without even knowing them. Men who were fighting for Vietnam's independence when I was just opening my eyes . . . thirty years ago in the Mekong Delta village of Cai Von.

◇   ◇   ◇

There's a story that I've heard from my mother a hundred times and that I've played in my mind hundreds more. It takes place in the summer of 1945, in Cai Von. A young man is gripping a long knife. His face is hard, threatening. Several steps away, staring at him wide-eyed, is a woman clutching a newborn infant to her breast. A little girl of seven huddles against the woman's legs.

"Where's your husband?" the man asks.

"In Saigon. . . . He works there. I've already told you," says the woman.

"You're lying! He's joined the underground. I know he has," says the young man.

"I swear he hasn't! He works for a French company . . . in Saigon."

The woman is my mother. I am the infant, and the terrified little girl is my sister. The husband in question is my father. A few months ago the hard-faced man with the knife was still a harmless neighborhood adolescent.

The next morning at dawn, taking nothing with her except her two children, one in her arms, the other clinging to her peasant pajamas, my mother left the village—a village gone mad. For her, the momentous national and international events of spring and summer that year had no meaning. In

March the Japanese had eliminated the Vichy French colonial
authorities who had ruled Vietnam under their tutelage for
five years. French troops were massacred or herded into prisons. Then, in August, the Nipponese Empire crumbled under
the atomic bomb, and the French came back to reclaim their
colony. But by the time they returned, Vietnam was no longer
the same. On September 2, 1945, Ho Chi Minh had declared
independence, addressing a huge crowd from the balcony of
Hanoi's National Theater. A new war was about to begin.

But to my mother, as to the other inhabitants of Cai Von,
these events were somewhere out there, in the invisible distance. The Japanese, like the French, kept to the cities and
were known mainly from hearsay. The real enemies of the people of Cai Von came from Tra On, the next village over. Tra
On was real.

The Tra On villagers were ethnic Khmer*—numerous in
our part of the delta. Between Cai Von and Tra On a very particular kind of war had been going on for as long as anyone
could remember. In Vietnamese eyes, the Khmer were ferocious barbarians. The Khmer thought the same of us. From
time to time one village would launch a murderous raid against
the other, then gird itself for the inevitable reprisal. Life went
on in a permanent state of fear and hatred. Guards watched
the approaches to both villages, ready to signal the enemy's arrival by beating on hollow bamboo trunks. Sometimes the
raiders would flee; other times there would be vicious battles.

Then there was the war between the Vietminh guerrillas
and the Hoa Hao, a religious sect with its own private army.
The sect's founder, Huynh Phu So, had been born near Cai
Von and made his first converts in the region. At first, Hoa
Hao was simply a more accessible form of Buddhism, its simplified and poetic rites more appealing to the peasants than the
traditional, intellectual doctrine. But Huynh Phu So also had
political ambitions. At first he directed his movement against
the French colonialists. Later, he allied himself with the

* The Mekong Delta had originally been part of Cambodia and in some areas was
still densely populated by people of Cambodian ancestry—the Khmer.

French against the Vietminh insurgents, whom he saw as his most formidable enemy. Differences between the Hoa Hao and the Vietminh were always settled in a bloody fashion, and Huynh Phu So himself was killed by a Vietminh assassin. But the sect outlived its founder. And so did its war against the Vietminh.

As early as 1943, my father had joined the Vietminh underground—the maquis. My brother, twelve years older than I, had joined him. My mother stayed behind in Cai Von and cultivated her rice paddies. At times my father sneaked home to see her. Always secretly. My mother had explained to the neighbors that Father had gotten a job in Saigon, and that my brother had gone to live with him. But the Hoa Hao militia suspected she was lying. Their threats, vague at first, became more explicit. She didn't take them lightly. The Hoa Hao had a long record of settling accounts with their enemies, and relatives of other Vietminh fighters had recently been murdered. After the visit from the young fanatic with the knife, my mother decided the time had come to get out.

When I was born, in March 1945, I was so weak that no one thought I would survive. So when my mother left the village, she told the peasants she met that she was going to the early-morning market to buy some medicine for me. The explanation seemed plausible. At the market she lost herself among the early-morning shoppers, then reappeared on the other side looking like someone on her way to the fields. Walking through the mango groves, she followed the dikes out into the flooded paddies. Beyond them was the road to Rach Ranh, about twenty kilometers away. As she walked, she thought about her house, about everything she had left behind. She also thought about the long knife, and the eyes of its owner.

She had walked this road several times before—to visit my father, who in fact was living in Rach Ranh, a center of Vietminh activity. By sunset she arrived exhausted at a small roadside pagoda, next to an arroyo. As she expected, a few Vietminh men were there. Like the Hoa Hao, they carried long knives in their belts, but these knives were reassuring. The men prepared tea for her, and something to eat, while one went to get my father and brother.

Father and brother arrived to tears and embraces. It seems that I started crying too, as I opened my eyes in a strange place, in the arms of a strange man. Cradling me back to sleep, my mother explained what had happened. "They suspect you're maquis," she told my father. "They're after everybody. Three days ago they dragged Mrs. Vinh behind our house and beat her to death. She was back there screaming and crying. I couldn't do anything for her, I couldn't even go out. They would have done the same thing to me. Then yesterday Nam Lua came over to ask where you were and threatened me. Of course I told him you were in Saigon. He didn't believe me, but I could tell he wasn't sure. I thought he would probably go ask the French if you were really there, since they're supporting him now. He's turned into a real big shot. He's a horror."

"Nam Lua!" my father exclaimed. "Nam Lua is an illiterate idiot. That's the kind of person the French are using. What a disgrace!" "Illiterate" is the worst insult my father can bestow on someone. He's a teacher who has always respected the peasants who haven't had the chance to go to school. But an uneducated hoodlum, especially one with pretensions to leadership, deserves only scorn.

"It's good you left," he told my mother.

A few days later news came that the Hoa Hao of Cai Von had gone on a rampage against local Vietminh partisans and their families. More than fifty people had been massacred and numerous houses burned down, ours among them. When my mother heard the news she burst into tears.

"We've got nothing left," she told my father. "What are we going to do?"

My father took her hand in his.

"The ones who died don't even have their lives left. A house we can always rebuild. In the meantime, we'll live here. In the pagoda."

That's how, at the age of about six months, I became a citizen of Rach Ranh, one of those "rebellious villages" France was to hear so much about for the next ten years.

By the time my mother brought us to Rach Ranh, the Vietminh already controlled hundreds of similar villages in the delta. For the French, the term *Vietminh* quickly became a synonym for *Communist*, a useful pretense in France's struggle to keep control of the country. *Vietminh*, short for "Vietnam Cach Menh Dong Minh Hoi," literally meant "The Unified Association of Revolutionary Vietnamese Forces." Initially, the Communist party (founded by Ho Chi Minh in 1931) was only one component of the association. The Vietminh president was Nguyen Hai Than, and Ho himself was only a member of the movement's executive council—as was Ta Nguyen Minh, whom I was to meet in prison in 1976, when he was over eighty years old.

But unlike his nationalist competitors, Ho Chi Minh had a doctrine—Marxism—that explained the world. And he had a method—Stalinism—that taught him how to use, then eliminate, allies. All this was topped off by a finely honed sense of human psychology and almost preternatural guile.

In the beginning, when talking to the other resistance fighters—romantic nationalists whose only doctrine was getting rid of the French—Ho never referred to communism. "Dialectical materialism" was not a cause that would appeal to the people. Nor would its tenets sit well with the ingrained Buddhism of their lives. Not communism, but the struggle against French colonialism, was Ho's great theme, as it was for the other factions that made up the Vietminh.

Communism was not a word I remember hearing as I grew up in the delta. People spoke of "patriotism" and "independence," but never communism or class warfare. It was not because the peasants were in love with communist ideals that they hated the big landowners, but because such individuals were the creatures and protégés of the French. All this Ho knew, and used, as he strove to assert his dominance over the resistance.

Rach Ranh, where I grew up, was not a village in the European sense. To picture it, you must first envision the Mekong Delta, which surrounds it. Carved by innumerable branches of the great Mekong River and watered by thousands of streams and arroyos, it is an immense plain, shimmering with rice fields and sectioned by low dikes. Interspersed among the paddies are groves of mango, coconut palm, and mangosteen with their leathery bark and sweet fruit. In this region there's no jungle; that occurs only to the north, near the Cambodian and Laotian borders and in the center. Just the irrigated plain stretching out as far as you can see.

The province of which Rach Ranh is part is called Vinh Long. Its chief city, also named Vinh Long, is about 30 kilometers from our village, 130 from Saigon, the capital. The single road connecting Vinh Long and Saigon threads between the river's branches, which at intervals must be crossed by ferry. Clusters of houses bunch together at the intersections of highway and waterway. In this country people get around mainly by boat. It's the only way into the backlands, which exist behind the main thoroughfares of road and rivers. The Vinh Long–Saigon road is guarded by the French, who have built blockhouses at strategic points. The road is their lifeline. They believe that whoever controls the road controls the country-side. But the backcountry people are unaffected by what the French think.

On the banks of one of the arroyos, about fifteen kilometers from the Vinh Long–Saigon highway, Rach Ranh spreads itself out. Alongside the village's main street the land is cultivated without interruption. Farther in, the fields are less accessible, and more of them lie fallow. Houses are scarcer too, sometimes more than a kilometer apart. Rach Ranh has no town center, except perhaps for the ancient pagoda that my father made into a school, and that was now our home as well.

About twenty children attended my father's school. Most of them lived too far away to go home at the end of the day, so they stayed with us, eating and sleeping as well as studying in the pagoda. Each day's meals were augmented by fish caught fresh from the arroyo. When the children did go home, they would return loaded down with provisions, which would go into the common larder.

In the Mekong Delta life was easy. It was a blessed land. Rice grew well in the rich, alluvial soil. Fruit abounded and was available for the picking. The streams teemed with fish. As a child I would watch them swarming around my legs when I went wading. To help out the dinner table, it wasn't even necessary to have a pole. Like all the other children, I learned to catch them in my hands. Chickens were allowed to live free, pecking out their own sustenance from whatever the ground offered. Catching one for dinner was a simple matter of scattering some rice grains around, then grabbing one of the takers by the neck.

When I was about five years old I started school. It was the most natural thing in the world. Having been brought up on the singsong of older playmates learning the rudiments of the alphabet under my father's quiet authority, I simply joined them. We wrote on small hardwood boards, with terra-cotta sticks that were made in the village. Sand was used as an eraser. Real pencils were rare, paper a treasure. Pens were unknown, except for the one my father owned, a Kaolo brand fountain pen that everybody considered a marvel. We would all gather around him in a circle when he filled it, watching wide-eyed as he slowly unscrewed the top and filled it with ink from a special bottle, which he would close carefully afterward. My father also owned a Printania watch with a luminous dial. These two objects were unique in the region, and they added no little to his prestige, as did the few books that he kept in a corner of the pagoda.

But even without these paraphernalia, my father would have been revered by the country people. Vietnamese peasants have a profound respect for learned men. In their scale of values the intellectual ranks first, followed by the farmer, the craftsman, and the shopkeeper (*nhat si, nhi nong, tam cong, tu thuong*). Soldiers, if they are mentioned at all, come last. The Vietnamese inherited this scale from their Chinese neighbors, along with other Chinese values and institutions, including the mandarinate, made up of scholar/administrators who had passed stringent academic examinations.

Little by little, the native intellectuals were supplanted by graduates of French schools and French universities, who were themselves eventually replaced by more au courant graduates of American institutions.* But my father had nothing in common with the elite who went on to finish their studies in France. He was the son of a delta peasant who had fifteen children . . . thirteen of them daughters. With that kind of luck, my grandfather was determined to give at least one of his sons an education. And so it was that my father had managed to get a teacher's certificate from the Can Tho Normal School.

But his learning, though it came through the French, did not cut him off from his roots. He was still a peasant's son, completely at home with the region and its people. French history, however, had taught him some valuable lessons, particularly the lesson of 1789, the French Revolution. Ironically perhaps, he learned from the colonialists to be a republican, and a nationalist . . . as did most of his fellow students in Can Tho. Among these were Pham Van Dang, later to become a Communist Central Committee member, and Dang Van Quang, for a time the NLF representative in Moscow. More famous men had also learned to be revolutionaries from the French. Both Pham Van Dong (prime minister of the Hanoi government) and General Vo Nguyen Giap (the victor of Dienbienphu) had achieved the sacred *baccalauréat* (high school diploma)† prior to World War II, their imaginations fired by the events of 1789.

But my father remained a man of the delta, living the kind of life everyone led in Rach Ranh, a Vietminh village apart from the world. Like other delta peasants, Rach Ranh's inhabitants produced almost everything they needed. And like their compatriots, they were uncommonly skilled at using all of na-

* Under Thieu, the sarcastic Vietnamese reorganized the traditional hierarchy to *nhat tuong, nhi cha, tam ma, tu di*; that is, generals, priests, puppets (i.e., those with American university degrees), and finally prostitutes.
† In the French system the *baccalauréat* is awarded to high school graduates who pass a comprehensive final examination.

ture's bountiful resources with the least possible amount of effort. They would, for example, bore a hole in a coconut still hanging in the tree. Through this hole they would insert a tiny young frog. Then they would poke through a couple of breathing holes and stop up the main opening. Inside, the frog would feed on the rich coconut meat and grow so fat that after a short time the hole could be unstopped. Before long, the frog would fill up the entire coconut, which was then opened, presenting its owner with a delectable and substantial dinner.

There is also the local coconut wine, made right in the tree. With the correct amount of yeast injected into the trunk, the coconut sap begins to ferment, transforming itself after ten days into a tangy and delicious wine. Following the "least effort" principle, baby ducks are raised in the cut-off trunks of large bamboo trees. Immobilized like this, they grow especially fast (though horribly deformed) until they are considered fit fare for the table.

The only items that had to be bought outside Rach Ranh were tea, salt, and cloth, and we didn't need large quantities of these. My mother would purchase whatever was necessary at the market in Song Phu, her native village, halfway between Vinh Long and Can Tho on the main highway. Because a military post guarded the intersection of the highway and the Rach Ranh arroyo, only women could go to Song Phu. Any man coming from the direction of our village was automatically considered to be Vietminh, and rightly so. In the Song Phu market, the women would sell fruit and perhaps some ducks. My mother would stop to see her family there, bringing us back such delicacies as French candy and chocolate.

People lived easily, but at a subsistence level. There was no money and no luxuries. One joke of long standing was that a wife and husband only had a single pair of pants between them. When guests came, only one spouse would be seen at a time, while the other waited for a turn at the trousers. The caricature was not really an exaggeration. There was more than one family in Rach Ranh that could boast only a single pair of pants.

But in spite of, or perhaps because of, their poverty, people helped each other out. They frequently ate at each other's homes and shared what they had. All the villagers, whether related or not, felt like family. Nothing was ever paid for with money. I remember when one of my uncles had to put a new roof on his house. On the appointed day, dozens of men came over to lend a hand. Some ducks had been killed and coconut wine had been fermented to fortify the troops' morale. But my uncle turned out to be the first one to overindulge, and he fell asleep. When he woke up, the roof was finished. Everyone made fun of him and had a good laugh. But they knew that later my uncle would work for others as they had worked for him, and that he wouldn't count his time or trouble any more than they were counting theirs.

Everyone took part in such exchanges all the time; they were part of the pattern of life. Some gave more, some less, but the talent of one would make up for the hard work of another. In the end it all seemed to even out. People either belonged to the community, or they didn't.

If anything, the war magnified this sense of the village as family. Passions were focused on the common enemy, who threatened everyone alike. In the war against the French, the bamboo drums were Rach Ranh's early warning system. *Bam-bam-bam . . . BAM . . . bam-bam-bam . . . BAM*: Three quick, short beats followed by one loud one meant the planes were coming. Carried from one drum to the next, the signal would wake the whole village or send the peasants scrambling from the paddies toward the concealed trenches. One loud beat followed by two short ones warned that a column of French soldiers and their Vietnamese auxiliaries had been seen approaching.

The French idea of bombing had nothing in common with the air war later carried on by the Americans. From a distance, two or three planes could be seen and heard as they lumbered in our direction—slow, heavy, World War II Dakotas. At some point they would haphazardly release their bombs; exactly where didn't seem too important to them, as long as they fell within the "Vietminh Zone"—that is to say, almost anywhere at all. Here and there they destroyed a few houses. Rarely were any people hurt. By the time the planes appeared overhead we had long since hidden in the trenches dug under the shelter of the orchard trees, far from any building.

But despite the drums, death occasionally came close. I can still feel my father's strong grip as he held me close to his chest in the bottom of a trench. I couldn't have been more than six or seven. But I can hear him muttering faster and faster: "*Nam do a di da phat, Nam do a di da phat, Nam do a di da phat,*" a Buddhist invocation meaning roughly, "May God protect us." Over the sound of this chanting came the roar of bombs exploding around the trench and the rain of dirt spattering onto us.

One particular day the drums had sounded too late, and many of the villagers—including my father and me—hadn't had time to take cover. One of the two planes spotted us and changed its bomb run, flying in low, right over the treetops. Little geysers of earth puffed up near us as my father dove for the trench, sweeping me up in his arms. The thunder overhead terrified me. Were we going to die? I hugged my father as tightly as I could and squeezed my eyes shut.

Suddenly, the racket went away and was followed by shouts of joy, coming louder and closer. My father jumped up and yelled, "It's been hit!" Everyone piled out of the trenches, running, shouting in delirium, "It's falling, it's falling!" Fingers pointed upward as the bomber, one engine on fire, swept across the sky in a relentless downward arc. The unbelievable had happened; a lucky gunshot had brought the monster down. As we ran, a fiery ball roared into being two or three kilometers away.

From everywhere the villagers raced toward the explosion: the young men out front, pursued by the children, the women and older men somewhat behind. I felt as if I had wings. When I caught up to my father he was pumping the hand of a beaming young man, his other hand on the young man's shoulder.

"Hey, you're the one who got him, aren't you? You're the one who did it! Wonderful, that's just wonderful!"

Then father held up the young men's hand, which was still

holding firmly onto his rifle, waving it against the sky. Turning toward the gathering crowd, Father shouted, "Brother Hai has brought honor to Rach Ranh! It's a great revolutionary victory! Let's all congratulate him! *Vietnam, Muon Nam, Vietnam, Muon Nam!*" ("Long live Vietnam!").

"Long live Hai! Long live Vietnam!" we screamed back.

"*Da dao de quoc Phap!*" shouted Father. ("Down with the French colonialists!")

"*Da dao de quoc Phap!*" we yelled.

All around people were overwhelmed with joy: laughing, talking, congratulating Hai and each other—then gazing at the flames that were now burning themselves out around the Dakota's black and twisted skeleton. The heat was still so intense no one could get near it. Pieces of the plane had been strewn around by the explosion. At first children were darting everywhere, exploring. But they were quickly brought under control when one of them seriously burned his fingers trying to pick up one of the shiny metal fragments.

A few yards away from what had been the cockpit lay a black shape, curled up and shriveled: the remains of one of the fliers. The other must have been incinerated inside.

"They were too low to jump out with their parachutes," one of the guerrillas said.

"Do these people even have parachutes?" I thought, marveling at the idea of people jumping out of planes.

Hai, the hero of the day, was not too long ago one of my father's students. He hoisted me up on his shoulders for the walk back to the pagoda. Riding high, I felt as if I was the hero of the day too. Later, at dusk, the whole village filed past on the low dikes, singing "*Quyet tien, ta giong dan lac hong.*" ("Forward, we are the heroes.") How could I know that this song was written by the uncle of my future wife, who had just then been born in Saigon? I sang as loudly as I could. We, the revolutionaries, had just shot down a French plane. What a glorious day it was. A time to rejoice.

Within a few minutes, a platform was erected in front of the pagoda, in the usual place. Often in the evening the villagers of

Rach Ranh would gather here for a theatrical performance, or for a concert by the small village orchestra, in which my brother played the mandolin. My special job was to open and close the curtains.

But that evening there was no curtain, no organized performance. It was a spontaneous celebration, improvised and a little crazy. Everyone was shouting, "Long live Hai! Long live Vietnam! Long live the Vietminh! Down with the French!" The whole village milled around in front of the stage, singing, "Forward, we are the heroes." Then my father got up to speak: "Our village has taught the enemy a lesson. The French Empire must be brought down!"

"Long live Vietnam! Down with the French!" from the cheering crowd. Again Hai hoisted me up on his shoulders so that I could see. A hero was my friend; my father was making a speech; my brother played mandolin in the orchestra. I was lost in a swirl of happiness, and pride that I was connected with the men Rach Ranh admired most. Since Rach Ranh was my universe, I couldn't imagine a higher honor. Nobody celebrated the victory over the airplane more enthusiastically than I did.

But such glory did not come to Rach Ranh every day. Whenever the bamboo drums announced the approach of a French army column, the day was more likely to end in tears.

The Vietminh fighters never sought a direct confrontation with the French. They weren't well enough armed for that. In the entire village of Rach Ranh there were only five guns. Not a single machine gun, not even a modern rifle. The guns we did have were entrusted to the best marksmen, like Hai. The others had only knives.

For the children of Rach Ranh, the war was a periodic, natural catastrophe—a little like a bad thunderstorm. There were long stretches when life was normal. Then suddenly there would be war. Afterward things would go back to normal, but the thunderstorms could break out at any moment. That was life. Except for the day the bomber was shot down, I don't remember ever having been afraid. The helter-skelter flights away from planes or patrols I thought of as a game of hide-and-seek, more exciting because it was dangerous.

For the older people, of course, it was a great deal more. One evening, a few days after the bomber was shot down, I saw my mother stumbling back to the pagoda surrounded by a group of armed men. They were helping her carry a body, the body of one of her younger brothers. She was crying, and the men and women around her were also crying, and praying. My uncle had died in an ambush. As far as I understood, we always won in these ambushes. But our men died in them too, just as the French and their mercenaries did.

My uncle was only a teenager. Staring at his lifeless body that day, I began to feel the first stirrings of hate. Why had the *Phap*, these French white men whom I had only seen from a distance, killed my uncle? Why did they hunt Vietnamese down? And why did other Vietnamese help them? What were they doing here anyway, since they had a country of their own on the other side of the ocean? Until then I had never understood much about the words *colonialism* and *independence*, which I heard over and over at the village meetings. But my uncle's death was a revelation. Unnoticed, my childish view of the revolution began to slip away. And I sensed a new dimension to my admiration for the men who were fighting it.

3

Tran Hung
Dao Prison

Solitary confinement. No letters, no books, no pen or paper. Three paces up, three paces back. Each day becomes a slow-motion nightmare that has to be lived to its end. But the end brings no relief. Day and night merge.

Like prisoners the world over I count the days, scratching a line each morning on the back wall near the corner. I force myself to keep up the memory exercise, but it becomes an act of will. My yoga is going downhill too. I tire quickly. It's the food, I think: two bowls of rice a day, no vegetables, no meat. I have less and less energy, and find myself growing apathetic.

But my mind is wonderfully focused anyway, preoccupied with the same questions: "Why have they put me here? When are they going to question me?" I develop a monomaniacal urge to explain myself, going over and over the phrases I will use, honing them until I think I've found the exact wording that will be most effective, then changing it as yet a more felicitous expression or tone occurs to me. I imagine a scene with a high-ranking prison official and try to divine if he will be sympathetic or cold as I sit opposite him, cogently describing my meritorious life—making it easy for him to acknowledge the mistake that's been made. "If a mistake has been made, the revolution will acknowledge it." Isn't that how the duty officer put it before they locked me up?

Every time I hear a *bo doi* in the hall I ask to speak to someone in charge. But they always have the same answer: "Be patient. You're not the only one. The officials are very busy."

"How busy can they be?" I think to myself. "How many souls do they have dying by inches in their cells, waiting for a turn?" I've just scratched the forty-fifth nick on my wall calendar. Have they had forty-five days' worth of prisoners to talk to before me?

Yoga still helps me fall asleep, but it's becoming increasingly difficult. I begin to feel a despair I have never experienced before, a choking sensation in my upper chest and throat.

Then, on the morning of the forty-sixth day, there's a knock on the door and the peephole opens.

"Number five! What is your name?"

"Doan Van Toai."

"Doan Van Toai, prepare yourself to go to work!"

Work is the Tran Hung Dao term for interrogation. I can't believe it. Suddenly the *bo doi* looking in through the peephole shouts: "*My nguy* [American puppet]! You're naked! What do you mean by that? Are you a dog?"

The fact is that I have only the shirt and pants I was arrested in. To keep them clean I sleep naked. And sometimes I don't bother to put them on at all. It's not exactly as if I'm on display to the world in here. But the idea of a naked prisoner has upset the *bo doi*'s sense of propriety. He's furious at this breach of good taste.

"Get dressed! Now!" he hisses.

I do, as fast as I can. Then the door opens, and the *bo doi* pushes me roughly down the hall. I begin to sway, dizzy from walking straight ahead for more than three paces.

An iron door swings open. We go left, then left again, stopping in front of an office door, which the *bo doi* opens gently, announcing, "Prisoner Toai."

"Bring him in," says a voice.

"Attention!" shouts the *bo doi*, turning toward me. Then, looking important, he signals me to go in.

As I step into the office I feel a wave of relief. The scene I've been imagining for a month and a half is about to take place. Finally I'm with someone I can talk to, someone who will tell me I don't have to stay here anymore.

This someone is sitting behind a desk at the back of the room, thumbing through a sheaf of papers. I greet him respectfully: *"Kinh thua Bac."* Literally, this means, "I salute you, Uncle." There's no family relationship implied, only polite deference. But my greeting elicits no response, just a continued leafing through the papers—my file, I suppose. I can see it's quite substantial already. Then, without raising his eyes from the file, the *can bo* tells me to sit down, indicating the chair seven or eight feet in front of his desk.

I sit. Several minutes go by, the silence broken only by the shuffling of papers. At last the *can bo* raises his head and smiles at me. He's about fifty years old, with a pleasant, friendly face.

"How are you?" he asks solicitously. "Are you sleeping well? Is your appetite all right?"

I feel almost as if I'm in a doctor's office. I hear myself say, "My appetite's all right, *bac* [uncle]. But there's not enough food." Then I catch myself. My appetite's hardly the issue I want to discuss. Still respectful, I say, *"Bac,* I'd like to know why I'm here! I haven't . . ."

With a quick gesture, the *can bo* cuts off the complaint that is starting to boil up inside me.

"You must understand, prisoners eat the same food we do. Our country is poor . . . you know that. Good. Now, are you ready to answer my questions?"

"Ready? *Bac,* I've been ready for forty-six days! Every time I could, I've asked to speak with someone, to prove that . . ."

Again I'm cut off.

"Perfect! You must answer honestly all the questions I'm

going to ask. One of these days you will be released. I'm absolutely sure of that. But it all depends on you, on your sincerity. The revolution is lenient with those who recognize their mistakes. But we are harsh with those who are obstinate and lie to us."

I restrain myself from jumping up and attacking him. Instead, in the most measured terms I'm capable of I express my indignation.

"What mistakes? My father was a teacher in the underground. I organized demonstrations against Diem when I was in high school. I was one of the student leaders against Thieu. I even went to jail for it. I didn't break any laws after liberation. What mistakes are you talking about?"

Again the hand raises, signaling me to be silent. I'm at this smiling *can bo*'s mercy. I shut up. All patience, all gentleness, he explains that he is acquainted with some of my activities against the old regime. But "certain points" have to be clarified.

"Which points?" I ask.

He smiles. "What's important here is that you tell me everything, truthfully. I understand you were born in Cai Von . . ."

So it begins. I start with the Hoa Hao, then tell him about the flight from Cai Von, about Rach Ranh and the Vietminh, my father, the French bomber. I talk for hours. The *can bo* writes down everything, asking questions from time to time, about my father, my mother, my grandparents, my brother and sister. Occasionally he switches to more recent years. He wants to know about the girlfriends I have had, how I met my wife, what my in-laws are like. But then he goes back to my childhood again, meticulously examining everything I say.

Finally we get to my adolescence.

"You say you organized demonstrations against Diem? When you were in high school? Describe that to me, will you please?"

For some time now the *can bo* has been calling me *anh*, which I've taken as a sign of respect. It's one of the things that's put me at ease, draining my anger. The man is charming and courteous. He's also a southerner, mercifully free from the arrogance of almost all the northern Communist officials. Sitting here talking about myself, I've begun to feel more like a witness than a suspect. It's true that I'm imprisoned, but obviously not for long. My whole past speaks in my favor to this sympathetic listener.

So I tell him about my adolescence—from the time Ngo Dinh Diem came to power in 1954 until his fall in 1963*— dates that correspond to my starting high school in the provincial capital of Vinh Long to the time of my passing the *baccalauréat*. These were the years right after the French defeat at Dienbienphu, and the Geneva peace accords that followed, which called for a temporary division of the country at the seventeenth parallel, with elections after two years to decide on a government for the entire nation. No one could have predicted that this temporary division was to last not two years, but twenty.

Before the unification elections, the Vietminh army was supposed to regroup north of the seventeenth parallel, the French south of it. In Saigon, Ngo Dinh Diem was appointed premier by the playboy king Bao Dai, himself a tool of the French. Diem, however, was no French puppet. He came to power with American backing, which he had cultivated while living in the United States during the early fifties. And with this support he deposed King Bao Dai and transformed South Vietnam into a republic, with himself as the first president. Having dissolved the South Vietnamese government that signed the Geneva agreement, the new president made it clear that he would not abide by Geneva's requirement of unification elections.

So officially there was now peace. But though the last French troops would soon be leaving, the people knew that the war against France would almost certainly be followed by a war

---

* Ngo Dinh Diem became the first president of South Vietnam in the period following the Geneva accords. He was overthrown and assassinated in a coup that took place on November 1, 1963.

among Vietnamese. Diem's rejection of the unification referendum virtually guaranteed it.

Another agreement reached at Geneva allowed for the free
movement of people north and south, depending on which regime they chose to live under. From North Vietnam, where
Ho Chi Minh was establishing a Communist government, a
million refugees flooded southward, many of them Catholic
villagers led by their priests. There was also a movement from
south to north, though this was a good deal smaller and has
been less well documented. Though difficult to estimate, the
number was probably over one hundred thousand. In addition
to the Vietminh regular army personnel, many southern Communists fled north with their families. So did others who were
not Communists, but whose passionate nationalism persuaded
them to live under Ho Chi Minh's government rather than
under that of the Western-backed Diem.

◇   ◇   ◇

After Geneva, a number of families from my village decided
to go north. Others, who had come to Rach Ranh only for
protection from the French, also left, moving back to their
home villages. With each passing day, my father saw the number of his students dwindling. But he couldn't take his family
back to Cai Von, where the Hoa Hao were more powerful than
ever, and where his house was a charred ruin anyway. So he
decided to move us all to the province capital, Vinh Long,
hoping to find a teaching position there.

It was not an easy trip. On our first attempt, we pushed off
down the arroyo in two boats. In the first boat was one of my
maternal uncles and most of our belongings. My mother, father, sister, and I rode in the second amid the extra bundles.
(My older brother had left earlier to try his luck in Saigon.)

But the new government was already taking measures to iso-
late (eventually to eliminate) people suspected of Communist
leanings. We were coming from a Vietminh zone; that was
enough. At Song Phu, the market town where the arroyo inter-
sected the national highway, shots rang out, and soldiers came

running down the bank toward my uncle's boat up ahead of ours. I saw them point their guns at him, and I saw the boat being pulled onto the bank. Meanwhile, my father was hurriedly turning our own boat around. Cradled in my sister's lap, I could hear them shouting, "Stop! Stop!" Then they were shooting at us, and the water splattered around the boat. My mother made a sound and reached down to hold her leg. But now we were moving quickly down the arroyo back toward Rach Ranh, and the soldiers' shouts were more distant. Soon I couldn't hear them at all.

My mother wasn't hurt badly, and in the several weeks it took her wound to heal my father had figured another way to get us to Vinh Long. This time we took one of the smaller arroyos that passed under the national highway in the outback, some distance from any town. There we pulled the boat onto the shore and flagged down the bus when it eventually clattered into sight. Assuming we were peasants who lived nearby, the bus driver asked no questions, and by the end of the day we were settled in my mother's aunt's house in the province capital. Before long my father found a teaching position in a private school whose principal had been a Vietminh sympathizer. Mother added to the family income by becoming a fruit-and-vegetable vendor in the market.

For me, Vinh Long was astonishing. Having seen nothing but the scattered huts of little delta villages, I thought it immense. (In fact, Vinh Long probably numbered fewer than fifty thousand people at that time.) Here I was, in the middle of modern civilization, marveling at such wonders as streetlights, cars, and buses. At night it seemed the entire city lit itself up, a startling contrast to the thick curtain of black that fell on the countryside when the sun went down.

Equally miraculous were the city buses. Each one had a driver who performed his duties wrapped in an aura of imperial dignity, and two conductors who were only a degree less impressive. These two would hang out the back door and yell at the traffic, making the cars and scooters keep clear. When passengers wanted to get on or off, the conductors would bang loudly on the side of the bus, signaling the driver to stop. Then, with an air of brusque authority, they would assist their charges to negotiate the steps. The first time I saw them I knew I could aspire to nothing higher in life.

But most intriguing of all was the movie theater where I saw my first film, in Chinese. That was another surprise: Vinh Long was full of Chinese. They owned practically all the shops, drugstores, and restaurants.

For the first time, too, I saw French people close up. But the ones who were still living in Vinh Long hardly resembled the cruel warriors I imagined all French to be. Instead they seemed fat and harmless. Most were teachers at the high school, a few more part of the city administration, in such departments as electricity and water.

But in the school I began to attend, all the teachers were Vietnamese. The curriculum too was being "Vietnamized," especially the history classes. I was among the first generation of Vietnamese students who missed hearing about "our ancestors, the Gauls," who had blond hair and fought the Romans. The French language, though, continued to be taught six hours a week.

To the delight of most students, our studies were often interrupted so that we could participate in political demonstrations on behalf of Ngo Dinh Diem, who had already launched his drive to depose King Bao Dai and change South Vietnam from a monarchy to a republic. For hours we would march through the streets waving pictures of Diem and shouting, "Down with Bao Dai!" "Down with French colonialists!" At some point an effigy of Bao Dai would appear, and we would beat it with our fists and trample it into the street before setting it on fire.

We were part of Ngo Dinh Diem's campaign to rouse the people. But in fact, most people didn't need rousing. Bao Dai was said to be living in luxury on the French Riviera, gambling huge sums of money and callously ignoring the needs of his people. Diem, on the other hand, was a new man, energetic, educated, without any link to the former colonial hierarchy.

Many considered him a nationalist, even a revolutionary. In any case, he seemed patriotic—and honest.

Independence was again the magic word. And at the beginning we heard nothing at all about fighting against communism. It was not the northern regime, but the leftover French colonialists and the distant Bao Dai, living it up at our expense on the Riviera, who were the targets of the new government's campaign to consolidate power. Diem was portraying himself as an intransigent nationalist, eager to sever the last links of Vietnam's colonial servitude.

On October 24, 1955, when I was ten and a half years old, the long-touted referendum took place. The next day South Vietnam was declared a republic. Diem had defeated Bao Dai, winning 98.2 percent of the vote. Like many Vietminh veterans in those days, my father was living in expectation. He was not in favor of Diem, who, after all, had spent the war in safety abroad while my father and his friends were risking their lives in the underground. But neither was my father actively opposing the new president, at least not yet. Diem had come to power on the promise of eliminating French colonialism. Besides, the unification elections were supposed to be less than a year away.

These elections, of course, were never to be. Whether the signatories to the Geneva agreement ever really expected them to be is anyone's guess. With Ho Chi Minh establishing a rigid communistic state in the North and Diem setting up his own stridently anti-Communist government in the South, the very idea became wildly improbable. Yet that was not how my father saw it, and not how most other Vietnamese saw it either. For the former Vietminh in the South, the permanent division of the country brought bitterness. For some, particularly the Communists who had stayed, it was an intolerable betrayal of hopes.*

* The southerners who had regrouped north were dismayed as well as angered. Many of them felt displaced and unhappy in the bleak austerity of North Vietnam, among people whose psychology and habits differed significantly from their own. The vast majority had left their families in the South. As their transports had left from Vung

For a while after Geneva, at least there was no more war. In Vinh Long we lived quietly, even taking occasional trips to visit friends and relatives around Cai Von and Rach Ranh. But before long the atmosphere began to change. The government-sponsored street demonstrations took on a more overtly anti-Communist tone. Attendance was now mandatory, enforced by ward leaders and government-paid street informants.

Every few days the warning drums would sound, announcing a new demonstration. The hollow knocking would resonate first from the street chief's house, then build up as the other households chimed in on the wooden drums everyone had to keep in their living rooms. At the signal, each household was required to send at least one representative to the political rally forming up in the city center. My father hated it. Everyone did, as their family evenings and weekends were disrupted time and again by the beating drums and the peremptory commands of the street chief.

As popular resentment grew toward the government's impositions, armed opposition also reappeared. We would hear of attacks against bridges or isolated guard stations around town. Anti-Diem political tracts secretly began to circulate. A heavy, charged air of impending conflict spread through the city.

At the age of twelve I was excited by all this. Even then, some instinctive sense of combativeness was coming to life inside me. I was neither old enough nor sufficiently sophisticated to understand national (let alone international) politics. But my street instincts told me to hate the "little leaders" who were becoming so obtrusive in everyone's lives.

From day to day the government's men on the street were more arrogant and obnoxious. They would buttonhole people, asking pointed, threatening questions: "Why weren't you at

---

Tau and other southern ports, they had wildly waved a victory sign—two fingers (for two years)—at the crowds of relatives seeing them off on the docks. All had steeled themselves to accept a two-year separation, but permanent exile was more than they could bear. These displaced southern fighters were among the most active proponents of the northern march to the South that would be under way by the early sixties.

yesterday's demonstration?" "You went out of town yesterday? Where did you go?" "I heard you had guests last night. Who slept at your house?" The mounting inquisition worried my father and made him nervous. He knew too well where all this was leading. I too became increasingly impatient and angry as I began to make some political connections for myself. Certainly the harassment and intimidation did not have anything to do with the "independence" for which I had been screaming my lungs out in demonstration after demonstration.

One day at school as I was walking into class, I noticed a hand-written leaflet on one of the benches. "To the Vietnamese People" was all I had a chance to read before my heart started racing. I buried the paper inside my shirt. When I got home I took it out and read it over and over—until I had memorized the words:

To the Vietnamese People!

Our people have paid a high price to expel the French colonialists and bring peace to our country. But we have won only a partial victory!

In the northern half of the country there is democracy and freedom. But the southern half is ruled by the colonialist puppets.

Ngo Dinh Diem's government oppresses the people, jails the patriots, and violates the Geneva agreement.

Down with Ngo Dinh Diem!

Down with the Saigon puppet government!

The revolution will triumph!

This message moved me in a strange way. At school the next day I couldn't resist talking about it to one of my friends, Minh. Minh was three years older than I, and often spoke about politics with other older students. He was noncommittal about the discovery, though, treating my excitement in a casual, offhand manner.

But during recess a few days later, Minh took me aside and

asked me quietly if I wanted to help him distribute leaflets.

"Leaflets? What leaflets?" I asked.

"The one you found the other day. I have a whole package of them."

I stared at him.

"A whole package? But . . . how come? Distribute them to whom?"

"Don't worry about that. Do you want to come or don't you?"

I was itching to get in on this secret action, but frightened too.

"What if we get caught?"

"We won't get caught. I've already done it a lot. Don't tell me you're chicken."

I shook my head.

"Okay! Good! I'll pick you up tonight at your house."

My parents didn't have anything against the little bike trip that Minh came over to propose after dinner. So off we went, Minh pedaling while I sat on the luggage rack over the back wheel. I could feel the package of leaflets pressing against my stomach under my shirt, and I could feel my heart pounding, pounding. Minh joked the whole time, laughing nervously, like an adolescent running away from trouble. My throat was so constricted from street dust and fear that I couldn't answer. When we'd come to a spot where no one was in sight, Minh would say, "Now!" and I'd let a few leaflets slide from under the shirt down my thigh. The first time I did it I almost blacked out. The second time, it wasn't so bad. Little by little I got bolder, and soon I began to feel a crazy kind of jubilation each time I let a few of them slip to the street.

Over the next few weeks I helped Minh "distribute" leaflets several times. Each time I went I felt an adrenaline rush. The danger and secretiveness were exhilarating.

But it didn't last. One day my father found a stack of leaflets I was hiding at home. He didn't reproach me for what I was doing. But he did advise me, in his firmest tones, to wait a few years before plunging into politics.

In Vinh Long at the age of twelve with my older brother visiting from Saigon

By and large I followed my father's advice, but by now my feelings about Diem and his government were wide awake. I listened intently as the adults discussed their grievances, feeling their anger as my own. The excitement with which I had first greeted the marches and ceremonies turned to loathing. For a demonstration at nine in the morning we would have to gather at six, waiting hours as the rest of the crowd was mustered, then hours more as the speeches and political harangues droned on.

Diem's older brother, Ngo Dinh Thuc, was bishop of Vinh Long, and twice Diem himself came to town. The first time we gathered at our assigned spots along the motorcade route early in the morning. For an eternity we stood by the roadside complaining, then suddenly the convoy of limousines and police cars rushed past and was gone.

The second time, though, we actually caught a glimpse of the president. This was a special occasion, and we reported to the school early in the evening, dressed in the new clothes our parents had been instructed to make or buy. There we labored over bamboo lanterns for the nighttime parade in which we were to march.

When the time came, we filed out of the school and down to the province chief's house, where a small, rotund man was standing on the balcony. Waving our lanterns at the distant figure we shouted in unison: "*Hoan Ho Tong Thong Ngo Dinh Diem*" ("Bravo President Ngo Dinh Diem"), "*Lanh Tu Anh Minh Va Vi Dai*" ("The Brightest and Most Sacred Leader").

Forced participation in the rallies was annoying enough, but it was really just a small part of the emerging pattern of government intimidation and control. The street leader made it his business to know everything that went on in each house. If a family member went off for a visit or on business, or if a guest was staying overnight, that had to be reported. And once or twice a month the police would come, always in the middle of the night. The neighborhood dogs would start barking in chorus, and I would hear banging on the doors of the houses around us. Soon, I knew, they would be at our door shouting, "Open up! Open up! Mr. Teacher, open up!" Then they would come inside with their flashlights, searching the corners and under the beds for unauthorized visitors.

On our way to school the next day the neighborhood kids would talk it over angrily, cursing out the police, the street leader, and the fat neighborhood chief. But there was fear

mixed in with the anger, especially when the night searchers
had taken someone away, perhaps a relative visiting from the
countryside, or perhaps someone who had slipped into a house
late at night after the children had gone to sleep—someone
maybe from the shadowy maquis.

Now and then one of the neighbors would disappear as well,
and when that happened those who heard about it were
gripped by a silent anxiety. Those were my feelings when Tri,
an older friend of mine, suddenly dropped from sight.

Tri was about eighteen, one of the neighborhood boys I considered an "older brother." As secretary of the block committee, he was already a prominent person in my eyes. Beyond
this, his idealistic nature attracted me, and I was proud that he
considered me a friend.

For the most part, talk among the neighborhood kids ran to
girls and sports, with the emphasis on girls—what they were
like, how you chased them, and what alluring possibilities presented themselves should you ever actually catch one. Of
course I was as fascinated by these topics as anyone, but inside
I was also disdainful. I hated the idea of being like all the
others. I already saw myself as different, the kind of person
who might do something extraordinary with his life. And Tri's
talk appealed to that side of my personality. We played bad-
minton and soccer together, and afterward we would share
long conversations in which he would do most of the convers-
ing, telling me about the young men who had performed heroic acts during the French war and prior to that, during
Vietnam's long and turbulent history.

When Tri didn't come around for a couple of days, I went
to his house to ask for him, thinking that perhaps he was sick
or had gone off on a visit somewhere. But his parents were
strangely evasive, unwilling to say anything specific. Later the
rumor spread that he had been arrested. When I heard this I
went to talk to his mother, to tell her that I wanted to see Tri.
Finally she agreed to take me with her on her next visit to the
Vinh Long prison.

On visiting day the prison courtyard was crowded with in-

mates and their relatives sitting on the ground and talking together or walking slowly in the hot sun. Around the courtyard
lounged lackadaisical policemen watching everything in a half-
hearted way; others slouched lazily through the crowd. When
we finally found Tri, his mother, he, and I sat down together.
Tri looked so pale to me, so sad. He told his mother he had
been beaten, and she said that the police were asking for
money before they would release him. She told him that the
family would sell everything to get him out, that they had already started with the household furniture. When his mother
said this she began to cry, then Tri joined her, and I too began
to feel the tears welling into my own eyes.

That afternoon in the prison courtyard made a lasting impression. I simply could not understand why they had arrested
Tri, and why they were beating this person, whom I thought
the most admirable of all my friends. After a time Tri was released, but before long he disappeared again, this time for
good. The street talk was that he had joined the maquis.

Though I was not explicitly aware of it at the time, the night
searches and arrests were part of what Diem was calling the *To
Cong* (Denounce Communists) campaign—his attempt to
smash the underground infrastructure the Communist party
had left behind, and along with it any other elements that
might present a challenge to his control. In the process he
spread terror among the veterans of the French war and an-
tagonized all who sympathized with them; that is, the better
part of the population.

The *To Cong* campaign was followed by measures that an-
tagonized other groups. Peasants were forced into militarily se-
cure, newly built villages called agrovilles that had little to do
with their traditional way of life. Buddhists felt aggrieved by favoritism toward Catholics. Even the army was in disarray over
Diem's habit of advancing selected cronies over competent officers. Of these things I knew nothing at the time, but I listened to the older people talk, and along with everyone else I
could feel the temperature rising.

As tension throughout the country grew, certain elements of

the South's army decided to take matters into their own hands. On November 11, 1960, several paratroop colonels in Saigon staged a coup against Ngo Dinh Diem and his brother Ngo Dinh Nhu, who had become the president's closest adviser. They besieged the Ngo brothers inside the presidential palace and began negotiating terms with them over a telephone hookup. Sometime during the night Diem broadcast by radio that he would bow to all the demands of the rebel leaders.

At Vinh Long High School the next morning, the excitement was electric. Ordinarily, all the students gathered in the courtyard at 7:30 or 7:45, talking and playing until eight o'clock when the caretaker beat the giant tambourine mounted behind the gate to announce that school was in session. At the tambourine's call, we'd line up in double file outside of our classrooms, everyone standing rigidly at attention.

When the class was sufficiently in order, we would march two by two past the teacher, who stood there glaring at us, without acknowledging in any way the bows that each pair of students paused to render. Once inside we would come to attention next to our seats and wait silently for the teacher to enter and bestow on us, again without a word, his most baleful morning stare. Then, with a wave of his hand, he would allow us to sit.

That was the usual procedure. On special days and just before vacations discipline was relaxed. Instead of holding ourselves stiffly upright in strict parade order, we could mill around and talk, even after the tambourine sounded. The teachers too were easier, as if pleased that they could neglect for a while the hopeless and perpetual labor of improving our decorum. On those days we would wander haphazardly into the classroom and quietly amuse ourselves until the teacher's sense of duty called him back from enjoying the company of his colleagues.

November 11 was that kind of special day, and a great deal more. Discipline was not just ignored for a few moments, it was tossed to the wind. The teachers were as excited as everybody else. Ours never did come into the classroom. Many of the students were yelling to an enthusiastic audience of their peers, "Down with Ngo Dinh Diem." In the midst of the uproar I decided that the time had come for a speech. I climbed up on the teacher's chair at the front of the room and launched into a spontaneous denunciation of the supposedly deposed president. Then I tore Diem's picture from the wall and smashed it to the floor, to the unrestrained cheers of my classmates.

But by the next day it was evident that the coup leaders hadn't planned very well. Diem's radio broadcast and all his conciliatory talk over the phone had simply been a ruse to buy some time while loyal forces were brought into Saigon from the south. With their arrival, the rebellion dissolved and its leaders fled to Cambodia.

In Vinh Long, my ill-considered outburst at school threatened to bring unpleasant consequences. The security police began an investigation of what had happened, and since I was considered to be one of the leaders, I was questioned for most of the day in the principal's office.

Fortunately for me, the officer in charge wasn't too concerned with the events themselves. What he really wanted to know was whether I had acted spontaneously, or whether someone had pushed me into it. Naturally, I didn't say a word about Minh, the leaflets, my friend Tri, or my burgeoning dislike of the government. To every line of questioning I responded that I had simply wanted to cause a ruckus.

Finally convinced that I had not been used by any organized group, the officer put the affair down to my natural unruliness and merely upbraided me, warning me to keep busy with my studies and stay out of politics. There the matter rested. But the experience in the principal's office frightened me and made me more cautious.

During the next few years I was approached from time to time by older students and other acquaintances who urged me to get involved in action against the regime. "You have ideals," they would say. "Come with us. We're the revolutionaries. We're the youth. We have to do something for our country." I loved the country, as they said. And I too believed, or came to believe, that the peasants were miserable, poor people, like us, who were exploited by the wealthy bourgeois in Saigon. But as far as direct involvement went . . . I was not yet ready for that.

In the years following the abortive coup, violence spread. Opposition to Diem's increasingly dictatorial rule coalesced under the banner of the National Liberation Front, a new version of the previous war's Vietminh underground, with widespread roots in the South, but dominated by the northern-based Communist party. But though the NLF, the "Front," was founded in 1960, in Vinh Long we never heard anything about it as a formal organization. Even its name was unfamiliar. We spoke instead of the *Cach Mang* (The Revolution) or the *du kich* (the guerrillas). We heard that they were everywhere, and we rejoiced in their victories, the ones we heard of from visiting relatives and the ones we knew of ourselves, such as the assassination of the Vinh Long province chief.

By the early sixties I was following political developments avidly over the BBC, the VOA (Voice of America), and Radio Hanoi. I listened intently as civil unrest flared throughout the South, spearheaded by Buddhist protests and demonstrations, which included the fiery suicides of several monks. The political and religious repression through which Diem and Nhu were striving to maintain a grip on power increasingly alienated their popular support. Even their American allies began to consider them a lost cause.

On November 1, 1963, several high-ranking generals engineered the overthrow of Diem and his family. The generals had been careful to block off any rescue attempts by loyal forces. They had also cleared their action with the United States embassy in Saigon. Diem and Nhu were captured in a Saigon church to which they had fled for asylum, then shot to death as they were being transported to the coup leaders' headquarters.

At the Vinh Long High School these events triggered an explosion of joy. This time I completely let myself go. We decided on a general student strike, and I spoke before the student body assembled in the courtyard: "The corrupt dictatorship is dead! The people were oppressed and living in poverty. Here, in this school, the curriculum is still under the influence of French colonialism. All this is going to change!"

In my harangue I used the political jargon I had picked up listening to Radio Hanoi. Almost everyone I knew tuned in to the northern broadcasts, either out of sympathy or just plain curiosity. The Communist radio programs extolled patriotism, independence, revolution, freedom, the struggle against colonialism, and the heroic exploits of the people. These were rousing, epic themes that appealed to the idealism and emotional fervor of the young—quite different from the insipid popular songs broadcast continuously by Radio Saigon.

North Vietnamese radio also provided information about Diem and conditions in the South that fit in all too well with the peasant unrest, assassinations and civil oppression that everyone could see in their own neighborhood. As for the North, we were told it was experiencing an economic miracle, news that my high school friends and I took as gospel truth. Up there at any rate, we told each other, they were governed by Vietnamese, not some American puppet (*My Diem*— "America/Diem" was Radio Hanoi's way of referring to the Saigon government.)

But though I considered my speech in front of the students a grand success, for the next few months I kept quiet about politics. It was my turn to prepare for the *baccalauréat*, the comprehensive, nationwide final examination.* American high school students would find it difficult to imagine the importance of the "*bac*" for Vietnamese students at that time. It was like the college boards and a high school transcript rolled into one—but because of its immense prestige, it was more than that.

Only two or three thousand of us in the entire province even took the exam. Those who did were participating in one of the French cultural rituals that had become ingrained in Vietnam-

---

* For us, the *baccalauréat* was the *tu tai*, the "talent." One who passed it was a "talent man."

ese thinking. The *baccalauréat* had always been a young Frenchman's entrée into society. For colonial high school students, it was a coveted golden key to privilege and status. The solemnity of the event was underscored by the fact that the examination was to be held in Can Tho—the administrative center for the entire delta, about fifty kilometers to the south of Vinh Long.

Fortunately, my father had a relative living there, and in June of 1964 I arrived at her house, equipped of course with the necessary provisions. This distant relation and I had never seen each other, and she made it clear she was putting up with me out of courtesy, nothing more. But when news came that I had passed the first part of the exam I was suddenly transformed into a prized possession. When I emerged victorious from the second round, I was the pride of the family, nothing less than a budding mandarin. I would be going to the *university*. People around me would pronounce the word carefully, rolling it on their tongues, as if savoring its magic. Of course my father was a teacher—so it ran in the family. But how many barefoot boys from the delta had ever actually gone to study at Saigon?

◊   ◊   ◊

In the Tran Hung Dao interrogation room it is eleven o'clock. I've been talking for two and a half hours. The *can bo* has written down the entire monologue, taking time out only to ask a question here and there or to momentarily work his cramped fingers. Now he stands up, stretches out his right arm, and looks over the pile of papers in front of him. There are fourteen closely written sheets. He hands them to me.

"You can check them," he says.

I'm not interested in checking them. For one thing, I want to let him know that I trust him. For another, if he's written down things I haven't said, to whom am I going to complain? I take the pen he holds out to me and quickly initial each sheet, then sign for them all. My attitude seems to please him. So I take advantage of the moment to ask again the uppermost question: "Why am I here? Why have I been arrested?"

"You'll know in due time," he says. "You can be sure you weren't arrested for nothing. The revolution does not arrest people arbitrarily. We are clarifying the reasons now"—he pats the papers on the desk—"and that will take time. The revolution has just begun. It has many urgent problems to solve, much more important than yours."

"But at least tell me what my mistakes were, so that I can think about them. I want to know if I've been irresponsible or harmful in some way. I don't want to be mistaken for an enemy of the revolution."

Apparently he's surprised that I am using this sort of language. This is the kind of thing he would expect to hear from some party veteran, not from me. He stops tapping his fingers on my file and looks at me for a moment, reflecting. "Well, for example, why was it that you never joined the Front? Millions did . . . why not you?"

"What does that mean," I ask, "that all those who didn't join are traitors? That almost all southerners are reactionaries? All the people who did business with the Americans, and the ones who were dealing opium . . . they're all going to do one month of reeducation, while people who were against the regime but didn't join the Front are going to do long prison terms?* I've been here forty-six days already, and I don't know why. Do you consider that just?"

Just then the bell rings throughout Tran Hung Dao, announcing lunchtime. The *can bo* dismisses me: "Go back to your cell. If you haven't committed any mistakes, you have nothing to fear. But we have to clarify your case, and we'll take as long as we need for it. One year, two years, three years if necessary." He motions for the *bo doi* to take me away. But I throw out one last request: "At least transfer me to a collective cell. I've been alone the whole time. It's too harsh!"

"I'll talk to the director," says the *can bo.*

---

* In the middle of June 1975, former officers and mid- to upper-level people in the Saigon administration were called up for what was ostensibly to be thirty days of "reeducation camp."

On the way back to the cell I ruminate on what I've just heard. There's a little optimism: "If you haven't committed any mistakes, you have nothing to fear." But a lot more pessimism: "One year, two years, three years if necessary." The *can bo* was "absolutely sure" I'd be released. But in three years?

It was less than three and a half months ago that I (along with almost everybody else in the South) was trying to decide what to do, what attitude to take toward the triumphant revolution. I had asked myself, "Should I join them wholeheartedly? Or should I wait and see what is going to happen?" At any rate I was not about to leave the country, as my older brother had pleaded with me to do. "If it turns out to be good," he had said, "we can always come back. But if it's bad, we'll never be able to leave." "No," I had thought, "I should not abandon the country."

But I wasn't ready to give the revolution my unreserved allegiance either. Rather, I would wait for developments to give me some hints about the right course. I considered going back to the land. I even went so far as to buy a small motor cultivator, telling my wife, "My ancestors were peasants. We can find some land around Vinh Long and take the children there." In my mind's eye I could see my parents going back to the delta with us, finding their old friends and relatives there. We would build a house, and the children could play in the arroyo, catching fish.

It was a pipe dream. And now, one and a half months later, I'm walking in front of a teenage *bo doi* dressed in green fatigues who's impatient to have his lunch: "Let's go, number five, move it faster!"

But I didn't move fast enough. And since I wasn't in the cell at sandy-rice time, I wasn't entitled to any. In place of the meal I indulged in a little extra meditation.

4

First Foray
into Politics

Not long after my return to the cell I make a discovery. Hien—the former Communist official—is no longer in number eight. At least there's no response to my repeated whispers. I feel his departure as a loss, not that he participated much in the under-the-door gossip sessions. But I appreciated his strength of character and the dignity with which he bore his imprisonment. His mere presence was a lesson in courage and bearing.

That night I'm awakened by loud scuffling and the sound of voices in the hall. New prisoners coming in: Women are pleading about something, and there's a baby crying. Then a door slams shut—cell number eight. From behind the door comes a muffled crying. Everyone's awake, listening intently.

"Psst! Number eight! Hey, number eight! Who are you?"

At long last the new number eight understands what's happening. A voice reaches out from beneath the door—a woman's voice! They've put one of the women in there. I can sense that everyone is holding his breath, as I am. Somebody asks her why she's been arrested, and right away she begins telling her tale of woe. At first it's difficult to understand; her voice keeps breaking into loud, hiccuping sobs.

"Shhh!" from the prisoners. "Not too much noise. They'll come and punish everyone."

For a bit she's silent, stifling her tears. She's terrified, but wants desperately to talk to someone friendly.

"Can you hear me?" she whispers.

"Yes! that's fine. You can talk like that."

She begins again.

"We tried to escape in a boat . . . there were eighty of us. But somebody denounced us and we were caught. They took my baby. . . . You heard? He's only eighteen months old. Why didn't they leave him with me? The guards put him with my mother, over there with the other women who were with us."

"How come they locked you up alone?"

"Because I was one of the organizers."

This young woman has a refined manner of speaking. It turns out that her husband is the manager of one of Saigon's biggest banks. A friend of theirs told her about someone in Rach Gia who was willing to sell his fishing boat. At a huge price, as it turned out. Several families got the money together and made arrangements for a pilot and provisions. On the set day all the families got to Rach Gia by separate routes, and by nightfall everyone was on the boat, anchored in some isolated spot on the river. Just before they were to leave, two police boats pulled up alongside, and the whole group was arrested. She thinks that either the owner was in collusion with the police all along, or maybe they had attracted attention in Rach Gia, with their city clothes and all the luggage. Either's a possibility. Things like that happen every day.

Long into the night I hear the woman crying to herself. I wonder if she'll be released soon because of her baby. What would they do with a baby in prison? Regardless, by now her house and possessions have already been confiscated. I didn't quite understand whether her husband had been with her.

Even if he hadn't, he has some long reeducation sessions in front of him.

I am moved by the young woman's misfortunes, especially because of her baby. But I don't feel any deep sympathy. She is one of the wealthy people who were trying to get out with what they had instead of staying to help. (This was before the mass exodus began that included people from every economic and political background.) As far as I am concerned, these people are not much better than my immediate neighbor in cell three, Nam Theo. Just a few months ago, he was king of Cholon, Saigon's Chinese quarter, where he controlled many of the movie theaters and nightclubs, and also the gambling dens and brothels. This immensely powerful man has now become meek as a lamb, cringing obsequiously before the least of the *bo dois.* Him I'm not surprised to see in prison. Nor does it surprise me that this woman is here.

But what am *I* doing here?

When someone is arrested for what he considers no reason, his first reaction is indignation. He loudly protests his innocence and demands nothing less than to be released, with apologies. As time passes, he becomes more reasonable. Now he would welcome freedom even if it were accompanied by a kick in the ass. After six weeks of isolation with only sandy pig rice to eat, his vision of happiness consists of a bit of meat or sugar. Or forget the meat and sugar, just give him someone to talk to.

It's like the old Vietnamese tale of the family of twelve living in a one-room house. Tired of listening to the complaints, the father brings a horse into the house. After a few days he takes the horse away, and everyone is ecstatic at the amount of room they never knew they had. It is the same in Tran Hung Dao: The more freedom they take away, the less you desire. I am so alone, and now for some unknown reason they've chained me up again. At this point joy would consist of free hands and companionship.

That happiness comes to me on August 10, 1975, at the end of my seventh week. Tha, one of the *bo dois,* comes into my cell and unlocks the handcuffs, saying, "Get up and get ready. You're going to a collective cell."

I'm in bliss. I stretch my arms, put on my shirt and pants, and walk into the hall. Tha is by far the kindest of the guards I've had to deal with. He talks and laughs easily. He's about my age, and I have the impression that he feels some sympathy for me. I decide to risk a question:

"Sir, can someone stay in jail for three or four years if they haven't committed any crimes?"

Tha turns his head slightly and looks at me with surprise.

"What? Three years? Never! One year at the most. The revolution forgives those who have only made some errors."

We turn left, then right (away from the interrogation offices), then go straight. There's a door on the right hand side of the hall, and here we are: collective cell A. When the door opens, I'm almost knocked over by the stench that pours out of the room. The cell is long and narrow, with dozens of prisoners standing at attention, packed together like sardines. My first reaction is a fervent wish that I were back in number five, where at least I had a couple of square meters of space. Suddenly I feel very tired.

"So," says a voice from the crowd, "a new guest for our luxury hotel!"

Then another voice cries out, "Hey, I know him! That's Doan Van Toai. . . . He's a Vietcong sympathizer." I can place that voice, and I know the face attached to it: his name is Rang, one of the secret police who used to follow me around occasionally during the student movement days.

Tha, the *bo doi*, shuts everybody up.

"The new prisoner will sleep here," he says, pointing to the place nearest the door on the cement bench that runs the length of the room. This is the choicest spot in the cell because of the draft that comes in under the door.

"The new prisoner is a special case," announces Tha. "He is exempt from any tasks."

Everyone is surprised by these declarations, no one more than I. I am mortified and stare at Tha. Why is he doing this to me? Again Tha indicates the spot next to the door. "The prisoner who used to sleep here will sleep somewhere else. This is Doan Van Toai's place!"

I am completely flustered. I don't know what kind of attitude I should take, or what I should do. As I set my bundle down I can hear the murmuring of my new cellmates: "He's an informer, a *cho san.*" How can I possibly get out from under this lovely introduction?

Then a familiar voice pulls me out of my anxiety: "Well, number five, so here you are too!" The voice I recognize immediately, and now I have a face to put with it. Nguyen Van Hien, the party veteran from cell number eight. He's unusually short, maybe four feet ten—and his smile sparkles: Every single one of his teeth is capped with gold. Afterward you notice the eyes, hard and penetrating. They seem to unmask you.

"Hah!" says one of the prisoners. "The informer's talking to the informer." Hien turns toward the speaker and fixes him with those eyes. His past and his dignity are such that the entire group is cowed into silence.

"Toai is a patriot," he says simply.

The tension suddenly dissolves and is replaced by a loud hubbub of talk, the normal noise level in this packed cell, as I will learn. The man whose place I'm supposed to take stoops to remove his things from next to the door. But I stop him, determined to recover from the "blessing" the *bo doi* Tha has bestowed on me.

"*Ong,*" I say, "stay there. It's your place. I'll sleep on the ground."

The prisoner, a man of about fifty, objects: "The *bo doi*'s order has to be obeyed," he says.

"I'll be responsible for it," I tell him, sitting down on the floor to claim a place. "This is fine, I'll wait until something else opens up on the bench."

My attitude further reduces the distrust Tha's introduction has sown and wins me a friendly welcome from the cell leader, an older man by the name of Nguyen The Thao, whom I will eventually get to know well. Thao has spent twenty-seven of his sixty-two years in prison, a guest successively of the French, the Saigon dictators, and now the revolution. "My father," he is fond of saying, "is Chi Hoa; my mother is Con Son"—Chi

Hoa is Saigon's central prison; Con Son, the infamous prison island that was home for Thieu's tiger cages.

Collective cell A is long and narrow, about fifty feet long by fifteen wide, with a high ceiling. At the far end is a tiny room with a hole in the floor and a faucet. Down the length of the right wall is the cement sleeping bench, which takes up almost two-thirds of the floor area, leaving a corridor six or seven feet wide in which cell A's inhabitants may take turns standing or walking a few steps. The cell might once have housed twenty prisoners without too much squeezing. My arrival has raised the population to an even sixty.

As I look around, it dawns on me that I have been here before. This is one of the places I was locked up in briefly by Thieu's police. I remember having carved my name on the wall somewhere, and I begin to search. A third of the way down the wall I find what I'm looking for. An accretion of grafitti has obscured "Doan" and "Van," but "Toai" is still just about legible. I am struck by the weird coincidence, and the irony. I turn to Hien, the Communist with the gold teeth, "You know, when I was locked up here in 1970 I was proud of myself. Now I'm not even sure whether I should be proud or ashamed. It's the strangest feeling."

"Tell me about it," he says. "It'll do you good to talk it over." And so, leaning my head close to his, in a low voice I begin to tell him about my hectic life as a student in Saigon.

◊   ◊   ◊

After passing the *baccalauréat* in 1964, I left Vinh Long for the great adventure of Saigon. My older brother was now established in the capital, and I was to live with him and his family for the duration of my studies.

When the semester started I registered at the school of pharmacy. It wasn't that I felt any particular vocation to be a pharmacist. But the course of study there was shorter than in the medical school, and jobs were a good deal easier to find than they were for graduates in humanities or law.

But I found out quickly that it wasn't a good choice. The

spirit of the pharmacy school was unbelievably antiquated, to say nothing of its curriculum and pedagogical methods. The whole enterprise was a carbon copy of the French system of the thirties, which itself probably dated to the nineteenth century. What was worse, almost all the courses were still given in French. I was unhappy with this for practical reasons (I had found that my French was not as good as that of students who had gone through school in Saigon). But more significant, here was another instance of the colonial mentality that France had left us with. My increasingly nationalistic sensibilities were outraged by this kind of proof that we were still subservient to the foreigners who had enslaved the country for so long. The pharmacy professors were like trained parrots, who went on repeating the formulas left to them by a departed master.

These professors constituted a small and jealous caste, vastly more interested in preserving their authority and in limiting the number of graduate pharmacists than they were in teaching. So they assiduously multiplied the obstacles facing the students. One of their methods of making things more difficult (and more profitable for themselves) was to duplicate sheets of their lecture notes and sell them at a good price. From one year to the next they would change a few segments of their courses, so that lecture sheets from previous years could not be used. It was a system that favored the students with money and penalized everyone else.

Examinations too were arbitrary and unfair. At the end of the first year, only two out of the eight examination topics were common to all the candidates. These two were tested in writing. Then individual students were tested on other topics chosen by lot. And these other examinations were oral, in French of course. The whole system was designed to favor those who could afford lecture notes and those who had attended the better French lycées—also those toward whom the professors felt indulgent. And this was no small matter in the rigidly stratified social world that South Vietnam was in the nineteen-sixties. In Vietnam, unlike the United States, a pharmacist was a person of considerable wealth and prestige. The professors, almost all of whom came from the monied and educated classes, recognized some of the pharmacy students as their own people. Others clearly were not.

This situation might have been especially created to excite my indignation, and to start me thinking about what might be done. The first thing that occurred to me was that the students didn't have to be reliant on the professors' note sheets; there was no reason we couldn't produce our own. Before long I had organized note taking, and we were copying them commercially ourselves.

That started the ball rolling. Once we realized we could organize ourselves and raise a few dollars it was a short step to the idea of a student newspaper through which we could voice our complaints and mobilize support for other reforms. And so *Hoa Sung* was born, the pharmacy students' newspaper, whose name was an untranslatable play on the words *flower* and *gun*. The name alluded to plants, the pet subject of every pharmacy student; it also suggested our aversion to the military rule that had emerged from the debris of Ngo Dinh Diem's government.

Since the coup, South Vietnam's political life had become a military carnival. Diem had been followed by a triumvirate of generals (Tran Van Don, "Big" Minh, and Le Van Kim), who were themselves overthrown several months later by another general, Nguyen Khanh. Khanh had first established a civilian government under his control. Then he set up a trio of military people, including himself, "Big" Minh—whom he had recently unseated—and yet another general, Tranh Thien Khiem. After several months these new rulers had fallen out, and Khanh alone remained. But not for long. His own turn came in February of 1965, when enemies (this time a colonel and a general) toppled him.* The leaders of this coup never took power, though. They were outmaneuvered by Nguyen

---

* The colonel was Pham Ngoc Thao, one of the most fascinating and enigmatic figures of the time. Thao had been a province chief, head of the "strategic hamlet" program and one of the leading anti-Diem plotters. After the Diem coup, he was promoted to chief of military security for South Vietnam's army. Unknown to either his army colleagues or the American reporters for whom he was a major source, Thao was all along a Vietcong agent. His story is told in *A Vietcong Memoir* by Truong Nhu Tang, the Vietcong minister of justice.

Cao Ky and Nguyen Van Thieu, who were to run the country until its final debacle.

Each of these generals had his own entourage of politicians and military people, and each clique labored mightily to woo the Americans. With such a succession of nonentities, play-boys, and corrupt botchers ruling the country, Doc Lap (Inde-pendence) Palace had become entirely dependent on the United States. To those of us watching this pitiful farce from close up, it seemed that the whole fragile edifice of government would have collapsed in a welter of incompetence except for American aid, military support, and (beginning in March 1965) active intervention. Without it, the southern regimes would likely have given way to the NLF by default.

Curiously, these developments gave rise to a certain nostal-gia for Ngo Dinh Diem. For all his faults, in retrospect he began to seem like a patriot. At least one could say that he hadn't kowtowed to the United States. "The Americans got rid of him"—that didn't sound like too bad an epitaph.

At any rate, it was glaringly obvious now that a "recoloniza-tion" was going on, different from French colonialism in many ways, but the same in essentials: Vietnam was again dom-inated by foreigners who were using the country for their own purposes. The Americans, it was true, were not economic plunderers, as the French had been. They had come, as they put it, "to protect South Vietnam's people from Communist aggression." In fact, it seemed clear to me and to my friends that they were here because Vietnam had a role to play in America's own worldwide confrontation with communism. As far as we could see, care for the Vietnamese people had pre-cious little to do with it.

After Nguyen Van Thieu took power in 1965, that impres-sion was driven home. Before then, the Americans had tried hard to remain in the background. Then came the invasion of GIs. Tens of thousands at first, then hundreds of thousands. They urinated from the tops of their tanks and littered the streets with Coca-Cola cans. Overnight there was an epidemic of bars. Prostitutes appeared in amazing numbers. The country was flooded with consumer goods that people hadn't even dreamed about before. Theft became a national industry. Goods stolen from the army PX stores reappeared in the heart of Saigon, in the famous "thieves market"—everything from sunglasses to refrigerators, from combat uniforms to the most sophisticated cameras. Everyone stole.

A story went around that always drew a laugh from Vietnamese, about a warehouse that had been robbed so often that the Americans decided to install an automatic surveillance camera . . . so the thieves stole the camera. There were other funny stories too: about the GI and his Vietnamese live-in girlfriend, who would first bring her poor sick mother to stay, then the children of a sister who had supposedly been killed in a bomb attack, and finally a "brother," who was in fact the woman's real lover.

But it was gallows humor. The humor of a country that was coming apart. Most people watched with dismay as their society began to disintegrate. But the sadness had no outlet, except for disgust at Vietnamese who took part in the pillage—and resentment toward the Americans. The French predecessors of these new Westerners had been domineering and bigoted exploiters. But while the Americans' motives might not have been so venal, their presence was proving even more destructive. The French at least had brought with them an ancient culture, which many Vietnamese found they could appreciate in some ways. French culture had indeed superimposed itself on upper-class Vietnamese life. But Vietnam's traditional social structure had been left largely intact. Now something else was happening, something more pervasive; less comprehensible and consequently more ominous. The Americans' material power was overwhelming, crushing, devoid of culture—except for a democratic ideal, which was grotesquely caricatured by Saigon's rulers.

One didn't have to be a Communist to feel frightened and humiliated by the degradation that was taking hold so rapidly. And angered. Among the students, there was continual discussion and debate about these things. As increasing numbers of

American troops poured into the country, the complexity of events seemed to present a simple choice: American recolonization, or Vietnamese communism. Many of the students distrusted the system that was operating in the North. But at least Ho Chi Minh was Vietnamese.

Since arriving in Saigon, I had been reading the more or less secret Communist literature that circulated from hand to hand. I was especially impressed by a biography of Ho Chi Minh; his austerity and idealism were such a contrast to the miserable opportunism of the Southern generals. Who had ever seen Ho or Pham Von Dong (North Vietnam's premier) scrambling to enrich themselves, or humbling themselves in front of Americans? Who had ever seen them humble themselves in front of anybody?

As the months passed, *Hoa Sung* began moving from professional issues to political criticism. It was inevitable. We were demanding a "Vietnamization" of education. But that presupposed a will to independence.

The magazine's sections on pharmacy and Vietnamese culture were complemented by a section that allowed students to express their political views. The overall theme was that at this juncture in the nation's history, students could not just sit around and study. They were morally obligated to involve themselves in the effort to "save the country" from the dictatorships that were destroying it (national salvation movements are a Vietnamese political tradition).

We translated articles from the foreign press that were critical of the Saigon regime, and we wrote our own. An early piece I wrote that made a strong impact and gave me a taste for the pleasures of writing was called "Peace on the Ruins." In it I pictured the war as two brothers fighting viciously and destroying their own house in the process. When they finally agree to stop they look around and see that everything's been lost in the ruin they've made.

For this article I drew on the vivid impressions of the war's devastation that I received as a student interviewer during the summer of 1966. Responding to an announcement on the student union bulletin board for a job that involved working with war refugees, I met several American students who had organized a research project. Their leader was a tall, humorous, quick-moving young man named Jerry Tinker, who indicated that the project had been initiated by the American Senator Kennedy. I didn't know which Kennedy, but I found the name impressive. Tinker seemed to be almost Vietnamese in his joking, talkative manner. I was also struck by his obvious interest in Vietnamese culture and by his care for the effects of the war—completely different from the GIs, so many of whom paraded their scorn for the country everywhere they went.*

The job required interviewing war refugees in central Vietnam who were sustaining themselves on government aid. I talked with hundreds and hundreds of people, walking into the shantytowns and refugee centers and identifying myself simply as a Saigon University student who wanted to understand their lives and aspirations. The more contact I had with these desperately poor people, the more I hated the government. I discovered that almost invariably they had been forced out of their homes by the Saigon army, and that even though they were being fed by the government, their hearts were clearly on the other side. Listening to them tell about their destroyed homes and the atrocities they had witnessed (and endured), I could feel myself becoming more committed to the need to "do something."

The most immediate path was through the pharmacy magazine, which was becoming ever more political. But though we were now intruding on dangerous ground, for the time being we were protected from official repercussions by the anarchy that prevailed on Saigon's streets. Several times my friends and I had joined the mobs of demonstrators, marching down Norodom Street, chanting, "Down with Khanh! Down with Khanh!" The police would charge, and we would scatter, regrouping to take up the march until the next police sally. Such

* Tinker later was to become an aide to Senator Kennedy and counsel to the U.S. Senate Subcommittee on Immigration and Refugees.

At eighteen, a first-year pharmacy student

confrontations were not terribly dangerous, yet. But that too would change shortly.

As political activism became more a part of my life, I began having serious second thoughts about becoming a pharmacist. I was not immune to the guarantee of a solid income that came with a degree in pharmacy. But the field offered none of the satisfaction that I was already deriving in a small way from political activity.

These considerations led me to register in the law school, which along with the school of letters was open to any high school graduate. Law students were required only to be enrolled and to take the examinations. Attendance at lectures was optional, and one could study from the lecture notes, which were published and circulated almost as a correspondence course is in the West. As a result, army officers, government functionaries, teachers, managers, and others looking for a second career or promotion through education enrolled. While I kept up with my pharmaceutical studies, I found both the courses and the professors at the law school far more stimulating, more in touch with the world as I was beginning to see it.

As the war escalated, Saigon's university students became increasingly politicized. Only five thousand or so (out of about thirty thousand) were politically active, but almost all of these more or less openly favored the National Liberation Front. There were also a few hundred anti-Communist student militants, but even they had nothing good to say about Khanh or his successors, Nguyen Van Thieu and Nguyen Cao Ky. By 1967 all the members of the union's executive board were NLF sympathizers. And so was I.

◊   ◊   ◊

Bowing his head in my direction, Hien is listening attentively to this story of my days as a fledgling student militant.

"And do you remember," he asks, "exactly what the Front was saying at that time?"

Do I remember? They were saying that there had to be negotiations to end the war. They were saying there had to be a coalition government that would represent all political opinions. They were saying that civil liberties had to be restored, and that there had to be talks on reunifying the country. Most of all they were saying there had to be a policy of national reconciliation. That was the major issue. Even the worst puppet collaborators had to be forgiven so that we could have national harmony when the fighting was over.

I remember all this only too well. I remember too the Front's insistence that unification could come about only after a long period of readaptation. The South and the North were "equal brothers" who had to respect each other's different social, economic, and political systems.

I'm running over the Front's program in my mind. Like everyone, I know it so well. "To promulgate all democratic freedoms," "To grant amnesty to all political detainees," "To abolish all concentration camps of any type whatsoever," "To strictly ban all illegal arrests and imprisonments." During the war it was a shining beacon compared to the dictator's paradise we were living in.

The corners of Hien's mouth curl up slightly in the hint of a smile. His gaze barely filters through his narrowed eyes. We are squatting next to each other, pressed close together by the crush of unwashed bodies in the cell.

"So? . . . so?" he says. "And what do you make of all that now?" Has it really taken this clear-sighted Communist fellow prisoner to get me to this point? To this question? I feel a flush of intense embarrassment, the dull student who has to be forced to see the obvious. But is this gold-tipped smile suggesting that we've *all* been taken in—the Front, the students, the "third force" nationalists,* the Buddhists? Look around you, stupid . . . what do you see?

See? I don't know what I see. But I can hear Mrs. Ngo Ba Thanh, the oppositionist international law expert, blasting the dictators in front of the foreign press. And I can hear the Buddhist leader Venerable Tri Quang electrifying the silent throng

* *Third force* was a term used loosely to describe political activists who were associated with neither the Saigon government nor the Front.

of believers before sending them down to the street. I can also hear my own voice breaking through . . . lecturing in my broken English about South Vietnam's right to self-determination to crowds of American university students in California at the end of 1970. And I can hear with special clarity Pham Hung, the politburo secretary, addressing the Great Spring Victory celebration crowd in front of Doc Lap Palace three months ago, on May 15: "All Vietnamese are the victors. Everyone with Vietnamese blood should take pride in the common victory of the whole nation. . . . Only the American imperialists are the losers."

"The only losers are the American imperialists!" But here I am, squatting inside this boxcar with a sweating horde of southerners—no, Hien's from Hanoi; how many others are?— guarded by these teenage northern army *bo dois*. My facial muscles must be doing contortions.

"I see you're doing some thinking," says Hien, flashing his smile. "Good, you've got a lot to learn. Just don't say anything out loud." And he turns toward his neighbor on the other side with a joke, as if we have just finished an ordinary conversation.

Time passes. My new knowledge has taken root and has begun to shoulder into previous convictions. Not that anyone can tell; the routine in collective cell A is always the same, and who knows what revolutions may be going on inside the head of one's fellow sardines? I've been sleeping on the floor here for two weeks now, still eating the two bowls of sandy rice a day, rinsing it down with water just like everybody else.

Every day is the same—except Friday. On Friday the cell wakes up to anxiety. That's the day a *bo doi* appears with a list of names to read out: "So-and-so, so-and-so, so-and-so! Prepare to leave the cell. Take everything that belongs to you!"

No one knows what happens to those who are called. The cell's optimists say they are being freed. Most think they are being transferred to a camp. Almost everyone believes in his heart that the camps are worse than the jails. But nobody says it. On the contrary, they all want to think that the camps are better, that those who leave the cell are better off. "Camp can't be worse than this! You can probably move around as much as you want. Being cooped up like this makes you crazy!"

But Hien whispers to me, "If they're going to a camp, they're going to die. I know. I ran a camp back in nineteen fifty-seven. I'd rather stay here the rest of my life . . . electric lights, toilets, food . . . you don't have to do anything and they still feed you, more or less. The camps are out in the jungle. You work like a dog for your food, and there's no medicine. Everyone gets sick—beriberi, malaria, dysentery, the worst. That means you die. There's no question about it."

On the third Friday Nguyen Van Thang's name is called. Thang is an ancient, white-haired Communist—eighty-two years old, he's told me. I've tried to engage him in conversation ever since I found out who he was. He's been a party member since the end of the 1920s, one of the historic leaders of Vietnamese communism. He had been in Hong Kong in 1930 with Ho Chi Minh, heading one of the factions that joined together to form the Indochinese Communist party. Thang seldom speaks, but on a couple of occasions I've been able to draw him out.

One of these times I've gotten him to talk about Ho Chi Minh. "A remarkable leader," he says, "a great militant! But, you know, the party history's been modified quite a bit so that he gets all the credit. Ho worked for the Comintern for many years—he lived all over: France, Russia, China. He didn't come back to Vietnam until nineteen forty-four when everything was prepared. Most of us had been fighting inside the country for twenty years and had taken a lot of risks. But he was only in jail for one long period, in China in forty-two and forty-three for about a year. But he was the one who took power—because he was the one Stalin trusted."

I am fascinated by this white-haired veteran of practically the whole struggle for Vietnam's independence. And by his present fate. What crime can he possibly have committed? What secret does he carry around with him? It occurs to me that perhaps Thang has already revealed it to me. Perhaps it's precisely because he's been a witness to so much.

But I don't know, and Thang hasn't opened up more. In spite of what has happened to him—and after the revolution's triumph at that—he's still a loyal party member. The old militant, resigned to being treated like dirt if it's in the higher interest of the party. He's a type I've never come across before . . . though I'll find out later they're not that rare.

When his name is called, he remains motionless for a moment, and I see his hands tremble. A few days earlier he has told me that the only thing he fears is being "displaced to the North." Seeing him gather his things and obey the *bo doi*'s barked order wrenches me. As he walks slowly out of the cell I remember something else he told me: "I've never eaten chocolate," he said. "I'll probably never know what it tastes like."

5

This Tet Is Different

Several days later the door opens and the *bo doi* Tha appears.
"Doan Van Toai! Follow me!"

I'm not sure what to make of him at this point. I had thought Tha was friendly, but his peculiar way of introducing me to cell A certainly wasn't meant to do me any good. On the other hand, I don't think he would have said those things gratuitously. I've already decided he was carrying out orders. Whatever the case, it looks as though I've got another interrogation in front of me.

To my surprise, instead of taking me to one of the interrogation offices, Tha asks me to sit down at a table in a hallway alcove. He wants me to help him copy lists of prisoners. Now I'm really perplexed. This is a sign of trust if I've ever seen one. But maybe he's got some trick up his sleeve. Experience has made me wary.

Later, back in the cell I ask Hien for advice. With each day he's become more of a friend and confidant.

"It means," Hien tells me, "that Tha probably handles a gun better than a pen, and he'd like somebody else do the work. But there's no way he could have made the decision himself. A *can bo* must have authorized it. So that means one of two things: Either they want to see if you can be trusted—in which case they'll try to use you as an informer. Or else they've decided your case isn't that serious—in which case they might be planning to release you soon."

Hearing Hien—the former camp chief—say this makes my heart race.

The next morning, and the mornings following, Tha comes for me to help with the transcribing. Until the eleven o'clock meal I conscientiously copy names, dates of birth, and dates of arrest, hundreds of them. Of course Tha has sworn me to absolute secrecy. But the fact that I am sharing forbidden knowledge helps my relationship with him grow into a kind of comradeship. I try my best to encourage this trust. In the back of my mind I've been mulling over a plan.

One day I decide it's time to broach the subject—indirectly.

"Brother Tha," I ask him, "are you by any chance married?"

"No," he laughs, "I never had time for it. What about you?"

"Yes, I've got a wife and three children." Now for the question. "I keep thinking about them. Especially my kids . . . they must be wondering where I've disappeared to. Do you know why it's forbidden to send a message?"

It's certainly not the first time Tha has heard this question. The answer is probably stated prominently in the elementary courses for prison guards—the 1975 version for liberated Vietnam.

"It's because prisoners here are only temporary. As long as their cases aren't clarified, they have to remain isolated. When their investigation is over, then they can write their families."

"But I've already been questioned, and I've been locked up for more than two months. My wife doesn't have any idea what's happened to me. At least if I could let her know I'm alive—only that I'm alive. What harm could that do the investigation? And it would be better for the revolution. Otherwise people think that prisoners are being secretly eliminated. People have got to trust the revolution."

This last is something Tha can understand. It's a militant's language, expressing the kind of attitude I picked up from old Thang. Whatever my own merits are or aren't, it's the revolution that counts. I can see Tha thinking it over. To make it easier for him, I take a slightly different tack.

"There's something else I'd like to tell you. . . . But I don't dare."

Happy for a chance to show his benevolence, Tha smiles at me.

"What's that? You have to dare! You were an activist, weren't you? Don't tell me you've lost your courage."

"Well . . . it's a personal matter."

"So?" He's indulgent now, "Don't worry about telling me. If I can help you, I will. If I can't, I'll say I can't."

"It's my mother, really. I'd like to get a few words to my mother." In fact, I've already managed to scribble a message to my mother during one of Tha's absences from the alcove. I hand it to Tha.

"Read it, see if you can accept it . . . out of humaneness. I have no one to help me but you. I trust you. It would mean so much to her."

It's a huge gamble. This is as dangerous for him as for me. He can denounce me immediately to the *can bo* for trying to corrupt him (even though I've promised nothing explicit—just that "it would mean so much"). Or, he can do it, out of kindness, and out of curiosity about just how "much" it might mean. He's hesitant to take the piece of paper in his hand. Just accepting it will make him my accomplice, which means I'd be able to cause him trouble.

I can see the caution in his eyes. He's almost visibly weighing the risks. There's no one around; I've chosen the moment carefully. I look straight at him, conveying all the friendship and trust I'm capable of. He unfolds the paper:

Dear Mom,
    I am in Tran Hung Dao. I am in good health. I need money and clothes. You can send them to me with the bearer of this letter. Don't worry. I think I may be released soon.
                               Toai

After scanning it quickly, Tha folds the letter up and shoves it into his pocket. In a low voice he says, "I'm not promising anything, but I'll do what I can."

I've won! I give him the name and address. He repeats them to me, making a mental note of them.

For the next few days Tha comes to get me for work as usual, as if nothing has happened. Then one morning while I'm copying one of the interminable lists, he slips a rolled-up paper to me. When he whispers, "Don't call me *bo* [the informal "you"] anymore," I know our clandestine relationship has been confirmed.

I wait on pins and needles all day, praying for night to come. It's only then, after the cell is snoring away, that I tiptoe through the bodies to the toilet room to examine this precious message. There are a few words from my mother, a short letter from my wife—the children are fine—and money. Thirty thousand piasters! A true fortune!

The next morning, sitting next to Tha at the table, I slip ten thousand piasters into his pocket.

"Don't refuse," I say softly. "You've helped me a lot. Let me help you a little, so that maybe you can get married one of these days. I can't do anything here with all this money anyhow." I'm calling him *bo*, ignoring the warning from yesterday.

"But it's not possible, not possible," Tha stammers. "That's corruption, it's a sin against the revolution."

I reassure him: "What do you mean, a sin? You didn't ask me for anything. All you've done is an act of kindness—delivering my letter and bringing me my mother's. So I've decided to share what I've received, out of my own free will. If that's a sin, it's mine, not yours."

For a moment Tha continues to act embarrassed. But it's

clear his scruples are dissolving fast. We keep working, and soon it's as if nothing has happened.

That night I have a hard time falling asleep. Ordinarily, I drop off easily, thinking about my wife and my boys. But tonight they are more alive than ever in the bedtime movies playing in my head. It's the letter, I know. I try to imagine what happened after they got my note. What did they say to each other? What has Yvonne (my wife) told Dinh (at four, my oldest) about why his father hasn't been home? I begin to wander through memories of other and better times: our marriage, the family celebrations, holiday gatherings, Tet—the Vietnamese new year. Then, unbidden, the memories come of Tet *Mau Than*, Tet in the year of the monkey. The terrible Tet of 1968.

◊   ◊   ◊

Tet! The whole country was on the move. By 1968 the war had emptied hundreds of villages and swollen the cities with refugees. It had scattered families and summoned more than a million men to arms. Tet was the time for the dispersed to regather. The refugee returned to his village, the civil servant disappeared from his office, the soldier moved heaven and earth for a leave. If necessary, he departed without one. In Vietnam, Tet is the time for family togetherness. Parents and children pray in front of the ancestors' altar, parade their new clothes, feast, and exchange gifts and visits. It's the time when people plunge into debt for the whole year so the family can flaunt the rarest holiday dishes. On Tet, everyone is rich.

Out in the countryside, New Year's Day can easily last a week. Why indeed should something this good end at all? The peasants spice up the holiday with cockfights and bullfights, pitting village against village in a raucous carnival of betting, arguments, and laughter. A popular song suggests that for some, Tet lasts four months:

January's the month for family rejoicing.
February's for playing card games.

March is the month that's meant for drinking.
April's the time for falling in love.
In May you have to go back to the fields.

I had left Saigon on my Suzuki motorcycle at about 4:00
P.M. the day before Tet, my little niece Ngan Khanh on the
back seat clinging to my shirt. Vinh Long was 130 kilometers
to the south, but I was fairly sure we could cover it in time for
a late dinner at my parents' house.

Traffic that afternoon was indescribable. Overloaded buses,
their doors open so that extra passengers could hang pre-
cariously from the steps, Lambretta three-wheel vehicles into
whose ten-passenger space fifteen or sixteen people were piled,
military trucks carrying as many women and children as soldiers, bicycles, pedicabs, taxis, private cars. A noisy, honking
armada converging on the two-lane highway connecting Saigon with the delta.

My little motorcycle managed to extricate us without too
much trouble from the jam in Saigon's outskirts. Zigzagging
around muddy potholes and hundreds of stalled vehicles, we
maneuvered along the narrow, half-flooded road until the traffic began to loosen up several miles out of town. Below My
Tho the rice fields glimmered a liquid bluegreen in the late afternoon sun, relieved here and there by groves of coconut trees
that we quickly passed as we picked up speed. Every two or
three miles came the observation towers, their sentries sil-
houetted against the sky. At longer intervals soldiers manned
checkpoints, cradling M16s in their arms and watching the
traffic flow by unhindered. Even they seemed relaxed, no more
than traffic cops now that the traditional Tet truce had set in.

We arrived in Vinh Long around 8:00 P.M. to find my
parents, my sister, and my sister's little boy Chung waiting ex-
pectantly. My mother delighted in having two of her grandchildren to play with and spoil, loading Ngan Khanh and little
Chung with treats and presents. My father seemed to find me
more mature, drawing me out about my studies and events in
the capital. We all listened to the radio as President Thieu

broadcast his new year's greetings, alluding to a verse in which the popular poet To Xuong hoped that "the king, the bureaucracy, and even the workers might live like human beings in the New Year."

We also listened in to Hanoi Radio's broadcast of Ho Chi Minh's new year wishes. Uncle Ho also turned to poetry for the occasion, reading a poem he had composed especially for this Tet:

> Xuan Nay Khac han cac xuan qua
> Tien len toan thang at ve ta.
> (This Tet is different from the others.
> Forward, march! Victory is ours.)

We should have listened more closely to the words, instead of just registering the familiar, martial style. But neither the Doan family nor anyone else knew that Ho's poem was a coded signal setting in motion a massive NLF and northern army offensive (much as the BBC's "long sobs of the violins" had announced the Normandy invasion to the French underground in 1944).

Happy in our ignorance, at midnight we ate the traditional "saying-good-bye-to-the-ancestors" meal. Afterward my father showed me the clothes he would wear to greet a teacher friend of his who was to visit in the early morning hours, the first guest of the new year. This friend's appearance would be auspicious, auguring good luck for the coming twelve months. If by some chance a person of less praiseworthy qualities happened by the house first, the whole year might turn out badly.

Tet's first visitors were not the ones Father expected. Several sharp cracking sounds had me bolt upright in bed before I even knew I was awake. Other shots were bursting as I rushed to the window to see what was happening. Peering over the sill, I made out black shapes hunching along the sides of the neighboring house. I thought to myself, "Troi oi [Oh, God], it's another coup," figuring that the shapes must be rebel soldiers on their way to attack the local army garrison.

My mother and father celebrating Tet

By this time everyone in the house was crawling along the floor, trying to find each other in the dark. I helped my father push furniture up against the door, then we gathered the family into the back bedroom. After a while the firing sounded farther off, but we stayed hunkered down behind the furniture barricades. The children lay still, frightened but woozy with sleep. From time to time one of them would open her eyes wide and ask why we were on the floor instead of in bed.

By dawn the sounds of shooting had been off in the distance for a long time, and I decided to look around outside to see what I could learn. Poking through the backyard down toward the arroyo, suddenly I found two AK-47 muzzles pointed at my stomach. Holding the rifles were two boys, maybe fifteen or sixteen years old. They seemed bewildered and afraid. Both of them were soaked up to the armpits of their black pajamas; obviously they had been hiding in the water for some time, maybe since the fighting had first flared up.

"Is there anyone in front of the house?" asked one.

"No, there isn't," I answered, trying hard to keep my voice calm. "Are you hungry, would you like something to eat?" I forced a smile, hoping a display of friendship might help quiet their nerves.

They glanced at each other and stared at me for a moment, not knowing if this might be a trick. But they were famished. Inside they wolfed down a couple of bowls of sticky Tet rice, then left without a word to search for their comrades. They were like apparitions, these Vietcong fighters, materializing from our backyard, then disappearing as if they had never been. It hadn't occurred to me that the Front's dreaded guerrillas might take the form of two frightened adolescents.

After that our neighborhood was relatively quiet. The battle had shifted to Vinh Long's downtown section, where it would flare, die down some, then flare again. But several hours into the morning the sounds started moving back in our direction. As we listened, the thud of artillery and the staccato hammering of small arms seemed to be walking slowly toward us. We had to make a decision about what to do. I went outside to see if I could find some of the neighbors, to see what they were doing, when a shell exploded about sixty feet away, hurling me to the ground. As I picked myself up, planes roared in, dropping bombs in the direction of the approaching battle.

I retreated hastily into the house and crawled inside the makeshift bunker we had built with our furniture, afraid to go back out. All that day and night we stayed where we were, eating what was left of our fancy Tet dishes while bombs and shells tore into the neighborhood. During one lull in the fighting, my father ventured out to bury some of his most valued possessions in the garden. Otherwise we huddled together, praying that the fighting would shift its course.

The next morning I made a quick reconnaissance of the houses around us and realized that all our neighbors had fled. The battle was dangerously near. It sounded as though the government soldiers had repelled the Vietcong from the center of Vinh Long and were pushing them toward us. Shells were now exploding closer to us and more regularly. It was time to get out.

As everyone got their things together, I put on the new clothes I had brought with me for Tet—three new suits, one on top of the other. My parents thought I was crazy. They were experienced at these things, and they always wore their oldest rags, afraid of robbers or desperate fellow-refugees who might attack someone who looked prosperous. But though I was sweating rivers, I was determined to save the suits.

Finally, we all managed to load ourselves onto the motorcycle. My sister straddled the gas tank in front of me with the children, my mother rode behind, and my father behind her, intermittently sliding off to run alongside when the overloaded machine threatened to stop altogether. I drove slowly down the path along the arroyo, listening to the straining engine and hoping it wouldn't give out. We had hardly gone more than two or three hundred yards when explosions rocked the area we had just left. For a brief instant we stopped, looking back. Tears streamed down my mother's cheeks. This was her third house to be destroyed. In a quiet, trembling voice she said to my father, "We're too old to start again." My father just stared, unable to find a word of comfort for her.

In a moment we were moving again, toward the arched bridge over the arroyo. Bursts of gunfire sprayed out from somewhere nearby, though I couldn't make out any soldiers. The area around our end of the bridge was alive with the whine and smack of bullets. Lying over to the left were several people, screaming. A man's shirtfront was stained crimson. A pregnant woman lay still on her back next to him, her belly protruding. Farther off other bodies were twisted into awkward positions on the ground. A bullet slammed into the motorcycle's rear tire, and we were crawling toward the bridge, trying to shield Ngan Khanh and Chung with our bodies.

We moved across the bridge on our hands and knees, no longer in the middle of the firing. On the other side we got up and ran, the shooting and cries for help receding behind us. I was bathing in sweat. Then we crossed a second bridge, finding ourselves in a quiet district where one of my mother's sisters lived. For the next ten days we stayed with her family.

Our cousin's neighborhood was an oasis, a kind of no-man's-land spared from destruction by fate. Vietcong troops in their black pajamas passed through, retreating from the government army. But there was no shooting, and we never saw the government soldiers from whom they were fleeing. The day after we arrived, a rumor spread that the Front was going to make a stand in the neighborhood. Everybody in the area crowded into the Catholic parish church, as if they believed its walls would offer protection. At midmorning three Front soldiers appeared in the doorway and stood there without speaking. Though older than the two Vietcong behind our house, they seemed just as much at a loss. After they left, people began filtering back to their homes.

The fighting went on for five days, as government artillery and planes blasted the Front back from one position after another. The radio reported that the Vietcong were being forced out of Saigon with heavy losses, and that fighting was still raging throughout the country, especially around Hue.* Another week and a half passed in relative calm. Then the Front army attempted another assault on Vinh Long. But within a few days this too petered away.

When we were sure the fighting was over, I went back to the old neighborhood to pick through the ruins of our house and see what might be salvaged. But except for some blackened debris there was nothing left. I was glad my parents hadn't come.

---

* Hue, the ancient imperial capital, was held by Vietcong and North Vietnamese forces for twenty-three days.

It would have broken their hearts. The house next door had also been hit, though some of it was still standing. In what had been the front room I made out the remains of a coffin still enclosing the charred and fragile form of its occupant. The old woman whose house it was had died just before Tet and had been awaiting burial when the battle started. There was no sign of any of her relatives. Corpses with swollen bellies lay everywhere, in the streets and in the wreckage of their homes. The stench was intolerable. It clung to my nostrils. The city was an eerie and strangely quiet ruin. Most of its people had fled to the countryside.

With nothing left for us in Vinh Long, we decided to go to Saigon. From the central post office I called my brother and listened to him say, "Bring everyone up." At least our mother and father could live in my brother's house while they decided on the next step.

When we got up to the capital, fighting was still going on in some of the outlying districts. Tet had treated Saigon even more harshly than it had Vinh Long. Deaths numbered in the thousands. Back at the university I found that perhaps fifty of my more militant fellow students had joined the Vietcong, believing that this would be the ultimate battle, the "general offensive and general uprising" that the Front had promised for so long. Like the Vietcong fighters, they had believed the people were just waiting for an opportunity to rise up. That was why the battles had gone on for so long, far beyond the point at which common sense should have dictated withdrawal. Day after day the Front soldiers hung in, awaiting the promised mass revolution that never happened. Instead, the city's inhabitants remained neutral, locking themselves up inside their houses and waiting to see how things turned out. Exposed before the murderous firepower of the South Vietnamese Army (ARVN) and the American forces, the Vietcong were massacred.*

---

* In fact the Front army never recovered from the disaster of Tet. About thirty-five thousand guerrilla regulars were killed. Subsequently the bulk of the fighting was taken over by North Vietnam's regular army. My cellmate Hien was political head of a five-thousand-man unit that attacked Saigon. He told me that after three weeks of

When the fighting was finally over, I was left with very mixed feelings. I had great admiration for the Vietcong forces that had given everything in their attempt to get rid of the American-sponsored regime. The government's reports of civilian massacres by Front forces I considered to be straight propaganda.* On the other hand, there had certainly been no outpouring of popular support for the revolution. That I saw with my own eyes, both in Vinh Long and Saigon. And it was only too clear that the guerrilla soldiers were not the heroic figures legend made them out to be. On balance, Tet did not change any fundamental attitudes. But I was coming to see that the situation was far more complex than I had believed.

◇   ◇   ◇

Every three weeks or so many of Tran Hung Dao's collective cell prisoners are shuffled off to other rooms, the idea being that this will prevent the formation of support groups, which it does. The transfers also upset the equilibrium that asserts itself when the same people are jammed together for long periods. Just when you've gotten used to the habits and movements of your numerous cohabitants, a new bunch comes along for you to adjust to. But the transfers also wash the cells with news from the outside world. Up-to-date information from the newly arrested makes the rounds of the entire prison much faster than it would otherwise.

At the end of August, about forty prisoners leave cell five, and their places are taken by an equal number of newcomers. Among these are ten who have just been arrested. Some are wealthy ethnic Chinese merchants. Their incessant wailing

---

continuous combat he was left with exactly *sixteen* able-bodied men. The rest had been either killed, wounded, or captured.
* Several thousand noncombatants had reportedly been murdered during the twenty-three-day Vietcong occupation of Hue. Later these charges were fully corroborated, though in the West this atrocity never received the coverage that the later, and far less extensive, massacre at My Lai did. In any event, at the time many Front sympathizers, myself included, were convinced the Thieu government had manufactured this incident out of whole cloth. Considering the blatantly false information the regime habitually issued, there was nothing improbable about this conclusion.

contributes as much to the cell's noise level as the rest of the denizens do put together. Apparently this unlooked-for separation from their property requires the loudest public lamentation.

I am now near neighbors with (among others) Tran Tranh, the notoriously corrupt "textile king" and Hoang Kim Quy, ex-senator and "barbed-wire king." Ly Sen is also here, owner of more than fifty companies, and reputedly the army's silent partner in anything that could be stolen or sold.

A few days after these unwelcome guests arrive, a tall, fat man is brought in, assisted by two *bo dois*. He moves heavily, stiffly, his right leg encased in a solid plaster cast. This individual had owned a large plastics company. When he realized he was going to be arrested, he tried to kill himself by jumping out a four-story window. But he only succeeded in breaking his leg. Now he's here, in pain. But it's obviously not severe enough to keep his mind off the losses he's sustained. "They took two thousand gold luongs,"* he moans, joining the chorus. "They took three hundred thousand in dollars, my factory, my home, my cars. . . . Why. . . . Why didn't I leave in time?"

My earlier career as a pharmacy student encourages the cell leader to choose me to tend the broken leg and help its owner to the bathroom. I'm afraid I fulfill these tasks without much grace. All number five's political prisoners grumble about our new cellmates. Having to live with these people is repugnant.

But if the profiteers and their constant whining arouse contempt, other new arrivals wrench our hearts. A number of village peasants have come in with this crowd, teenagers for the most part, with looks of hurt incomprehension in their eyes. In their naiveté they can't imagine what twist of fate has lifted them out of their villages and flung them down here in Tran Hung Dao. We decide that most of them have been victimized by false denunciations. It's simplicity itself these days to get rid of a rival, or someone you feel has wronged you.

One of these peasants is a sixteen-year-old named Du, who

---

* One luong equals thirty-three grams of gold.

never tires of repeating his story—as though he thinks that if he tells it enough he will eventually understand what has happened. Several months before the final collapse he had been drafted into Thieu's Popular Forces for Local Defense, a kind of untrained village militia made up of old men and boys. When the war ended he had been promptly remobilized into the revolutionary government's People's Militia. One night after a few drinks too many Du had fired off a couple of celebratory rifle rounds into the air. Suddenly he found himself under arrest, accused of being a CIA agent. Badgering him to confess, they had told him, "It's your choice. Either the tiger cages on Con Son or the death penalty!" His denials aggravated the village militia leader, and now he's here. He doesn't know what the CIA might be, and thinks that if he did he might understand his mysterious imprisonment. If only someone could explain it to him.

Du is also trying desperately to remember what else he might have done while he was drunk, what crime so abominable they won't even tell him about it. He doesn't see his present predicament as an injustice; it's more like some kind of incomprehensible catastrophe. He keeps repeating to himself, "The tiger cages or the death penalty; I might as well die now."

His utter simplicity makes the cell veterans smile. But it also tugs at your heart. How could they put this defenseless child in the same boat with the barbed-wire king and the whining plastics magnate?

Shortly after the new influx, the political prisoners have a meeting and decide to demand a transfer away from the "enemies of the people" and the war profiteers. The resolution is rejected contemptuously by the *bo doi* to whom it is presented. "You're all prisoners," he replies curtly. "You have no civil rights. So what makes you think you have the right to petition for anything?" That's the end of that.

But a few days later the fat plastics man is transferred out, most likely to the infirmary. That's a big relief, to me at least. And after the September 2 Independence Day holiday, the rest of the profiteers are also taken away. The cell seems livable again. It's certainly quieter.

September 2 is a memorable day. It commemorates the day, back in 1945, when Ho Chi Minh declared Vietnam's independence from the French, beginning his speech, "We hold these truths to be self-evident, that all men are created equal." In 1975 September 2 will be celebrated for the first time in the South—even in the South's jails. But the real reason September 2 is memorable is that for the first time since my arrest, meat appears on the Tran Hung Dao menu. Even more extraordinary, number five's prisoners are treated to a special hors d'oeuvre, a comic number performed by a northern party official.

Two days before the holiday, we are visited by Captain Hai Phan of the North Vietnamese Army. He is here to make a speech that he has already presented in several other collective cells. An unforgettable speech. It goes something like this: "You southerners think that you're civilized, don't you? But if so, how come your bridges are all made of cement? In the North, all the bridges are made of iron. This is proof that the North is more civilized!"

Smiles begin to appear on the prisoners' faces. There's a scattering of applause. The captain goes on: "Uncle Ho was very wise when he chose the North over the South in 1954. The American Seventh Fleet could have sailed right up the Mekong to Phnom Penh." By now the prisoners are winking at each other in amusement. The applause is more vigorous. The Seventh Fleet sailing up the Mekong to Phnom Penh! What an idea!

Delighted with the response, Captain Phan continues, raising his voice: "The neocolonialists wanted to bomb Vietnam back into the Stone Age. But they failed! Under the party's leadership, our country is now in the Rubber Age. We now make our own truck tires!"

The entire cell bursts with laughter and applause. Hai Phan hasn't noticed anything funny in his remarks, and he's disconcerted for a moment. But he recovers swiftly and concludes his speech: "You are temporarily incarcerated, and therefore you do not have the same rights as citizens have. But on the occasion of the national holiday, the revolution will allow you to have a meal with meat. Furthermore, you will be allowed to buy certain products, in particular candy and sugar."

This time the applause and shouts of joy couldn't be more sincere.

When the day comes, several kilos of cooked pork show up at the cell door along with the usual red rice. The smell makes me salivate uncontrollably. It takes all the authority the oldest inmates can muster to prevent a riot and to divide up the meat equitably among the sixty drooling prisoners—an especially difficult task without a knife.

Everyone gets two pieces of pork about the length of a finger. It's the most exquisite dish I've ever tasted.

6

Delegate from the School of Pharmacy

The elderly Nguyen Thc Thao (whose "mother" is Chi Hoa and "father" Con Son) is transferred out the day after the national holiday, along with the profiteers and several others. His place as head prisoner is taken by a young man named Khanh, formerly a musician. It's an exchange we regret immediately.

Khanh is not only a former musician, he's also a former Communist who quit the party in 1972 to join the Thieu government. That makes him an archtraitor, one of those who owes what's called a "blood debt" to the people. If he's alive at all, it's due only to the revolution's boundless mercy. That's why the *can bos* have made him head prisoner. To keep earning his forgiveness, Khanh enforces an iron regime in the cell. Apparently Tran Hung Dao has regulations whose existence we never suspected under the amiable Thao.

Prior to Khanh's advent, cell five's inhabitants passed the time talking and playing Chinese checkers. Now the checkers are confiscated, and we learn there's a rule of silence, every infraction of which earns a denunciation to the *bo dois*. It's unnatural. Sixty souls sharing 100 square yards, and you can hear a pin drop. Every now and then there's a furtive whisper; other than that it's quiet. Even our sandy rice has to be eaten in silence, and in place. No moving around at mealtime.

Fortunately, I'm not subject to this dictatorship for long. On the morning of September 5 a *bo doi* appears, list in hand. Card shuffling time. But now my name is one of those read out for transfer "elsewhere." To my joy, golden-toothed Hien is also among the chosen. We stand next to each other, hoping to increase our chances of staying together. It turns out to be a wise precaution. The *bo dois* go through the group, handcuffing everyone together in pairs, right hand to left hand.

On our way through the prison corridors we are joined by inmates from other cells, also handcuffed. Suddenly we are outside. I haven't seen the sky for eleven weeks. The fresh air is making me dizzy. Several prisoners stumble, their legs wobbly. Waiting for us in the courtyard is a line of dark green prison trucks, exactly the same ones the old regime used. We are herded toward them like animals, packed in until they can just close the door. About forty of us are pressed tightly together. I feel nauseous from lack of air. It's impossible to tell where we are going, no way at all to see outside.

We travel like this for about an hour, then pull to a stop. As soon as the door opens, Hien whispers in my ear, "Le Van Duyet." We're in a courtyard—squat brick buildings on three sides, on the fourth a wall about twelve feet high. We are told to sit on the ground while a man in civilian clothes walks by, looking us over. "Toai!" He stops in front of me. "Don't you recognize me?"

I don't. His face is vaguely familiar, but who he is or where we could have met is a mystery.

"I'm the one who wrote the poem in *Tin Sang*. You remember . . . 'Blood'!" Of course. Now I know who it is: a former student activist with a flair for verse. So the poet has now become a policeman. A curious transformation, not that I'm in any position to comment on it. I address him politely.

"Of course. Sure I remember. And now you're an official . . . and I'm a prisoner."

He appears concerned. "But what happened? I heard you were working for the finance committee. What's going on? Did you get caught violating the curfew or something?"

So there's still a curfew. (It's been four months since liberation.) Out loud I say, "No, to tell you the truth, I don't know why I was arrested. I *was* working for the finance committee, but I was planning to quit. I haven't done anything wrong . . . I really don't understand it."

The author of "Blood" stiffens perceptibly. If I'm maintaining that I don't know why I'm here, it's got to be more than some simple violation. Toai *was* working for the committee. Then the party's probably involved in this. Better to avoid him.

By now it's obvious he regrets having recognized me. He glances around uneasily. Mumbling a few words about telling my family I'm in Le Van Duyet, he disappears.

We remain sitting in the courtyard under a blazing sun until midafternoon, with no food or water. At last we're sent off to be searched before being shown to our new quarters. Stark naked, our clothes bundled up in our hands, we file singly past a lieutenant assisted by two *bo dois*. They inspect every item of clothing meticulously. But they don't find the twenty thousand piasters that are rolled up tightly inside my anus, a trick I've learned from Henri Charriere's *Papillon*, a Saigon best-seller.

Thanks to the handcuffs, Hien and I are taken to the same cell: Le Van Duyet collective cell number two. It's as if we've never left Tran Hung Dao. The cell has about the same dimensions as our old number five: long, narrow, and high-ceilinged. The wall with the door, however, is a metal grill that allows plenty of air circulation. At the far end of the room are a toilet hole, a faucet, and a water tank. Running down the left side from front to back is a brick sleeping platform.

As we come in, a man near the front makes a correction in chalk on a small board. He is Nguyen Dich Nha, head prisoner. The board has marked on it the number of his charges. Hien and I are numbers sixty-one and sixty-two. That means, as we will soon learn, that each prisoner has a space of approximately six feet by one and a half feet on which to sleep. In other words, it's impossible to lie on your back or stomach. In Le Van Duyet number two, one sleeps on one's side, like a domino lying on edge among a row of dominoes on edge.

Since Hien and I are the most recent arrivals, we get to sleep in the back, next to the toilet.

Our fellow prisoners in number two are in no hurry to get acquainted. As was the case in Tran Hung Dao, they belong to several distinct groups. And they observe each other carefully before deciding who fits and who doesn't. Communists associate with Communists, though they're also willing to accept Front sympathizers like me. But they shun like poison ex-Communists or former Front members who at some point had rallied to the old regime. The ralliers in turn consider themselves political prisoners and are determined not to be mistaken for the war profiteers. For their part, the profiteers display the most profound aversion for all the "politicals," whom they hold directly responsible for their present unhappiness. This stew is further spiced by the addition of a number of actual thieves and murderers, and of course by a sprinkling of informers who might belong to any of the groups.

So it is that new arrivals are observed suspiciously until their status is determined, and Hien and I remain carefully on guard that first evening.

But if the makeup of the cell's inhabitants is no surprise, the food when it finally arrives is a great improvement: the same rice, but without the sand. With a quick flash of gold, Hien observes, "We've changed hotels, and it looks like we've got a better cook. Unfortunately the beds are just as hard." In any event, it's a pleasure to be able to talk once more, after the Trappist regime of the last few days, and we quickly take up our discussion. My discussion, anyway. I've been busy telling him about my deepening involvement in the opposition. He's the best listener I've ever come across. His questions are few, but each one makes me focus my experiences better, understand them better.

"After Tet I had some doubts," I tell him. (I wonder for an instant whether he did, with sixteen men left.) "But they weren't nearly enough to make me change sides. Anyway, the regime was so corrupt and stupid that you had to be corrupt or stupid yourself to join it. . . ."

◊   ◊   ◊

After the Front's Tet disaster in 1968, the Saigon government seemed to be on the high road. With the Americans' help, Thieu's army had decimated the guerrillas, while the population had for the most part remained firmly neutral. Now it was time for the regime to capitalize on victory and eradicate the vulnerable remnants of communism south of the seventeenth parallel. Other thorn-in-the-side opposition elements would have to look out too.

In Saigon, Nguyen Cao Ky, commander-in-chief of the air force and vice-president of the republic, was given the job of straightening out that wrong-thinking little world, the university.

Ky was a South Vietnamese phenomenon. Nobody could quite figure out how this playboy with no visible qualifications had gotten to where he was. In 1968 he was not yet forty years old. He strutted around in specially tailored flamboyant uniforms, surrounded by a personal bodyguard corps of young men in tight black pants, red scarves, and tinted glasses. It was like a rock movie fantasy come to life. Ky liked women, gambling, and showing off—in no particular order. The clever and secretive Nguyen Van Thieu probably found his brash, outspoken ways useful. And Ky was too young to seriously disturb the older generals who watched the throne so jealously. As far as the Americans were concerned, they had dealt with so many bizarrely inadequate Vietnamese leaders that this new one in the masquerade outfit no doubt seemed nothing special.

Getting used to being a political leader, Ky began to take himself more seriously. He divorced his French wife (who had

borne him five children) and married a pretty Vietnamese woman, thus distancing himself from the French colonial taint. He began making sweeping public denunciations of Vietnam's colonial inheritance, attempting to project an image of himself as a confirmed nationalist. His approach to the troublesome university students was characteristically direct, and characteristically ill conceived. The students were to become part of the national struggle by joining paramilitary units, donning uniforms, and patrolling the streets.

Predictably, this idea got a sour reception at the university. Students were furious at the thought of being militarized. Making night patrols around the relatively peaceful capital had nothing to do with how they thought they ought to spend their time. Their parents concurred, insisting loudly that the new plan would jeopardize the students' work.

To capitalize on the unrest, the Front mobilized its agents, working to sharpen the conflict between students and the regime. One of these agents was Nguyen Tuan Kiet, whom I had been close to for some time. Together we organized protests at the school of pharmacy. Not only were the students especially vocal about this issue, but even the leading generals had begun to have second thoughts. After all, what might Ky be able to make out of a student militia under his personal command? Between the protests and the lack of government support, the militarization program quickly deteriorated, and was finally dumped altogether.

This outcome boosted my popularity among the students and propelled me toward the life of an activist. Politics began to take more and more of my time and pharmacy less.

It didn't take me long to realize that, though I loved the give-and-take of politicking, I wasn't extremely well prepared for it. In particular, I needed to educate myself on issues and to train myself for public speaking. I began reading deeply in history and politics, and I undertook to make myself into an effective orator. At home I practiced for hours at a stretch, thinking about how to organize speeches, then delivering them in a semiwhisper, hoping no one would hear or walk into the bedroom and surprise me. At rallies and meetings I watched speakers carefully, noting their gestures and styles of delivery. I considered how best to begin a speech, and how to conclude most effectively.

And all the while I was putting what I learned to use in my own talks. I lost my nervousness about appearing before large groups, and I discovered how to draw attention to myself among the various speakers that might be addressing a meeting. Almost always I found that there was some volatile issue that no one was touching on, and I would make that the center of my speech. I developed a knack for extemporaneous speaking and began to attract a reputation as someone who was not afraid of controversy.

This reputation took a leap forward at the funeral of Phan Khac Suu, who had been the figurehead civilian chief of state for a short time several years back. Suu had died in his seventies after a long career as an ardent nationalist. He had struggled against the French and had opposed Diem, and his funeral brought together all of Saigon's major opposition figures, as well as the governmental leadership whom they opposed.

The funeral cortege was accompanied by crowds of marchers from various opposition groups, including close to five thousand students I had helped to muster. With our pennants and banderoles flying we moved along the street chanting, "Down with the militarists!" "Down with corruption!" "Peace now!" and "Self-determination!" In front of the presidential palace we forced a stop for a few minutes and shouted out our slogans.

At the cemetery, though, the students were kept out, as was the rest of the unruly crowd. Inside were President Thieu and Vice-President Ky among a small throng of dignitaries from across Saigon's political spectrum. Finally, one of Suu's relatives arranged to allow a group of student representatives in and gave us the chance to say a few words after the formal eulogies were completed. So it was that Thieu and Ky spoke, as did Tran Van An (Thieu's chief political adviser). Then it was my turn.

I had nothing prepared and I was shaking with excitement and fear. But once I stood in front of the crowd, the nerves disappeared. Suddenly I was outside of myself, propelled by anger over the official tears shed by the very element Suu fought so vigorously most of his life. I took as my theme the fact that we were standing in Mac Dinh Chi cemetery where the French colonialists had been buried, a rich man's cemetery, a collaborator's cemetery.

Though I had prepared nothing, the words came easily.

"When you were alive," I said, "they oppressed you and deceived you" (alluding to Suu's earlier struggles and to his consent at the age of seventy to head a token civilian government). "Now that you are dead, they bury you here with traitors and lackeys. Then they read hypocritical statements over you and cry their crocodile tears. I do not cry before your soul. I do not regret your passing. But I swear, for the youth of the nation, that we will take revenge for you!"

As I was working myself up to this fine rage, I noticed Thieu and Ky leaving with their retinues. When I was finished, there was loud applause from the opposition people among the mourners. But as it died out, I was again afraid.

In front of the crowd, I had been brave and happy. As was to happen so many times in the future, when I began to speak I no longer had any real sense of my individuality. It was as if I had become for those moments a man of the people. And feeling that way, I had no caution in what I said.

But now that it was over, I wondered how I would get away from the secret police in the crowd, whose masters I had just finished maligning. Then I was surrounded by a dozen students and hustled out through the gates. It wasn't until several days later that I stopped expecting to be arrested momentarily.

As my role in student affairs grew, I found myself being courted by various Saigon political figures, especially those in opposition to the regime. And I wasn't alone. The student organizations were able to mobilize the large, noisy street demonstrations that were a vital element in the political warfare of the time. As a consequence, all the student leaders were sought after.

Sensing that my own future path might lie in legal political opposition, I went about establishing close ties with several leading antiregime personalities: Tran Van Tuyen, Nguyen Long, and Mrs. Ton That Duong Ky, among others.*

---

* All of these were NLF sympathizers who managed to survive as open opposition leaders. Tran Van Tuyen was the dean of the "anti" bloc in the National Assembly, Nguyen Long was a prominent lawyer, and Mrs. Duong Ky was the wife of a prominent Front figure who was living in the jungle.

My new friends encouraged me to begin a new magazine, for which they would provide support and financial backing. Together we invited young, opposition-minded professionals and students to join the editorial board. Mrs. Duong Ky offered the use of her printing house. The result was that after several months of organizing, *Tu Quyet (Self-Determination)* came to life.

As its title indicated, *Tu Quyet* espoused the right of South Vietnam to determine its own future, without interference from anyone—not from Hanoi, and especially not from the United States. Though the first issues were impounded by the police, before long *Tu Quyet* had found its voice, publishing articles by South Vietnamese intellectuals who were closely related to the NLF and by foreign personalities who advocated the same line of thinking. (Noam Chomsky was one of our favorites.)

I was, I knew, steering a dangerous course. I was not a member of the Front, but now I had become an open sympathizer. Each month my articles appeared in *Tu Quyet,* and each month the magazine was read by the police. Nguyen Tuan Kiet, one of the Front's agents in the student movement, was a close friend who from time to time attempted to persuade me to join formally. A year before he had even arranged a meeting for me with one of the Front's urban proselytizers.

The meeting took place at a *pho* (soup shop) on my own street, to which Kiet had taken us on a circuitous route to make sure we weren't being followed. The Vietnamese *pho,* like a French café, is a lively place, ideal for people who want to talk without being noticed. The proselytizer had told me that the Front had noticed my activities and was following them closely. He also told me that I must see my actions as part of a larger plan whose goal was the independence of South Vietnam. This was the Front's overall aim in coordinating the efforts of many very different individuals, people like me, making their individual efforts meaningful. Outside the Front I would be waging a solitary battle that would lead nowhere. With the Front I would be able to realize my own ideals and work for the country's future at the same time.

TựQUYết

TẠP CHÍ XUẤT BẢN HÀNG THÁNG

QUYỀN TỰ QUYẾT CỦA NHÂN DÂN M.N *THANH SƠN*
THỰC TRẠNG VẤN ĐỀ TỰ QUYẾT *THẠC BÁCH*

❖

ĐOÀN VĂN TOẠI — NGUYỄN VĂN THẮNG — TÓ THỊ THỦY
viết về
CUỘC TRANH ĐẤU VỪA QUA CỦA S.V.H.S
HOÀNG THÁI NGUYÊN VẤN ĐỀ TỰ TRỊ ĐẠI HỌC

❖

NGUYỄN BÌNH TUYỀN HOÀ BÌNH VÀ VIỆT NAM
BÙI CHÁNH THỜI RUỘT ĐỨT VẪN NHÌN NHAU
TRƯỜNG SƠN VỤ TỐ CÁO MUỘN MÀNG TẠI MỸ LAI

❖

Những mẩu chuyện miền Tây ly loạn
Thơ Trần quang Chúc

THÁNG TÁM BẢY MƯƠI

Cover page of *Tu Quyet* for August 1970. The two lead articles are entitled "The Vietnamese People's Right to Self-Determination" and "The Nature of the Self-Determination Question." Following are three articles on "The Recent Struggle of the Students," by Doan Van Toai, Nguyen Van Thang, and To Thi Thuy (another member of the student union board). The last article (by Truong Son) is on "The Crimes of My Lai."

I had found this pitch disappointing. My romanticized picture of the NLF had led me to expect a fiery leader of men. Instead, this proselytizer seemed quite ordinary, mouthing someone else's arguments. I told him that I agreed in general with the NLF's objectives, but that I needed time to think things over before committing myself further. And whether I joined or not, I intended to play an active role in the student movement, and I was ready to work closely with the Front while I did.

So while I hadn't accepted the proselytizer's invitation, I stayed in close touch, receiving Front publications and documents, and introducing into my own articles and political talks the Front's unswerving line: Hoa Binh, Tu Do, Doc Lap, Trung Lap, Hanh Phuc (Peace, Freedom, Independence, Neutrality, Social Welfare).

By the beginning of the 1969 academic year, the student union was in desperate need of reorganization. The last election had been two years ago, and most of the leaders had by now disappeared, either into the resistance or into prison. I immersed myself in the work, helping to prepare elections throughout the seventeen schools of the university.

By late September each school had chosen a delegate, and the delegates had in turn appointed an executive board. I was elected from the pharmacy school, becoming the second vice-president of the board—in charge of foreign affairs. An agronomy student with a quiet and conciliatory nature was made president.

Typically in Vietnam, the official head of an organization is a malleable individual with no real authority. Power lies in the hands of someone behind him, or perhaps someone even farther behind the scene. Leaders (and organizations) have an instinctive tendency to protect themselves in this fashion, layering protective shields around their true identities.* On the

---

* Even ordinary people are commonly known by their nicknames, while underground cadres would often take a series of code names, utilizing their wives' and childrens' names or some conspicuous physical characteristic their friends could be counted on to recognize. One NLF leader, for example, was known as "Number Four Twitch," while another was "Number Three Slow." The safety provided by

student union executive board, it wasn't Quy the agronomist who provided the real leadership, but Huynh Tan Mam, a strong-minded medical student who was chosen first vice-president. It wasn't till after liberation that I found out who had been standing behind Huynh Tan Mam. For editor of the student periodical *Sinh Vien* I backed my friend Kiet. I knew full well who was behind him.

The union secretary was another friend of mine, named Nguyen Van Thang. Thang was one of my fellow editors at *Tu Quyet*. He belonged to a species not much known outside of Vietnam, the southern independent. He hated the Saigon generals, whom he regarded as puppets of the Americans. But he was also against all northerners, Communist or anti-Communist. To Thang, northerners were a different people, who richly merited suspicion and disdain.

Thang's feelings were hardly unique. Among the South Vietnamese there was (and is) widespread mistrust of, even hostility toward, northerners. North Vietnamese live in a harsh and poor land that has shaped their national character. Southerners think of them as calculating, austere people, with are ingrained love of authority, hierarchy, and order. They have little of the southerner's happy-go-lucky ways, his expansiveness, or tolerance. Their leaders give off an unlovely air of self-importance and contemptuous disregard for subordinates.

The northern stereotype of their southern cousins is of course no less acidulous. To them, South Vietnamese seem indolent, fickle, and careless, interested primarily in enjoying the good life. And the truth is that in the South life is easier, the land more bountiful, the climate more temperate. Southerners jest that northerners will throw a wooden fish into a pot to give themselves the illusion of having a feast.

Despite Thang's dislike of northerners, he and the rest of us knew that the immediate threat was closer to home. It was evi-

---

such embedded customs was considered far more significant than any public recognition an individual might feel he deserved. South Vietnamese officials were secretly amused by the Americans' bluff habit of introducing themselves to complete strangers by announcing their names loudly and distinctly, reinforcing the introduction with a hearty handshake.

dent that the government was keeping a close eye on the militant new student board, and we half-expected some kind of move to keep us in order. We didn't have long to wait. In early October Quy the agronomist received his draft notice from the army. This was the shot across the bow, warning us clearly that no militancy would be tolerated from the revivified union. Now we would have to respond.

Nature was not particularly kind to Huynh Tan Mam. He was cross-eyed, and had a delicate, sickly constitution. But he also had guts. He knew that if the union simply accepted this attack on its president, its independence would be destroyed, along with any potential it had to play a role in the nation's political life.

Under Mam's leadership, we called for a demonstration to protest the regime's intolerable effort to intimidate the students. More than two thousand people gathered at the school of agronomy for an event that we named "Sing for the People." Right in the middle of it, the police arrived, in massive force. Mam and twelve other board members (including me) were arrested and locked up in the First District police jail. We were there for three weeks awaiting trial. Three weeks filled with glory.

The jailing of the student union board quickly developed into a major political scandal. Not only the Saigon newspapers, but the foreign press as well began to report the story—the illegal arrest of student leaders meeting peacefully on the university campus. In the National Assembly, opposition deputies gave speeches demanding our release. Some of the Assembly deputies made it a point to visit us regularly, joining the relatives and lawyers who came each day to bring us food and prepare our cases. Cakes, fruit, and homemade meals abounded. Scornfully we rejected the prison food. (Though it included meat along with rice. Had I only known!) We knew we had become celebrities, public symbols of Saigon government oppression.

According to our lawyers (among whom were Nguyen Long and other leaders of the Saigon bar), the trial would be a triumph for the opposition. We prepared ourselves with a sense of jubilation, rehearsing the passionate answers we would hurl at the judges. It is *we* who would accuse *them*, not the other way around. The government itself would be on trial. And if they dared to find us guilty, we would become, not just celebrities, but heroes. The entire university would rise up, bringing the people along with us. We were swept up in a truly extraordinary state of exaltation.

On the morning of the trial we received a visit from the First District police chief, who spoke to us in a plaintive, half-apologetic tone:

"All you give me is trouble. If I arrest you, they call me a brute. If I don't arrest you, I get chewed out by the minister. Next time go and hold your demonstrations somewhere else, in some other district."

In the prison truck (precisely the same type that would later transport me and thirty-nine others from Tran Hung Dao to Le Van Duyet) we broke into song:

Prison is the place for purification!
In this fight we need no arms.
My heart is made of steel, my blood flows red.
My body is made of gold, death to all traitors.
My blood flows today for the sake of the flag,
For its shining future.
We are the heroes . . .

The presiding judge was an elderly man who seemed tired even before we started. Outside his courtroom, a crowd of several hundred angry students had gathered. Inside were dozens of lawyers, National Assembly deputies, and journalists. The scene was weighted in our favor, and the spiritless questioning (answered on our behalf by Mam) gave us the impression that the judge was primarily concerned with avoiding a complete public relations disaster.

"You organized a meeting in violation of the government's ban! Did you know about the ban?"

"First of all, the right of free assembly is guaranteed by the constitution. Second, our meeting was on the university campus."

"But it was a political meeting, not a meeting concerning university business."

"Yes, it was university business. Its purpose was to present the program of the student union board. Is it our fault if the union president was drafted? If the meeting became political, it's the government's responsibility."

More questions and answers in the same inconclusive vein followed. By now we were certain that the government had decided not to push things, not to give us a further opening that we might exploit. The judge refused to press hard, doing everything he could to avoid a controversy. Frustrated, Mam looked for an opportunity to make the dramatic speech he had prepared, trying to provoke the court: "Before we were arrested we were afraid! Now we are not afraid of anything! We know our cause is just!"

"That's fine," said the judge. "The court has decided to grant you clemency. You are students. Your duty to the country is to continue your studies so that you can become useful citizens. Are you aware of that?"

"Yes," said Mam, nudging me with his elbow. "Say 'yes,' " he whispered. One after another we answered the elderly judge, who was looking at us with sternly raised eyebrows. "Yes, your honor, yes."

We left the courtroom free men, smiling triumphantly amid a crowd of friends and well-wishers. But Mam wasn't satisfied. "We should make some kind of statement against the police," he told me. "If we don't protest, they'll think they can get away with anything."

"Listen," I said, "We came out of it all right. They didn't even treat us badly. Let's leave it alone."

But Mam had his eye on the strategic opportunity. There was a crowd, and reporters—a perfect chance to rip into the regime. So as our spokesman, he made a declaration on the case and claimed that we had been brutalized by the police.*

---

* Strategically, Mam may have been right. Personally, his protest brought serious consequences. After his second arrest the police did torture him. While it was going on, one of them told him, "No one touched you the first time. But you said you got hit. This time we're really going to give it to you. At least that way we won't have to listen to your lies anymore."

Huynh Tan Mam (on shoulders) during a student celebration

Our widely publicized imprisonment, trial, and acquittal turned the student leaders into recognized figures on South Vietnam's political horizon. The episode had launched us as full-blooded opposition militants, on the lookout for more confrontation.

At the beginning of 1970, our next big issue was handed to us, this time not by the police, but by the minister of finance, who announced a substantial increase in the price of paper. The Saigon newspapers, all forty of them, exploded in a chorus of indignation, charging the government with a bald attempt to strangle freedom of the press. The student union joined the protests, unhappy about the rising cost of textbooks and anxious to use this opportunity to press home its attack on other government policies. I drew up a vitriolic declaration that Mam (now president) signed, then called a press conference to present it. Among other accusations, the declaration charged the regime with oppressing the poor and following the dictates of the Americans.

A week later, Huynh Tan Mam was arrested, accused of belonging to the Communist party.

Mam's arrest was, I thought, another blatant attempt to intimidate the union, as Quy's induction had been the previous September. The regime was obviously out to break the student movement by getting rid of its leaders. Two other board members disappeared at the same time Mam was arrested: Truc, the secretary general, and Yen, the treasurer. But as far as we could find out, neither had been taken by the police. What might have happened to them was an ominous mystery.*

At the union headquarters I was beginning to feel isolated. Mam, Truc, and Yen had been among the most energetic members of the board, and it seemed absolutely essential to take some kind of forceful action. I had to fight against what I saw as the step-by-step elimination of the student leadership, before I found myself sharing Mam's fate or whatever it was that had befallen Truc and Yen.

Believing that the most effective (and safest) course would be to mobilize public support for the imprisoned Mam, I composed an open letter to President Thieu and Prime Minister Khiem.† In it, I called Mam's arrest a "kidnapping" and demanded on behalf of the student union either the immediate liberation of our president or a full accounting of the case against him at a public trial to be held within one month. I concluded the letter: "The students have reached the end of their patience." It was published in almost all of Saigon's papers.

A few days later I received a formal invitation to meet with the chief of police, General Tran Van Hai. This was no peremptory summons, but the politest of invitations, hand-delivered and complete with a calling card. To prevent any surprises, I informed our lawyers of what was happening, along with a number of opposition Assembly deputies and journal-

---

* After liberation Mam emerged as one of the stars of the new regime. It turned out that he had in fact been a party member all along, part of a network that included Truc and Yen. When Mam was arrested, the other two had gone to cover. Even Kiet, my NLF friend, had not been aware of the trio's party affiliation.
† Khiem was a general who served as Thieu's defense minister and prime minister.

ists. Then, accompanied by a well-known reporter friend, I kept my appointment with the general.

Despite my obvious antagonism, General Hai received me (and the reporter) courteously, all smiles and friendship. Over tea, he got right to the point. We were badly mistaken about Mam. The government had no intention of making war on the students. Quite the contrary. After all, the students are the nation's future. But the government could not tolerate the activities of clandestine Communists who were out to destroy the country. Mam was a Communist who was using his student union position as a cover and the union itself as a tool.

I replied that if Mam was a party member (which I didn't for a moment believe), the government had better be ready to prove it publicly, and soon. Furthermore, union representatives must be allowed to meet with him to make sure his rights were being respected.

Annoyed, Hai answered that there was firm proof, but that it could not be made public yet. As far as a meeting with Mam was concerned, that was out of the question. The investigation was still going on and required secrecy.

I was unable to restrain my indignation at this. "So," I said, "the investigation requires secrecy! And meanwhile the police can do whatever they want, without any checks. And that's the way you're running the country!"

Although the general was still smiling, the smile was now decidedly less cordial: "Come on, Mr. Toai. You're not a child. You know our enemies don't use democratic methods any more than they use toy guns. Do you think we can get along without a strong police? It's fine that you're defending students' rights. But it will be better if you don't confuse that with political agitation!" With this not-so-veiled threat Hai stood up, indicating the audience was over.

Back at the union I was furious. I had gotten exactly nothing out of Hai—except a patronizing lecture and a threat. Angrily I told the others that the police took us for little boys who could be intimidated by yelling at them. We had to mobilize the whole student body. And for that we'd have to do something extreme and risky.

The next day the student union published an ultimatum to the government: Either Mam's trial would begin by March 20, or the entire university would go on strike. Of course we had no assurances from anyone that we could pull off a general strike. But it was a calculated risk. The students liked forceful language, and the fall's events had accustomed them to political action. Immediately we went about forming strike committees. At the same time, we began rounding up support among our political friends, opposition lawyers, and the media.

When March 20 came and went with no answer to the union ultimatum, we took the first step in our planned escalation. The medical school (where Mam was a student) went out on a three-day strike. That was our warning shot. It brought only continued silence from the government. After a week's wait, ten more schools went out, also for three days. Still the generals said nothing.

Sure now of enthusiastic student support, we were ready for our most dramatic move. At the beginning of April, all seventeen schools declared a month-long strike. At the same moment our supporters outside the university triggered off their own campaigns. Newspapers and lawyers challenged the government and brought the international press into the affair. In the National Assembly, the Interior Committee summoned the minister of the interior to give an explanation of Mam's case.

With the strike in high gear, the student union raised the stakes. Now we demanded not only Mam's release, but the release of *all* the students who had been arrested as "Communists" over the past years. To generate additional support, I visited the universities in Can Tho, Dalat, and Hue, spreading the strike.

Thang and I also started thinking about how we might take over the National Assembly.

7

The Students' War

The National Assembly met in a neoclassical building on Tu Do Street that had formerly been a theater and would be again after the war. Facing this building, the Thieu regime had erected a huge and hideous monument: A Vietnamese soldier wearing an American helmet and pointing his rifle toward the Assembly entrance. Quite a symbol!

Outwardly, the Assembly functioned according to democratic rules. There was a senate, with 40 members, and a house with 120, all elected by universal suffrage. Anyone could run, and there were plenty of candidates. In Saigon's voting districts it wasn't unusual to have ten candidates for each seat.

In the capital, a lively and obstreperous press kept a watch on political intrigues—to some extent controlling the regime's manipulations. In the countryside, ruled in effect by the army, it was a different story. There, with no press or independent bar to speak of, the government did whatever it wished with election procedures. In Diem's time an unwelcome candidate could even be murdered. But Diem's successors had found that simple intimidation worked just as well.

But despite fraud and threats, any given Assembly session would find only about 60 percent of the members to be unconditional government retainers. Another dozen or so—Buddhists, social democrats, self-determination advocates—were actually declared enemies of the regime. The rest tended to vote the issues. This hardly qualified the Assembly as a bona fide democratic institution, but it did manage to impose a certain minimal restraint on the regime's abuse of power.

On the other hand, corruption was massive. Although the deputies and senators received large salaries (140,000 piasters a month for deputies, 200,000 for senators—comparable to the earnings of chief executive officers in Vietnam's major firms), this didn't prevent a thriving trade in votes. One well-reported scandal, for example, was the 1972 electoral law debate, during which the regime paid up to a million piasters for individual votes in its favor.

Needless to say, it was the Assembly's abuses and corruption that engaged the students' attention, rather than the flickering gleams of democratic light it gave off. So none of us had any hesitation about attacking the institution in order to demonstrate the strength of our convictions and help weaken the regime.

In developing our plan of attack, at first Thang and I considered taking over the Assembly building. But as we reflected on the violence this might lead to, we decided to limit ourselves to a sit-in. And even a good-sized sit-in would be hard to bring off. The Assembly building was well guarded, and if any rumors got around beforehand, we'd be arrested immediately.

In the end, we involved several leaders from the schools of agronomy, pharmacy, and letters, which adjoined each other in downtown Saigon. They, in turn, mustered their forces.

One fine morning when everything was set, Thang and I were having a soda in the Givral Café, a favorite hangout of Saigon politicians, media people, and other luminaries. With some regularity friends would notice us and stop by our table to chat a moment. At least this was how it was supposed to look. In reality the "friends" were messengers coming in with reports about progress outside. Directly across the street from where we were sitting was the Assembly building, looming behind its giant stone guardian. As we sipped our drinks, four distinct groups of about a hundred and fifty students each were mingling with the crowds of pedestrians, converging unnoticed on the building's entrance.

At a word from one of our messengers, Thang and I got up and strolled as nonchalantly as we could out into the street. For a moment Thang stopped at the foot of the monument, looking up at its menacing bulk. Then he raised his right arm. As it went up, the bustling street scene erupted into four streams of running, shouting students. Coalescing into a giant, moving battering ram, they charged up the Assembly steps, brushing aside the startled guards.

In less than a minute I had burst into the office of the Assembly president, Nguyen Ba Luong, panting with excitement. "Who gave you the right to break into the Assembly?" he yelled, wildly indignant. "If the students come in here, why not the pedicab pushers, the fishermen, the . . . the . . . the police?"

I shouted back that the Assembly didn't represent the people, that Luong himself had just shown his contempt for the people he so piously pretended to serve, and that we were in control. The phrases were worthy of 1789, or 1917 anyway, when the Bolsheviks routed out the Provisional Assembly. At least it was the best leftist jargon I could muster—that is to say, my usual manner of speech. With this, Luong made a bolt for the door, but we grabbed him before he had covered half the room.

Meanwhile the reporters were already pouring into the building—their watering holes (the Givral, the Brodard, and especially the Continental Hotel) were only a few steps away. As they gathered, I read our communiqué, with its demands for unconditional peace, the immediate withdrawal of American troops, and South Vietnamese self-determination. When I was finished, a number of opposition assemblymen made their own statements supporting our demands.

Afterward we sat down in the halls and offices—singing, talking, chanting slogans, and waiting for the police to come and haul us off. By closing time nothing had happened, and more than half the demonstrators decided to call it a day. The rest of us bedded down wherever we could for the night.

Sometime in the very early morning, the police arrived in force. With everyone else, I was herded downstairs and outside. There the leaders were separated out and all the others sent home. The ten or twelve of us whom the cops recognized were booked, charged with "occupying government property" and "disturbing the peace." Then we too were released on our own recognizance. In the regime's on-again, off-again attitude about how much severity to use toward the students, we had obviously chosen a lucky moment.

But the strike was now in full career. With plenty of people available and emotions high, each day we'd try to do something that would make news. We organized teach-ins, sing-ins, marches, lectures, anything at all to get large groups of students together and keep things moving. All this the police watched carefully, though without intervening.

The fact was that police action was a two-edged sword that more often than not hurt those who wielded it as much as those against whom it was wielded. A far more effective weapon in the regime's face-off with the students was the military draft.

In 1970, South Vietnam was in the middle of an immense bloodletting, and few young men—students, peasants, or workers—were enthusiastic about taking part. While many were willing to fight against northern or Communist domination, few could generate a heartfelt commitment to the Thieu regime. It was not a government that excited hopes or ideals. In a nation just emerging from one hundred years of servitude to the West, the key ideal for many if not most Vietnamese was national independence. And in this regard especially, Thieu's government—with its American backbone—failed the test. So

One of the many demonstrations on the front steps of the National Assembly building. The one pictured is a protest during the 1971 presidential elections. The middle banner demands Nguyen Van Thieu's resignation "in order to save democratic government." The banner on the left reads "The October 3 election will establish an oppressive, foreign lackey regime."

the natural reluctance of young men to court death was enhanced by their particular antipathy toward risking their lives for the sake of a puppet general.

Now, with the student strike threatening real disruption, the government announced it would induct all those not attending classes. The effect was immediate, and chilling. Many students, zealous strikers the day before, grew quiet and thoughtful, then began filtering back to their studies. I could see the entire house of cards beginning to tremble. Somehow we had to change out tactics. We needed to extricate ourselves from the impending collapse without losing face, though how this might be done was anybody's guess. At this point fate intervened in the person of Cambodia's Prince Norodom Sihanouk.

Since 1941 Sihanouk had ruled the fragile Cambodian king-

dom on South Vietnam's western border. From time imme-
morial Cambodians have feared the Vietnamese, just as Vietnamese have feared their great neighbor, China—and for good
reason. If the ethnic Khmer villagers of Tra On hated the Vietnamese villagers of my native Cai Von and thought them ag-
gressive savages, it was because that entire region of the delta
had once been Cambodian.

By 1970, Sihanouk's reign was in serious trouble, due largely
to his steadfast blindness toward the North Vietnamese and
NLF armies that had in effect occupied the Vietnam-Cambo-
dia border regions and much of northeastern Cambodia as
well. These areas contained the Vietnamese revolutionaries'
supply systems, staging areas, and sanctuaries. Feeling incapable of controlling Vietnamese activities, Sihanouk acquiesced
to them. It was an approach that did not sit well with many of
his people, especially the civil servants, intellectuals, and military—guardians of the hereditary Khmer nightmares about
Vietnamese expansion.

On March 18 of that year, while Sihanouk was in France
taking his yearly obesity cure, the Khmer National Assembly
decided the time had come for a new ruler. In a bloodless coup
d'état, Sihanouk was replaced by his defense minister, Lon
Nol. For the Cambodians in general, Sihanouk's overthrow
signaled that it was now open season for Vietnamese-hunting.
Since their small and poorly equipped army could scarcely attack the powerful Vietnamese revolutionary forces entrenched
in the border regions, they turned instead on the civilian Vietnamese communities that had existed inside Cambodia for
generations.

Cambodia was racked by anti-Vietnamese pogroms. In an
explosion of hate, Vietnamese businesses were looted and
Vietnamese homes burned down. Thousands of Vietnamese
peasants and villagers were murdered, and tens of thousands
more fled in terror across the border into South Vietnam.
There the tales they told rekindled all the old hatreds.

While Cambodian villagers and peasants were terrorizing
the ethnic Vietnamese living among them, Lon Nol attempted
to get rid of the Vietcong and North Vietnamese troops occu-

pying his eastern frontier. With the new ruler's encouragement, and in concert with the Royal Cambodian Army, in late
March South Vietnamese forces launched attacks into the revolutionary bases and sanctuaries within Cambodia. These attacks were followed by the large-scale incursion of American
and South Vietnamese troops (also undertaken with Lon Nol's
cooperation) that took place on April 30.

But quite apart from what was happening in the war between the Saigon government and the revolution, public opinion inside Vietnam was inflamed against the Khmers. A cry to
revenge the slaughtered Vietnamese civilians rang through the
press and the streets. Strangely enough, this situation gave the
student union the tactic it was looking for and saved the general strike, which by mid-April was wheezing its last.

One of the activities the student union had organized for
this period was a peace songfest featuring several well-known
popular singers who were also antiwar activists. When Thang
and I saw the number of people who had arrived at the school
of science for this program it struck us as a good opportunity to
try and pump up the flagging strike. As far as we were concerned at that point, whatever issue we used to move a crowd
was not particularly important. It was the demonstration of
antigovernment energy that we were after, and the more energy the better.

With the level of emotion about Cambodia as high as it
was, it didn't take long for us to decide on our issue. First I
warmed up the crowd, telling them that we could all hear the
cries of our innocent countrymen who had been slain, slowly
building up until I could ask with real effect: "How can we sit
here, we young Vietnamese men, without doing something?"

At this, Thang rose to speak. He had a gentle, moving way
about him, less harsh and authoritarian than my manner. First
he said a few words, expanding on my theme. Then he started
singing "Xuong Duong" ("To the Street"), the student demonstration song: "Xuong duong! Xuong duong! Chung ta
cung, Xuong duong!"—"To the street, To the street! Let's all
go down to the street!"

Immediately the crowd took up the cry: "Xuong duong!"

The Saigon daily *New Saigon* reports student demonstrations against the Cambodian massacres. The photograph shows students performing public mourning for the victims.

The enthusiasm was tremendous. Thang and I were practically swept outside, heading by instinct toward the Cambodian embassy.

Nobody was prepared for this, neither the police, the Khmer diplomats, nor even the student union board. With a spontaneous surge, the students broke through the embassy gates and into the embassy itself. The only people there at that hour were a maid and caretaker, and we quickly hustled them out of the building. Over five hundred triumphant students were now the undisputed occupants of the Cambodian embassy. It was to be our home for the next month.

The rush of unplanned events that had started little more than an hour earlier now became a torrent. Just as we were figuring out how we might stave off attempts to get us out, the police arrived, quickly surrounding the building and lobbing in tear gas grenades, which we countered with showers of rocks from behind the barbed-wire fence around the embassy's perimeter.

Before long the police themselves were being surrounded and harassed by thousands of jeering students who had heard the news and were pouring into the area. In the confusion, new arrivals were breaking through police lines and climbing into the compound where the back wall abutted the rooftops of adjoining houses. Through the same back wall route I sent messengers out to begin mobilizing the media and our opposition allies, and to make arrangements to get food in to us.

To the government, the affair was an acute embarrassment. On the one hand they were reluctant to take any truly harsh measures. After all, public opinion was boiling against the Khmers, and it would hardly do to kill people who were expressing that opinion. On the other, how long could the regime tolerate such bald defiance of its authority? As the days passed in a standoff, the regime began to look ever more incompetent and silly.

Efforts to end the siege were simply not getting anywhere. By the end of a week the original 500 occupiers had dwindled to a 150 or so—but those were all militants determined to stay to the end. Of course our electricity, water, telephone, and gas had been cut off. But the embassy was set in a huge garden, and it was relatively simple to get messengers in and out over the back wall or through the thin line of police pickets. As for water, we managed to dig a well that went down almost thirty feet.

Every night the police would harass us, firing tear gas grenades into the compound. But by this time we had a well-planned defense. We kept a sharp lookout and responded immediately with stones and an occasional Molotov cocktail.

We also conducted an ongoing psychological war. Armed with a battery-powered bullhorn, I and others kept up a constant harangue: "You are underpaid!—You're being used by a corrupt government!—You're given the worst jobs!—If anything happens, they'll leave you holding the bag!—If you kill anybody, it's you who'll end up in prison!—Just as soon as the next regime comes in!—You can count on it!—So why are you fighting us?" A lot of this was just noise, but there was enough truth so that it affected police morale.

At least it didn't seem as if they had their heart in the nightly assaults. With no one really interested in hurting anyone else, little by little the besieged and the besiegers worked out a *modus vivendi*. Under the guise of "mediation," we were even allowed to receive visits from friendly Assembly deputies in cars displaying special insignia . . . their trunks secretly loaded with food supplies.

It wasn't until more than a month had passed in this fashion that the government finally decided to put an end to it. One day toward the end of June, the familiar police units posted around us were replaced by squads of special riot police. They attacked at once.

A barrage of tear gas blanketed the whole area, blinding and suffocating everyone. As we stumbled around gasping for breath, the new police charged, wearing gas masks and swinging their billy clubs and rifles viciously. We put up a gallant fight, with sticks, stones, anything we could get our hands on. In the melee, about fifty policemen were hurt—and perhaps twice that number of students.

Thang and I were among the last to be arrested. We had holed up in our second-floor "headquarters" when the police stormed up the stairs and broke through our barricade, shoving us out with their rifle butts. As we were pushed outside, all the students let out a tremendous cheer. Some of the police panicked. Thinking the riot was starting up again, they began firing their rifles into the air. Amid the din and confusion, I was arguing with the police commander. It was Thang and I who were responsible; the others had only been following our lead. We would accept full responsibility, but the rest should be released. In the end, the police agreed to free all but a few of the students, who were by this time sitting quietly on the ground, watching our deliberations. As Thang and I were led off, they broke into applause. The police had won the day, but I felt as though the honors had gone to us.

The prison they took us to that afternoon was Tran Hung Dao, where we were locked up in separate cells. Mine was a large common cell, cell number five—which for some reason I had all to myself. I scratched my name on the wall, wondering what might happen now, blissfully unaware that five years later I would be threading my way through sixty sweating cellmates to find this memento of former glory.

Sometime around midnight I was called for questioning. It was a thorough and unfriendly grilling that bore little resemblance to my experience the previous October. Several questions about my curriculum vitae, and then to the heart of the matter. "Whose idea was it to occupy the embassy? Who put you up to it?"

"Nobody 'put me up to it.' I'm Vietnamese, same as you. I think the government ought to do something about the massacres. But it's not . . . it's a disgrace!!"

The interrogator began to pick at my ideas about the regime. Did I have some problem with it? Didn't I think it was legitimate? Was I sure no one had suggested this embassy business in order to embarrass the government, to put it in a bad light? What about Huynh Tan Mam, for example? Of course he was in jail—but what about his friends?

"How did you get to know Mam anyway? Who introduced you?"

"Well," I answered, "Mam was elected to the union by the medical school, and I was elected by the pharmacy school. We met at the fist union meeting. We didn't need anybody to introduce us."

"Did you know Mam was a Communist?"

"That's what General Hai himself told me after you arrested Mam. Personally, I don't believe it."

Angry now, fist pounding the table: "Mam is a Communist. And so are you! You were in constant touch with him!"

"With that kind of reasoning, every medical student's a Communist, and so are all of Mam's friends. His family too, for that matter."

All night long the hammering went on about Mam, the Communists, the NLF, the interrogator trying to trip me up, find some inconsistency, some connection. The Cambodian business, as we both understood, was not the issue. The students were at war with the government. They were out to discredit it, to weaken it, to find ways to press home their political views. For the interrogator, these views—"self-determination," "independence from the Americans," "democratic rights"— played right into the hands of the Communists. Ergo, the student movement was a dangerous front, with implicit and no doubt explicit ties to the party and the NLF. It was dawn before the guard took me back to my commodious cell.

During the day I was left alone. But the next night the game started all over again, and the next night and the next—four nights of wheedling, cajoling, good-natured joking, angry browbeating, a determined assault to lay bare my secret connection with the revolution. By this time I was exhausted from lack of sleep. But mentally I was still sharp, and I couldn't have felt more confident. I knew, as the interrogator probably did, that there was nothing to prove. And all of Saigon was aware of my arrest. Although I was being held incommunicado, I had no doubt that people on the outside were working on my behalf, and on Thang's. The interrogator had even told me that I would be able to see a lawyer "sometime soon." Under these circumstances I was pretty sure they wouldn't torture me. It might be a long siege, but I felt up to it.

On the fifth day I was shocked to hear a guard announce that my trial would be held the following morning. That meant they had already given up trying to turn Thang and me into Communists. They also had to be experiencing a lot of pressure, enough so that keeping us in jail was becoming difficult.

The next day I joined Thang in the paddy wagon that would take us to court. As we drove up to the building we could hear what sounded like thousands of people chanting and shouting slogans. It was no wonder the government wanted to get out from under this situation as fast as it could. Inside, an even bigger surprise was waiting, a team of defense lawyers who told us that over fifty attorneys had volunteered their services, including such stars of the Saigon bar as Tran Van Tuyen (president of the League for Human Rights) and Nguyen Long. Not only was the university in a turmoil, but newspapers, politicians, and people in general were demanding that we be freed. How could the government want to punish individuals who were demanding the defense of the helpless Vietnamese in Cambodia?

The indictment was read quickly: illegal entry, damage to property, insurgency, attack on police forces, violation of diplomatic extraterritoriality laws. Some of these were serious indeed, but the indictment also made note of our "patriotic motives." The government attorney made his case in what might have been record speed. When he was finished, the presiding judge looked at our battery of lawyers and requested them to "follow the example of the prosecution and be brief." By this point there was no question in anybody's mind what direction we were headed in. The judge didn't want to hear any antigovernment slogans or declarations or condemnations, either from us or from the opposition orators who were defending us. He just wanted us out.

After deliberating for a few minutes, the panel of judges was ready with its verdict—guilty—and its sentence: a severe reprimand. Without a doubt, they were announcing a decision that had been made earlier at the interior ministry. We emerged from the courthouse through the main entrance to an ovation from the crowds of students.

8

"The Agony of Student Toai"

The events of the past year, the trial of the union board, the general strike, the Assembly sit-in, the embassy occupation, and the many smaller actions, had given the student movement a loud, prominent voice in Saigon's political world. We had proven ourselves to be organized, capable of damaging the regime, and difficult to handle. Having shaped the movement into an oppositionist political force with teeth, we were now ready to press forward with our agenda.

Part of the agenda was tied to the academic world: We wanted guarantees of the university's autonomy and permanent premises for the student union. Part of it straddled the political and academic worlds: We wanted all student prisoners freed. And part of it was purely political: protection for Vietnamese in Cambodia, affirmation of South Vietnam's right to self-determination, and recognition that United States involvement in Vietnam was antithetical to that right.

Recognizing the damage it had sustained in a year of encounters with the students, the government now responded to our initiatives by accepting the mediation of several mutually agreed-on professors. As a result of their efforts, in June a twelve-member union delegation was received by the prime minister himself (General Tran Thien Khiem), the vice–prime minister, the ministers of education and foreign affairs, and the chancellor of the university.

Our demands were formally presented by the union's new treasurer while Thang and I remained quietly in the background. Mention of the self-determination issue and of the American presence drew some involuntary winces from the ministers, but otherwise they maintained an air of attentive sympathy. Then, after glancing at Prime Minister Khiem for approval, the foreign minister, Tran Van Lam, launched on a little prepared talk.

Addressing us as his "dear friends," he said we should know that as far as Cambodia went, our troops had not been soft on the Khmer, but had repaid them in kind for what they had done.* Of course we couldn't say that publicly, since the Lon Nol government was our "objective ally." At any rate, the massacres were now over. As for the influence of the United States on our country, "dear friends," "Well, I ask you to consider what would happen if we should lose their support." Hanoi was aided by the Soviet Union and the entire international Communist movement. It was only normal that Vietnam should seek assistance from the United States. After all, South Vietnam was a small country that could not defend itself without help. In any case, that kind of matter was hardly within the purview of the students.

At that point Dr. Nguyen Luu Vien, the vice–prime minister, took over from Lam and gave a short paternal sermon: "You are students, aren't you? You have to study, to prepare yourselves for the job of rebuilding the country. When you've finished your studies, then it will be all right to take part in politics. Right now, perhaps you don't realize that all your enthu-

---

* The South Vietnamese–American incursion had taken place in May.

siasm and idealism are being exploited by the country's enemies."

By this time, Prime Minister Khiem had noticed that all
these gentle words were not having the desired effect. Inter-
rupting Lam, he laid the government's cards squarely on the
table. Our first three demands would be met. The student
union would have its own villa, the autonomy of the university
would be formally recognized, and the arrested students—including Mam—would be released.

Khiem was true to his word. A week later, Mam and the
others were assembled in the central jail of Chi Hoa, some of
them having been returned to the capital from the sinister Con
Son Island Prison with its famous "tiger cages." Before their
release they were allowed to talk to lawyers, and to receive visitors from the union.

At Chi Hoa, the director of the prison greeted the union delegation in person. We were authorized, he said, to meet with
Mam and the others. He had also arranged for us to meet with
two other student prisoners, Tran Khiem and Duong Van
Day. The first name meant nothing to me. Day I didn't know,
but I had heard his name mentioned as one of the Front contacts in the university.

Meeting these two turned out to be something of a shock.
Tran Khiem I had indeed met before, once. He was the Front
agent my friend Kiet had taken me to see at the *pho* shop three
years before. Duong Van Day was even more of an astonish-
ment. I did know him—as a fairly ordinary student at the university who sympathized with the Front and from time to time
took part in our activities. He was a supporter of Mam's, and I
always assumed that he was very much under Mam's influence. The shock was that I knew this inconspicuous person
under an entirely different name. Now I understood that not
only was he not one of Mam's followers, he was Mam's superior, the individual Mam got his instructions from.

Now I saw why this particular meeting had been arranged,
and why we were being allowed to speak freely to Mam and
the others before their release. All the students had been tor-

tured during their imprisonment, and some of them looked
just awful. Needles had been thrust under their nails, and they
had been forced to drink soapy water, killing off intestinal bac-
teria and causing agonizing stomach problems. All of them,
Mam included, had confessed to being party members. Of
course it was impossible to say how many really were, and how
many had simply confessed a lie. But there could hardly be any
doubt about people like Tran Khiem and Duong Van Day.

Now that he was obligated to release these people, especially
given the shape they were in, Police Chief General Hai wanted
everyone to know in advance that these really were Communists, not merely innocent student activists. In this way he
might head off, or at least undercut, the furor he could see
coming.

It was a stillborn hope. The moment the prisoners were released, we brought them before the public in a press conference the union called at the agronomy school, four hundred
yards from the presidential palace. Their mere appearance,
especially in that place, was damningly eloquent. Although
they had received the best care and food during the week or so
before their release, most of them were suffering visibly from
the effects of semistarvation and torture. Mam and several
others described the ordeals they had been through, and the
stories found their way into a number of Saigon newspapers,
despite the tight censorship. For the foreign reporters it was a
windfall; the Con Son tiger cages had recently been discovered, and indignant articles were appearing all over about the
inhuman conditions inside Thieu's prisons.

After Mam and the others spoke, I took the microphone to
ask that a thorough investigation be made into what had happened, demanding that the torturers be identified and con-
victed. A few days later a government spokesman stated that if
anything improper had happened while the students were in
jail, it was due to "mistakes" made by certain individuals. The
government itself both condemned and deplored torture.
Those guilty of acting beyond their authority would be found
and punished.

ÀI MỸ

và triển lãm

«chiến lợi phẩm»

- Sáng 14-6-70 một chú MP bắn 6 phát súng Colt về phía S.V.H.S. nhưng không trúng ai.
- Chiều 13-6, SVHS báo động dữ dội — Binh sĩ Dù gác đài Tivi mời C.S DC «đi chỗ khác chơi».

● LINH HƯƠNG

SAIGON 14-6 (SM). — Lối 9 giờ sáng nay, 2 xe díp Quân Cảnh Hoa kỳ (MP) đã chạy đến ngã tư Thống Nhứt —Cường Để. Hơn 20 HB thuộc toán «Sao xẹt» của đoàn xung kích SVHS tranh đấu đứng trên tàu (trường Đại Học Dược khoa phía đại lộ Thống Nhứt) liền reo hò inh ỏi.

Một ông MP đã móc súng colt 45 ra, và bắn về phía HS này 6 phát. Các em hoảng hồn hụp xuống tránh đạn. 2 đầu đạn của MP này trúng của sổ ngay đầu HS đứng, 4 đầu đạn kia bay lên mái nhà. Toán HS «Sao xẹt» có lượm 1 đầu đạn đem cho báo chí coi.

Theo các em thì MP hận SVHS hôm qua «bài Mỹ» kỳ quá bằng hành động ném bễ kính 1 số xe Mỹ và đốt 1 xe vận tải nhẹ của RMK, nên họ bắn các HS bạo động để trả thù.

Bạo động dữ dội

Như số báo qua SM đã loan tin đầy đủ, trên 200 SVHS đã «làm chủ»

(XEM TIẾP U TRANG 6)

CHINH QUYEN ĐÃ CÓ THIỆN CHÍ

SVHS học lại từ 22-6

★ CÁC SV CÒN BỊ GIỮ VÌ THUỘC THÀNH PHẦN QUÂN NHÂN ĐÀO NGŨ ?
(Xem D tiếp trang 6)

Hình ảnh «trận đại chiến» giữa SVHS và CSDC hôm 13-6
HÌNH TRÊN : — SVHS Trưng bày chi n lợi phẩm tịch thu được.
HÌNH DƯỚI : — SV Huỳnh tấn Mẫm (người cầm micro) và 5 SV khác vừa được tạm thích
(TH)

Từ đây đến 30-6 mà Bộ T. Chánh vẫn lờ

NGHỊ SĨ PHIỆT SẼ CÔNG BỐ

danh sách 800 ông bự thiếu thuế

Huynh Tan Mam (with microphone) and others on their release from prison

Neither I nor anyone else had any illusions about what would happen. But I hoped the uproar this was creating would inspire the police to be more cautious in the future.

At this juncture the prestige of the student union was at its peak. We formed the Committee against Repression to monitor arbitrary arrests and police brutality. We created the Committee for the Right to Live to campaign against more general infringements upon basic civil and human rights. On both of these committees I became responsible for foreign relations, the same job I held on the student union board.

◊ ◊ ◊

It was the heyday of the student movement, an intense and exciting time, when each day brought its actions and confrontations, and we knew we were effectively damaging the regime we so thoroughly detested. The proof of it was that early in the summer of 1970, the police decided to crack down. After a hectic day of meetings and planning for future actions, I had slept at a friend's house and was awakened the next morning by news that Thang and a number of other leaders had been caught in a police sweep.

Calling my brother's house, I learned that the police had come for me too, in the middle of the night. These arrests were clearly not standard police action, like the surveillance, threats, and occasional detentions that were ordinary fare. The midnight sweep of student leaders meant that a conscious policy decision had been made; we had finally crossed the line.

My first impulse was to get away, to find a way to protect myself from arrest. With this in mind I went to the offices of *Cong Luan*, a fairly moderate oppositionist newspaper that was owned by General Ton That Dinh. Dinh was a wildly eccentric individual, known for his unpredictable thinking. His editor in chief was a high-profile journalist and a good friend of mine named Le Hien. I could count on Hien to hide me for a while and to give me advice. I also thought General Dinh's name might help keep the bloodhounds away.

I slept in the *Cong Luan* offices for several days, going over the situation time and again with Le Hien. But as much as we talked, I couldn't see the next step. By this time, almost every one of the movement leaders had been tracked down, and I knew my time was coming. Finally I decided that if I was finished, at least I would go out in a blaze.

It didn't take much to organize what I saw as my final action. I called Duong Van Ba, the vice-secretary-general of the National Assembly (one of the opposition bloc), to arrange a press conference in his office. Then I got in touch with several of my activist friends who had not had leadership roles and so had not been arrested, asking them to put together a small sit-in at the National Assembly. Finally, I sat down to compose a telegram to Richard Nixon.

In the telegram I said that President Nixon and his government were supporting a dictator whose suppression of basic human rights was intolerable, that as long as the United States continued its support, it was not helping the Vietnamese people, it was betraying them. With that sent, I headed off to the National Assembly.

In the vice-secretary-general's office, I addressed the reporters, students, and opposition representatives who crowded in. First I gave a short speech, saying that the government had now arrested all the student leaders, that I was the last, and that I too would soon be taken. Then I read my telegram to Nixon. This, I said, was my final act, a last gesture on the part of those who had led the students in their fight against the dictatorship. Now, I told them, it was up to the next generation of students to carry the struggle forward . . . and to take revenge for us.

Almost all the next day's newspapers covered the event, calling it "The Agony of Student Leader Toai." Later I would be able to take satisfaction from the success I had achieved there, but as I walked away from the conference I felt an immense fatigue, as if I had just closed out a chapter of my life on a note of dejection. Walking down the steps with some of my supporters—assemblymen and journalists—I was sure I would be arrested within minutes.

As we crossed the street, the police were already arriving and beginning to grab the sit-in protestors. Looking back toward the building, I saw a line of students snaking down the steps in single file, their hands clasped on top of their heads. I could hear the police barking their orders, and I stood there a moment, undecided about whether I should just walk back and give myself up.

Before I could bring myself to take the first step back, a red Citröen braked to a stop in front of me. Out of the window a reporter friend of mine* stuck his head. "Toai!" he shouted, "don't go back! Get in the car, quick!" It was all I could do to wrench my eyes away from the scene before opening the door and jumping in next to Bong.

But I wasn't quite fast enough. As Bong threaded his way through the traffic, I saw behind us a Honda motorbike with two plainclothes policemen. Bong swerved down the packed streets, but the Honda got closer and closer, slipping through traffic we could only honk at. "Kieu Mong Thu's house," I gasped at Bong, realizing that we were very near the in-town villa of one of the Assembly opposition leaders. A few seconds later, Bong pulled up, and I sprinted across the pavement and knocked frantically at the door. It was opened just as the Honda bounced to a halt at the curb.

Kieu Mong Thu was one of those women one often sees in Vietnam, her feminine charm complemented by a powerful and determined character. In 1970 she was one of the best-known women in the opposition, representing the militantly antiregime Buddhists. In the temporary shelter of her parliamentary immunity, I managed to rest a while, talking things over with her and trying to come up with some sort of plan. I even got a few hours of sleep, waking just before dawn, when I thought the police surveillance might be relaxed enough for me to slip out of the house and go into hiding.

At about five o'clock I left through the back door, thinking that if I could get a couple of blocks away I'd try to find a pedicab. The street, lit faintly by the early morning sky, was

* Bach Huu Bong, who worked for CBS.

still, deserted. I walked slowly away from the villa, alert, keeping in the shadows of the walls. About a hundred yards down the block, two men jumped out of the dark and pinioned me in an armlock. I didn't struggle. I couldn't really imagine staying free for long anyway.

A few moments later a car pulled up, and I was shoved roughly inside. At police headquarters I was booked, then marched down the hall between two rows of cells. Voices called out to me, welcoming me, voices of my friends who had been arrested earlier in the day. Inside the cell it was like nothing so much as a family reunion.

Two days later, Police Chief General Hai came to visit. He had a strangely perplexed air about him, much different from the friendly menace with which he had greeted me in his office five months before. Hai ate dinner with us that evening, and on the next several evenings, engaging us in discussion and asking questions. He even allowed us out into the prison courtyard to walk with him, the disconcerted guards looking on nervously. He seemed to be searching for answers, trying to comprehend the rationale behind the student movement's bizarre (to him) activities.

Those talks were, I thought, a sincere—if odd—dialogue, just the opposite of my grueling interrogation sessions after the embassy takeover. To the interrogatoi then, everything had been simple. The students were fighting against the regime; that meant they were either Communists themselves, or were being led by Communists. But General Hai couldn't quite believe that. In the sharply stratified world of South Vietnam, students were the elite; they stood to inherit the best that society offered. What could be possessing them to spurn their heritage of wealth and ease, to oppose the order that insured it?

Among the participants at these colloquia with the police chief were some dyed-in-the-wool Communists such as Nguyen Tron Quang Nghi, a student ideologue several years older than I. For General Hai, arguing with a convinced Marxist like Nghi was like preaching in the desert. But he had no better luck with the rest of us. We were in fact not much different from so many resisters of the older generation. The bulk of them had had no clear vision of the future; neither a Marxist vision nor any other. Their motivating passion had been to liberate the nation. "Nothing," they believed with Ho Chi Minh, "is more precious than independence and liberty."

It was true that our circumstances differed from theirs. The parasitic colonialism of the French was now history, and so was the moral simplicity of the earlier rebellion. But since the shameful French era had been brought to a bloody finish, Vietnam's identity, its indigenous culture, had not been given a moment to revive itself. Instead, the Americans had descended on us, bringing with them forces vastly more destructive than the genteel rapacity of their predecessors.

Caught between the NLF and northern melange of communism and nationalism on the one hand and the Americans and their servitors on the other, I and others like me supported the Communists. At least they were Vietnamese! Amid the quicksand ambiguities of the war, here was a principle one could grasp hold of. Careful, afraid, unwilling to commit myself, unsure about what kind of future I wanted, or about how to get there—with all these doubts, I knew a couple of things clearly: I too was Vietnamese, while those whom General Hai represented had created a government of treason. Like so many of his colleagues (including Generals Thieu and Ky) he had been an officer in the French colonial army committed to preserving the colonial status of his countrymen. Trained in that spirit, there was simply no way for him to understand our motives, let alone to dissuade us from them.

We spent a week in Chi Hoa jail, then we were released. There was no hearing, no trial, nothing. The entire world had eyes and ears in Vietnam, its attention fastened on the Thieu regime's excesses. Amnesty International, the Red Cross, American congressional committees, and the international press were all spreading their indictments. To the besieged government we were nothing but a liability. So in the end they just let us go—though not without a strict warning about what would happen if we resumed our subversive activities.

9

End of a Movement

It was now mid-July. Back at the beginning of March when Huynh Tan Mam was arrested, I had written letters to student associations around the world asking for support. One of the responses I received came from the Malaysian Students Association, inviting me to participate in the Asian Students Conference to be held in Hong Kong on July 26 with a follow-up session in Manila. On behalf of the student union I had accepted, and now Khac Do (the union's secretary-general) and I applied for permission to leave South Vietnam so that we could attend.

Our departure permits were eventually signed, but not until the day before the end of the conference. As a result, Do and I arrived in Hong Kong only for the last session. Nevertheless, when we were introduced there was a warm round of welcoming applause, showing clearly where the delegates' sentiments lay. I used my one chance to speak to say that unfortunately, we represented only one-half of Vietnam and that both halves should be in attendance. By the same token, I believed that a delegation from the People's Republic of China had a right to join the association.

My remarks occasioned some discussion from delegates who said that if students from these countries were invited, their own governments would not permit them to attend. In the end, my proposal was recorded and given to the executive committee to decide on before the following year's conference.

When we arrived back in Saigon from this perfunctory appearance, the student union was getting ready for the new round of elections that were to take place in September. But a listless and futile air enveloped the preparations. In fact, the events of the previous period had shaken the student union badly. Most damaging was that Huynh Tan Mam and his friends had been revealed as Communist party members. To make matters worse, a number of the most active non-Communist leaders had been shipped into the army after the wave of arrests earlier in the summer and so would not be available to balance Mam's faction.

Many of the militant nationalists were discouraged. Recognizing more and more clearly that they were caught between the government and the Front, they began to lose the hopes they had cherished for a third way. A real "third force," of which the student movement could be part, appeared less and less viable. Overwhelmed in the clash between the two real antagonists, the time was coming when the militants would have to choose between joining the Vietcong, joining the government side, or withdrawing from the struggle altogether. The new union election would hurry that time.

Huynh Tan Mam, now back at the medical school, was one of the candidates for president. His opponent was a science student named Pham Hao Quang. Quang was one of the thirty students our actions had freed from prison along with Mam. But though the police had arrested him as a Communist, he was in reality nothing of the kind. A passionate nationalist of mild leftist leanings, Quang had been approached by the Front, much as I had been. Like me he had deflected their overtures. Now he suspected that it was the Front that had secretly denounced him as a Communist, counting on police maltreatment to turn him into an enthusiastic partisan. With suspicions like these, he was a determined adversary of he Communist Mam.

With a vicious contest shaping up I decided against running myself, despite Mam's encouragement. I knew that if I won with Mam's support, I would be irrevocably beholden to him and to those who stood behind him. And without his support, I didn't think there was a chance. Even if I were to squeak by without his backing, I simply wouldn't have enough strength to maintain a neutralist position.

The duel between Mam and Quang was savage. Mam accused Quang of being a tool of the generals. Quang countered by charging that Mam was a mouthpiece for Hanoi. In the course of the struggle, Mam asked for my support, but our relationship had entered an ambiguous stage. Since his Communist affiliation was now known, any endorsement would have been practically equivalent to joining the party myself. That was a label I didn't want at any price. Instead I tried to speak for moderation and for the unity of the movement. But emotions were running far too high.

On the first ballot, Mam received votes from ten of the seventeen schools that made up Saigon university. Quang received seven. But the election resolved nothing. By this time the two groups were so antagonistic that they began meeting separately. In the end, the seven schools that supported Quang seceded from the union. It was the clearest possible declaration that as we looked toward the end of 1970, the student movement was incapable of sustaining an independent identity for itself. With this realization, deterioration quickly set in. Feeling undercut by the accusations that had been made against him, Quang gradually withdrew from active leadership, leaving his faction without direction. Not long afterward Mam was rearrested (he would be held until 1975), along with most of the others we fought so hard to liberate. This time the divided and disheartened union was unable to react.

By now my own vision was turning away from the student movement. I knew that my time at the university was nearly over. I had spent so much time away from the books during the last year that I was in danger of flunking out. On the other hand, I had made a name for myself in politics and political journalism, and I was attracted by the idea of a future in public life. Without having formulated any specific plans along these lines, I decided to take advantage of two more invitations I had received to travel abroad, this time to France and the United States. I knew that international experience would give me an unusual qualification for any future political activity.

The trip to Paris turned out to be uneventful. I met a good many overseas Vietnamese politicians and gave a speech before the Vietnamese Student Association, in which I denounced the corrupt regime and its oppression of the students. In public and private, I told the story of the student union's struggle over this past year and the progress we had made. I met too with people from various French student associations and answered their questions about conditions inside Vietnam.

In Paris I also made contact with the Front. Dr. Hung, the head of Vietnamese student groups in Paris, introduced me to a young Vietnamese student who drove me to a meeting on the outskirts of the city with two Front operatives. Our discussion proved inconclusive. For my own reasons I was anxious to find out about chances that the Front might support a more neutralist president (South Vietnam's presidential elections were coming up the next year, and "Big" Minh was already being spoken of as a candidate) in order to get direct talks going between the NLF and Saigon. For their part, the two cadres would have been happy to recruit me for the NLF. But when they realized I was probing just as much as they were, they turned distant. We parted after dinner, with no gain on either part.

After ten days in Paris I flew to the United States, where I had an invitation from several antiwar professors from Redlands University (California) with whom I had spent time while they were visiting Saigon.

My first stop was Washington, where I was met by an attractive young woman who showed me around the city and helped me make my travel connections. Everything in the United States seemed bigger than in France; the cars, the spaces, even the people. There was also an atmosphere of energy and purpose that I didn't sense among the Parisians. Though I had never been there before, France had seemed somehow familiar. The United States definitely was not.

My escort herself was an introduction to the strangeness of American ways. She had recently been divorced and was obviously still preoccupied by the trauma. To be polite, I told her that she seemed beautiful and intelligent, and that I couldn't understand how anyone would want to divorce her. To my shock, every time I said "beautiful" or "intelligent," she thanked me. In Vietnam such a response would have been impossible. Conditioned from childhood to modesty, Vietnamese have an unerring ability to deflect praise. Outright compliments, to someone of my background, are to be shied away from in the most self-deprecatory manner you can manage. Thanking someone for calling you beautiful is in Vietnamese terms the equivalent of trumpeting your own magnificence. It's just not done.

When I got out to California for my first antiwar speaking engagement, my impression of Americans as people of strange personal habits was intensified. At Redlands University the audience seemed full of young people with long and wildly unkempt hair. Many of them were wearing raggedy clothes, often with the sleeves cut out of their shirts. Some had pieces of cloth tied around their wrists and bright rags bound to their pants or wrapped around their heads. It was as if I had landed on another planet, full of creatures who found it impossible to take themselves seriously. After giving a speech to a small crowd in an auditorium and a couple of talks in classrooms, I headed north to San Francisco, where other dates had been set up for me at Berkeley and Stanford.

In San Francisco, one of the Berkeley organizers picked me up at the airport and took me first to his apartment so that I could wash up and leave my bag. As I walked into his place, I found myself looking straight at a giant poster portrait of Che Guevara. On other walls were equally big posters of Chairman Mao and Uncle Ho. I couldn't believe an American would have such things; not even the most leftist of my friends would create a display like this (even without the threat of police searches).

At the university I spoke about political oppression in South Vietnam, about opposition to the dictators, about the need for South Vietnamese self-determination. All of this was received well, but I had the feeling that the audience wanted more, that they wanted me to tell them that the Vietcong should win and that the Vietcong were going to win. While I spoke, I kept thinking to myself that if I were really a Vietcong they would go wild over me. I also had the sudden conviction that the southern regime could never succeed in this war, that if American young people were such partisans of the other side, it was just a matter of time before Thieu's ally and sole support began to back away from him.

From Berkeley I went to Stanford, where this conviction took root. First I had dinner with about thirty professors and students, to whom I gave a short talk on the Saigon regime and its opposition. Even though my English was broken, they listened attentively to what I said and obviously had a great deal of respect for me. Then I realized that it wasn't necessarily me; it was what I represented that elicited their respect. Standing in front of them, I had become to some degree a symbol of Vietnam's revolution. Given my own ambivalence on the subject, it was not a role I felt at all comfortable with.

After dinner, I was scheduled to speak at a large antiwar rally of perhaps a thousand people. A woman activist spoke before me, making an emotional appeal to the crowd to stop the war and get American soldiers out of Vietnam. One of her main points seemed to be that major American corporations were profiting hugely from the killing. She ended with a rousing appeal to "stop America from selling war!"

My first words as I got up to speak were to the effect that

"America can't be allowed to sell the war, and Vietnam can't be allowed to buy it!" At this the audience broke into a roar of applause, standing up to cheer and clap. With such a response, I discarded my prepared speech and told them I would just answer questions. A great many were about the NLF, about how strong they were and about how well they represented the people of South Vietnam. Mostly, the questioners wanted me to tell them what they already believed, about the great strength of the Vietcong and about the validity of their cause.

I was no expert on American politics or culture, but I was an expert on student movements and the disruption they could cause. Interpolating from my own experience, I concluded that these committed and enthusiastic antiwar people would eventually have a powerful affect on events in Vietnam. With these thoughts to keep me company I embarked on the long flight home.

10

Phan Rang

Shortly after I returned, my girlfriend of several years and I got married. Yvonne Vo Duc was, almost literally, the girl next door—her family's house was directly across from my brother's. After I moved to Saigon in 1964 we would see each other on the street and wave or say hello. I thought of her as one of the neighborhood kids. But Tet *Mau Than* changed our relationship, as it changed so much else.

As the offensive raged, sputtered, and then died, the number of corpses littering Saigon's streets grew. With the corpses came the threat of plague. From some of his doctor friends, my brother had gotten hold of several lots of cholera serum, and it fell to me to administer the inoculations. In Vietnam, unlike the United States, injections are not given by medical personnel, but by local people trained in the art. One of my father's roles in Vinh Long was that of "injector," and he had passed his knowledge on to me. From time to time I would administer shots to neighborhood residents who had heard I was gentle with the needle, and now there was a lively demand for cholera vaccinations.

I gave the injections to family, friends, and neighbors, including the Vo Duc family across the way. As I was preparing Yvonne's arm for the shot—pinching it, plumping it up, rubbing it with alcohol—something happened, some electricity that I never expected. That was the beginning. She was my first date, and after three years our relationship had survived other friendships and ripened. Before I left for France, we decided to get married as soon as I came back.

I had debated this decision with myself for a long while. Vietnamese politicians, especially militants, are better off single. It was a dangerous profession, with long jail terms common, and torture or death distinct possibilities. Beyond these things, political leaders welcome the aura of self-sacrifice and devotion to the people that comes with denying themselves family comforts. Ho Chi Minh had never married and had never (as far as anyone knew for sure) had a serious attachment.

I was beginning to think seriously about a political career, and I certainly regarded myself as a militant. So the decision to marry hadn't been easy. There were other obstacles too, foremost among them my mother. Yvonne's family was Catholic, which didn't sit well with my mother's deep-seated Buddhism and her feeling for Vietnamese traditions. (It was only in the last few years that Catholics had been given special dispensation to take part in ancestor veneration. Marriage with non-Catholics had also only recently been permitted.) My father accepted the situation more easily. An old teacher of French, he was not at all upset by the prospect of an alliance with the French-educated Vo Ducs. The fact that my future father-in-law was a well-known composer and conductor also attracted him.

Eventually my mother allowed herself to be persuaded, though her tolerance did not extend so far that she would come to church for the wedding. Out of consideration for her feelings, my father also stayed away, leaving my brother and sister to represent the family. Another hitch developed at the restaurant where both families finally gathered to celebrate the union. That night, the usual singer and band were supplemented by a surprise striptease act. Though the performance was fairly tame, it sent some of my older aunts from the delta into shock. "Toai, this is decadent! What kind of tradition is this?" They had certainly never seen anything like it in Rach Ranh.

After the wedding, Yvonne and I settled into marriage at her parents' house. Slightly larger than my brother's, it was home to only Yvonne's mother and father and their two daughters. Across the way, we were eleven in all. Already my brother and his wife had given my parents six grandchildren, with a seventh on the way.

While I enjoyed the relative quiet and began to think hard about the future, Yvonne changed jobs. Marriage to me had put her in a difficult situation at the government ministry where she worked, but her boss had helped her to find another position at a private bank. It was the first problem that life with a militant gave her. Perhaps she sensed it would not be the last.

Although technically I was still a student, my thoughts were further and further from studies. I realized I was at a turning point in my life, a time to take stock of where I was and think hard about the future. In the crowded drama of the previous year and a half, events had come so fast there had been no opportunity to think beyond the moment. For the first time I began to consider how I might use my energies in some more decisive, more stable way.

It was not just a problem of energy; I also had to make a living. We were staying with my parents-in-law, getting along on my wife's salary and the money I earned as a tutor. But what was I to do? I was twenty-five years old. For years already I had been preoccupied with thoughts of the nation, the regime, the Front—and with where I stood in relation to the historic events into which I had grown up. In this I was no different from most Vietnamese of my generation. But I recognized in

Yvonne and I celebrating our wedding. Sitting directly in front of me (with the glasses) is Nguyen Van Thang.

myself certain qualities—fervor, combativeness, an ability to move people—that colored my own situation. I could not see myself taking some kind of ordinary job. Service in the government's bureaucracy or military was anathema.

The Front was a different story. In my heart I supported them. And my trip to the United States had convinced me that someday they would win. But I bridled at the thought of being controlled, of giving up my autonomy and consigning myself to life as someone else's agent, as Mam had done and as the Front operative in the *pho* shop had urged me to do.

I understood too that my recent experiences were valuable training, giving me the ability to speak and write effectively. I had been brought into close touch with most of the South's leading opposition figures—political people like Tuyen, Kieu

Mong Thu, Ngo Ba Thanh, and Nguyen Long, religious people like Thich Tri Quang and Thich Thien Minh.* I had also gained wide popular recognition, at least in Saigon. With national elections coming up in the fall of 1971, I began to devise plans for a political campaign that would take me to the National Assembly to join the small but vocal block of anti-Thieu deputies.

The first order of business was staying out of the draft, so often used by the regime to keep military-age opponents in line. To this end I took the standard route, finding an official to bribe for exemption papers. With this worry out of the way, I spent the days reading, writing, defining my ideas, and publishing them in *Tu Quyet*. I met with friends and mentors, gauging my support and looking for commitments. Each week I would stop by the student union to teach my class at the union-sponsored free school and to keep up my contacts. I felt I was off to a good start.

This "start," however, was quickly squelched by a new minimum age requirement that was pushed through the Assembly in preparation for the fall elections. I missed the cutoff by a couple of months.

With this news, Thang and I decided that he would make the run for First District representative instead of me. His constituency was exactly the same, and it was an easy matter to line up for him the support I had already rallied for myself. I became his manager. Ours was not the only campaign by student activists; in Phu Yen Province Nguyen Cong Hoan, a member of the Buddhist student opposition, was running against twenty other candidates in an election that was likely to be determined by regime control of the ballot boxes.

But in the end, neither campaign went as expected. Hoan won by a landslide so big that even the standard provincial election fraud was ineffective to prevent it. Thang also won a seat—on the first count when he was fourth in the running for five places. But the next day, it turned out that he was not fourth after all, but sixth.

---

* *Thich* signifies "venerable," the common title for Buddhist monks.

The aftermath of a student demonstration against government manipulation of the 1971 elections. I am on the left wearing an armband.

This was an election notorious for its corruption, one that became world news because of Thieu's successful machinations to keep Vice-President Ky and General "Big" Minh out of the running. But corrupt or not, the result was that we had lost. Thang was promptly drafted and shipped out to Ca Mau Province in the farthest reaches of the delta. My bought exemption saved me from that fate. But my future was now as muddy as the water in the Rach Ranh canal.

Watching me grope my way around in some desperation after our defeat in the fall of 1971 eventually proved too much for my brother Trung, watching all this from across the way. Twelve years older than I, he had always cared for me with what might have been called fatherly affection, except that he was far gentler and more openly loving than Vietnamese fathers generally are. Living with him and his rapidly expanding family after I first came to Saigon had only drawn us closer.

In his own career, Trung had studied agricultural science in Japan and had worked for a relative of ours who owned a thriving fishing business. He later set up his own consulting firm and developed wide contacts in Saigon's banking and business world. Now Trung decided the time had come to intervene in my unhappy situation.

One of his close friends was the president of the Nam Do Bank, a man I too had met on occasion. Trung prevailed on this friend to offer me a job, though what qualifications of mine they might have discussed I was never able to determine. The first I knew of it was when Trung knocked on my door and told me to change clothes—I was going downtown to talk with the president of Nam Do about a position.

My initial response was typical: "A job? I don't need any job! I'm doing just fine!"

"Okay," Trung said, smiling and philosophical. "Okay, there's no need for a job. A job isn't necessary. Maybe you'll want it, maybe you won't. All he wants to do is talk. Now just get changed and go."

So I went. The president made it clear that he wanted me, and I made it clear that I might be interested. "Maybe later," I told him. I needed time to think about it.

At home I did think about it, hard. I thought: I can't live like this, jobless, Yvonne pregnant by this time. My golden political future—where was that? Dried up, now that Thang had been "defeated." And even if Thang had won, Thieu was clamping down harder and harder on opposition, increasing the violence, the intimidation. With the Americans on their way out, Thieu was cleaning house, reverting to real Vietnamese politics and scrapping the concessions to form the Westerners had wrung from him. The political vista looked extraordinarily narrow, at least for the time being. Meanwhile, the bank was offering a good salary, and a manager's position. Of course it didn't have to be permanent. If I chose to see it as a temporary position, something to do while I figured out the future, that's what it would be.

Responsibility beckoned. I was, I knew, rationalizing my way into accepting the job. But neither did I know what else I might do. In the end, I took it, in time to start on-the-job

My brother Trung and I on Hong Thap Tu Street where we lived

training at Nam Do headquarters on December 1, 1971. Then I was sent for further seasoning to the branch in Bien Hoa, about twenty miles north of Saigon. After that I was judged fit to run my own branch, the Nam Do bank in Phan Rang, another two hundred long miles north of the capital.

Phan Rang was an impoverished backwater, noted primarily as the birthplace of Nguyen Van Thieu and as the capital of the ancient kingdom of Champa, which the Vietnamese had finished annihilating in the fifteenth century. One joke had it that Thieu was Champa's revenge on Vietnam.

But though Thieu was from Phan Rang, he was in fact ethnically Vietnamese. But racial Chams still lived in the region, distinguishable by their dark skins and small, black eyes. Some still spoke the Cham language, quite different from Vietnamese and totally incomprehensible to me. Monuments too had survived from Champa's glorious past, brick remains, some of them intricately carved.

But except for these odd bits of a vanished culture, Phan Rang had nothing to recommend it. There was little business to do at the bank, I had no friends, Yvonne and Dinh (our first-born) were still living in Saigon, and no one at all talked politics. I felt as if I had been cast into exile. I played tennis and went swimming. Most of all I tried to think up ways to relieve the stupefaction.

What business there was was entirely routine, primarily money transfers, deposits, and withdrawals—transactions for which a manager was hardly needed. With so little happening, I found myself initiating political discussions with my employees. Though it wasn't discreet, I could hardly help myself. I knew my views offended a number of the tellers and clerks, especially the chief teller, who would fume in silence over my analyses or my attacks on the corruption of the generals or the cynicism of war profiteers.

The oppressiveness of the place was enhanced by the sporadic meetings and social affairs called by the province chief for the city's leading businessmen, myself among them. With us the chief acted exactly like a king with his retainers. He was completely unembarrassed by the mulct, which he considered only his due. "You," he would tell us directly. "You, five thousand; you, ten thousand; you, seven thousand!" It was simply the cost of doing business, but it did its share in reinforcing my hostility toward the regime.

If his tone with the local establishment was imperious, the attitude he took toward ordinary people was insufferable. At one point I was in his office when several elders were ushered in to report an attack on their village. In front of me and other businessmen the chief broke into a tirade, using language and a tone that I would not encounter again until I heard the Tran Hung Dao and Le Van Duyet *bo dois* abusing elderly prisoners. "You are more worthless than dogs!" he screamed. "At least dogs know how to bite if they're attacked!"

As time went by I began to notice that not all the bank's business was as routine as it looked. From time to time we would exchange money for depositors; someone's son would be studying in the United States and would send dollars. Someone else's daughter would have married an American, and they too would have dollars. But when the same person would exchange one thousand dollars one month, then three thousand dollars a month later, I knew these were funny transactions. I began to identify certain people as finance officers for the Front, signs of a war that in Phan Rang at least was largely hidden. I also began to hear stories of road tolls and taxes on Phan Rang's shipments of onions and huge tomatoes that were the province's specialty, collections made by the Front shadow government.

My car trips back to Saigon every two or three weeks provided more dramatic evidence of war. On each trip, the national route would be cut in one or more places, the road blown up or a bridge destroyed. Hundreds of cars would line up, waiting for the army engineers to fill in the holes or bring in a temporary steel bridge. People would lounge on the roadside, or stroll back to the last coffee shop, where they'd pass the time eating, drinking, talking, and flirting. We were used to it. We had accommodated the war into our lives. Even if a car had been blown up by a mine, and its occupants' bodies laid out next to the wreck waiting to be carted off, even then people would just look and pass by. It was nothing special, just the conditions of life.

Sometime in August I was called back to Saigon for a meeting with Nam Do's president. This was unusual, and I wondered what might be brewing. In his office, he showed me a telegram he had received from the province chief demanding that I be replaced immediately. According to the telegram, I was a "Communist sympathizer," which was "inadmissible in the native province of President Thieu." The bank president was friendly, as always, and he proposed a solution. He would transfer me to Qui Nhon, a bustling port city of over a million people. I should go back to Phan Rang and get ready to hand over the branch to a new manager. Also, I should make an effort to restrain myself for as long as it took to show the new man the ropes, pack, and leave.

But I was seething with anger at the province chief. As far as I was concerned he was nothing but an armed robber and a bully, and at least I was going to express the resentment I had built up toward him over the preceding months. With my transfer already in the works, I was primed for a fight, without really fearing that anything serious would come of it.

Getting back in the evening, I drove directly to the province chief's house and insisted on seeing him. I had already concluded that my head teller had denounced me, and I knew that though my remarks to the bank's employees had not been tactful, they were hardly revolutionary. As soon as I was shown in I challenged him directly: "How can you, the son of a Vietnamese patriot"—his father had died in a French jail—"pressure a citizen who is only expressing his opinion? I'm not a government employee! I work for a private company! How can you demand that I be fired from my job? If you really think I'm a Communist, why don't you put me in jail?"

The chief was enraged by this intrusion and assault from the manager of a minor branch bank. Going to his desk, he opened a drawer and pulled out a dossier. From the stack of papers he took several and waved them in my face—photocopies of *Tu Quyet* articles I had written. "Here's proof!" he yelled, his face turning red. "Here's proof you're working for the Communists!"

"What? You think because I want Vietnam's independence I'm working for the Communists?" After some more inconclusive shouting and arm waving, he told me to get out, which I did, slamming the door behind me.

The next day I was summoned to the police station. I went without too much trepidation, fairly sure that the chief had just asked the police to intimidate me a bit. I was wrong. In the duty officer's room, two police grabbed my arms, and I heard the officer say, "I have received an order to arrest you." Then he showed me an arrest warrant, properly made out. Grounds for arrest: "illegal political agitation" and "being a pernicious influence on the public."

In the Phan Rang jail I was first given a single cell, and fairly decent food. But after ten days or so, they shifted me to a collective cell, a large cage about fifteen feet by fifteen that already housed twenty prisoners. Several helmets were available for relieving ourselves, and we were allowed to empty the contents and rinse them out at mealtimes. The food was more revolting than anything I had ever seen: rice with a little meat thrown in, served in a corrugated tub. Since we didn't have individual bowls, it was impossible to divide this repast equitably, and quarrels were always part of the feeding routine. We took turns eating, dipping our hands into the tub, those waiting their turn counting each handful jealously.

This disgusting manner of feeding us was not simply gratuitous. Most of the guards and their families lived in the prison compound, and we were not only prisoners but also an opportunity for them to make money. Several times a day the guards' children and wives would make the rounds of the cells asking, "You want some rice? Some chicken?" Everyone with the means got his food this way, and the wives' cookpots were always steaming. As a result, there were often leftovers of the revolting muck in the tub, and this too was utilized, going to feed the pigs the guards raised in the courtyard. Four years later in Le Van Duyet I would occasionally think back longingly on the leftovers I might have enjoyed at Phan Rang.

During the several weeks I spent in Phan Rang prison I was never mistreated. My stay there was more a personal punishment arranged by the province chief than a serious police matter. But many of my cellmates were not so lucky.

For the most part these people were peasants who had been accused of collaborating with the Front, more or less. Few were hard-core revolutionaries. They had simply suffered the misfortune of living in villages that were subject to the government by day, to the Front by night. Who in those places was not a collaborator of one side or the other? The Front meted out its punishment to those who too readily accepted the government dictates. The government applied its mercies to those suspected of revolutionary leanings.

My peasant cellmates had a hard time understanding what I was doing there; a "gentleman," a banker no less. Despite my denials, the consensus was that I must be a clandestine party official. Whatever they thought of me, to my eyes it was clear that most of these people wanted only to be left alone by both sides, that before their arrests they had not harbored strong political convictions. Like most peasants, their main ambition had simply been to hunker down, avoid attention, and get on with their farming.

Now they had failed at that goal, and life in Phan Rang prison had turned all of them violently against the government. Even the calmest were propelled by anger. They despised the police for taking them away from their families, and they expressed their defiance in any way they could, shouting, "Long live Ho Chi Minh" at the guards (though Ho had been dead two years already) and caring tenderly for those who were dragged back into the cell after interrogation, semiconscious and bloody from the beatings that were standard procedure.

Some had been there more than a year, held without trial or any other legal proceedings under Article Four of the constitution, which outlawed the Communist party and Communist activity. Suspects jailed under Article Four enjoyed none of the usual legal protection. They had no right to counsel, and their sentences were passed in secret by the committee for security of the province or town, a special court presided over by the police chief and the prosecutor. In the far provinces, mere suspicion could send a peasant to jail for years, with no possibility of defending himself. And that was the situation most of my cellmates found themselves in.

But at least one prisoner in the cell was a bona fide Communist, and his life appeared to me almost a symbol of what it meant to be Vietnamese in the twentieth century. Nguyen The Thao was my cellmate in Phan Rang in 1971 and was to be my cellmate again in Tran Hung Dao and Le Van Duyet five years later. While the irony and trauma of my own prison experiences ended by shocking me into a thorough reexamination of everything I knew or thought, Thao, when I met him, was far beyond shock of any sort.

In 1971 he was sixty years old and had been a party member for almost forty of those years. Under the French he had been imprisoned for nine years in the horrific Poulo Condor, where he shared a cell with Le Duan, who succeeded Ho Chi Minh to power in 1969. After his release he rejoined the resistance, where to his surprise he was met with suspicion. He hadn't yet learned that the party always distrusts its own after they have been exposed to the enemy and his nefarious blandishments. To reinstate himself into its good graces, Thai was put through a "reeducation" wringer, writing countless autobiographies, undergoing long interrogations, conducting his own detailed autocriticism. He accepted it all without complaint, until one day the party was sure he was once again pure in word, thought, and deed. It had taken two years. "After all I had been through," he told me, "it was humiliating. But I understood that the party had to be cautious. It's true there have been traitors."

Back in his role as a resistance operative, Thao became a baker in Tay Ninh, responsible for liaison between the city and guerrilla forces outside. After the war he stayed in the South, until in 1956 the hunt for Communists began once more. This time he was arrested by Diem's police and sent back to the familiar Poulo Condor, now called Con Son, a Vietnamese name instead of a French one. The conditions, though, hadn't changed.

Neither had conditions outside, as Thao found out in 1960, when once more he was released and once more subjected to the party's reeducation gauntlet. This time he was out for eight years before the government caught up with him again—

Thieu's police now. Thao was beginning to lose track. Another release and more reeducation. "It's an obsession they have. You're out of their sight for an instant, and they immediately suspect you've gone over."

Like the others in the cage, Thao was sure I was a secret cadre, though he let me know that he understood I couldn't reveal my secret. Still, he wanted me to tell him why they wouldn't trust a militant who'd grown old in jails and fighting. He was tired, but apprehensive too. Not about prison. The crowding, the food, the beatings—those he had learned to handle long ago. What worried him was getting out and facing the party again. Between jail terms he'd been able to marry and have children. "I hardly know them," he said. "They don't recognize me from one time to the next." He wanted to spend his last years with them, but all he could see ahead was reeducation and another assignment. "What would the party think if. . . ." He was afraid to say it out loud, to admit his weakness, this desire to be shut of the whole thing. But maybe I could give him a hint, without forcing him to actually enunciate the question. "What if . . . ?" But I couldn't—or wouldn't. Again I told him I wasn't party. But I could see he didn't believe me, that my reticence merely restated the answer that he already knew.

Later, in Le Van Duyet's Zone C, I heard the rest of Thao's story. In Phan Rang until 1973, then released after the Paris agreement was signed, he chose his family over the revolution. This time there would be no reeducation. Was he naive, or did he think he would have the luck to die in their bosom before anything more could happen?

Two years later the revolution arrived in Saigon, and Nguyen The Thao followed the same route I did, from Tran Hung Dao to Le Van Duyet: an old Communist jailed by young Communists whose fathers were not yet born when he started fighting. By then he had chosen resignation and black humor as his defense. Sure now that I was not a cadre, he talked softly about his life as we squatted next to each other. What else was there to do but talk? "Prison is my country," he said. "Every time I get out, someone recognizes me, and they throw me back in. I know all the cops. First there were the French cops, then there were Diem's cops. After that there were Thieu's cops, and now there are Pham Van Dong's cops. That's normal, I guess."

Before Tet in 1976 we were allowed to write a letter, ostensibly for delivery to our families. Thao wrote: "Forget me. Consider that I've died in combat." It went straight into his dossier.

◊   ◊   ◊

After I had been in jail for two weeks or so, the Phan Rang representative to the National Assembly came to see me, along with a couple of lawyers and businessmen I knew. They were willing to start agitating for my release. I told them not to. Back in Saigon Yvonne was pregnant with our second child, and so far I had managed to hide my imprisonment from her. I was anxious not to worry her. I also knew that Nam Do's president was working quietly to get me out.

Several days later his efforts bore fruit. The news came as an order of expulsion signed by the province chief. Not only was I to get out of jail, I was never to set foot again in the province. By this time I was only too happy to comply.

11

Qui Nhon

When I got back to Saigon, I received a long sermon from the Nam Do president, mixed equally of anger over the embarrassment I had caused and concern for my safety. The tone was more fatherly than castigating. "What did you think you were doing? Don't you know you could get yourself killed out in a province like that?" Afterward I was given a brief vacation, then sent off to my new post in Qui Nhon.

Almost exactly halfway up South Vietnam's long coastline, Qui Nhon in September of 1972 was a busy seaport and commercial center. Swollen with refugees from the countryside, its population was approaching a million people. A crowded and active place, it was as different from the torpor of Phan Rang as I could have wished.

In Qui Nhon I felt at home immediately, making friends and business contacts, excited by the bustle of the place. My position gave me quick access to the local establishment and political people and access to a wide range of information on the city's economic life. I rapidly discovered there was a lot to know.

The irreducible fact of life in Qui Nhon was the corruption that touched almost every single commercial transaction. What I had known before in a general way, I now saw in the most vivid and concrete detail. As cynical as I thought myself, my initial reaction was shock and incredulity. The prime cause (if indeed one cause could be singled out) was the government's failure to pay a living wage to its civil and military functionaries. The bureaucrats, the people around whom private enterprise turned (or didn't turn), simply could not survive on the money their jobs brought them. To get by, let alone to get rich, they had to cultivate other sources.

And of course they did. In Phan Rang when the province chief levied his personal tax I had been surprised he was so direct about it. After the first immersion in Qui Nhon's business waters, it was impossible to be surprised by anything. Innovative financing was a way of life, a commonplace that people discussed as freely and unashamedly as they did sports or their restaurant dinner the previous night. The old idea of government service as a trust was simply not part of the world I was now learning to chart.

The disappearance of the very concept of public trust or guardianship, which had been so prominent in Vietnam's past, I laid squarely on the doorstep of Nguyen Van Thieu and his lieutenants. It was the celebrated dealing and scheming at the highest levels in Saigon that set the tone for the pettiest bribes in Qui Nhon, five hundred miles up the coast. The entire country was like a broody sow upon whom everyone suckled who could. A job as captain, clerk, or general (or president, for that matter) was seen as a way of making money that provided access to other ways of making money. The businessman would come to the government official to facilitate a deal, and the official would become his partner. As the Nam Do manager, I often played banker to both parties.

One of my first experiences in this role was a bridge deal. A local businessman looking for steel had been able to buy an all-steel bridge from the army captain in charge of an outlying district. The bridge, which had been laid in to replace an earlier structure mined by the guerrillas, simply disappeared—dismantled and hauled off by the entrepreneur's workers. The captain's report described the new bridge as having been blown up, just as the old one had been. He asked for beefed-up patrolling in the area. Everyone was happy, except the peasants who used the bridge to get their crops to market. I couldn't even blame the captain. I knew that he needed money to pay off his commanding officer, who was blackmailing him by threatening a transfer to some active front. Who might have been doing what to the commanding officer, I didn't know.

More and more aware now of the systemwide rot, I was rapidly coming to the conclusion that there was no way out but to scrap the whole thing and start anew. For *Tu Quyet* I wrote a long article entitled "The Bankruptcy of Revolution," which argued the impossibility of any nationalist or reform-minded "revolution." My point was that the entire edifice had to be swept away and a new start made. American aid, I said, had been grossly responsible for much of the corruption. The more money and the more goods that were made available, the more rotten the Saigon government grew. And the corrupt government had spread its infection. At all costs we had to separate Vietnam from the source of this infection. Though the language may have been turbid, the analysis, I felt, was valid. It certainly corresponded to everything I saw in Qui Nhon.

At the same time, I began to look around actively for contact with the Front, and it wasn't long before I was able to identify certain customers who were serving as intermediaries. Apparently inadvertent hints allowed me to establish contact. When I felt comfortable enough that I was right, I began to talk more directly. Soon I had become friendly with a drugstore owner whose main business was supplying medicine to the guerrillas, and with a manufacturer of *nuoc mam* (the ubiquitous Vietnamese fish sauce) who served as a Front banker.

After the *nuoc mam* maker introduced me to a liaison agent

QUI NHON ◊ 169

from the Front's economics section, I began cooperating in small ways, handling discreet exchange transactions and responding to requests for economic reports. The subjects covered in these reports ranged from the specific impact of American aid and of the severe inflation to the effectiveness of South Vietnam's land reform program. I found it easy to acquire information. Friends in the National Bank, my own widening government and military contacts, and my brother's business associates all were unknowingly helpful. My job allowed me to circulate freely through the province to examine bank-related investments and potential investments, and these trips too added to my stock of knowledge. They also convinced me that South Vietnam was ripening to fall.

◊   ◊   ◊

On January 27, 1973, the Paris cease-fire agreement was signed. The night the news came out, Yvonne and I had dinner with friends, then went back with them to the house to monitor the radio. That night peace was in the air. But peace seemed hardly imaginable, unreal, visionary. None of us sitting around our radio had ever experienced a society at peace. We had been born into war. War had attended us in childhood and was the companion of our maturity. War was real, but peace (hoa binh) had an effervescent feel to it. We didn't quite believe in it.

When the terms of the agreement became known, our skepticism mounted. If indeed there was going to be some kind of peace, it would be the Front's peace, and the North's peace. In the circles I moved in, almost everyone thought that the government had lost. There was to be no withdrawal of the northern army from South Vietnam. On the other side, the Americans were really out, retaining only their power to threaten. The general sense that Paris had been a disaster for Saigon was reinforced by Thieu's attempt to limit publication or discussion of the agreement, while at the same time the Front was doing everything it could to circulate the text and publicize its meaning. Radio Hanoi and Radio Giai Phong

In front of the Nam Do branch in Qui Nhon

(Radio "Liberty," the Front station) celebrated Paris as if it were a victory rather than a compromise.

As time passed I sensed that a new mood had come over people. Somehow this war was going to be over, though how it might end nobody could say. Perhaps when the pressure mounted Thieu would agree to some form of coalition government as outlined in the agreement. (Chapter Four stipulated the creation of the National Council of National Reconciliation and Concord, made up of three equal parties: Saigon, the Front, and neutral third parties. This council was to arrange elections and settle all internal political matters.) Or perhaps Thieu's regime would simply collapse, leaving "Big" Minh or some other neutralist leader to negotiate with the Front.

I sensed this mood most strongly among my army friends and acquaintances around Qui Nhon. They were depressed about growing shortages of equipment, fuel, and ammunition. Underneath, they believed the war was being lost, that it could well be over in the foreseeable future. Like everyone else, they

longed to be done with the killing, to return home and live ordinary lives, to forget the strain of it all. And who in their right
mind wanted to be the last fool to die?

This was emphatically not the mood of my contacts in the
Front. They showed not fatigue, but enthusiasm. Paris had
brought vast new opportunities; the future, they thought, was
bright.

Through the remainder of 1973 and into 1974 nothing
much seemed to be happening on the war front. Instead the
two sides appeared to be testing each other, preparing for some
final drama. A ranger colonel friend of mine told me he had
watched, helpless, as a North Vietnamese armored column
rolled by his positions in the hills overlooking the approaches
to Qui Nhon. It was an ominous event, full of news about a
buildup of revolutionary forces and a decisive swing in the balance of power.

On the civilian front, rumors swept the city. We heard that
Kissinger had made a secret deal with Le Duc Tho to partition
South Vietnam right below Qui Nhon. We heard that Ky was
planning to overthrow Thieu, and that "Big" Minh had similar intentions, that the South would declare itself neutral.
Every wind brought its message, and no one could tell the true
from the false. Tension, uncertainty, and an incipient panic
made their way through the city. The anxiety of Qui Nhon's
several hundred thousand refugees, who had already lost everything, now laid its hand on the rest of the inhabitants.

In mid-December it began. Several North Vietnamese divisions struck the province of Phuoc Long on the Cambodian
border, crippling government defenses and besieging the province capital. From the Americans there was no response at all,
not a move toward implementing their threat about punishing
violations of the agreement. In three weeks the ARVN forces
had collapsed, leaving the Communists with their first trophy
of the offensive. Never before had the revolution controlled an
entire province.

Hearing about the defeat, I sensed that this was the beginning, that the premonitions of the last year and a half were

about to come true. I wasn't particularly unhappy about it, though now that it was happening I couldn't feel any enthusiasm either. It was, I thought, a classic dilemma. What sane person could want the Thieu dictatorship to continue? But who could see what shape a future without Thieu might have? There were too many factors swirling together: communism, nationalism, the northern army, the Front, the third force neutralists. And what about the Americans—would they eventually step back in?

I was awash in emotion; anxiety reached out toward hope, and expectation danced with fear. At Tet I took Yvonne and the children (three, now that Huy had been born) back to Saigon, and left them there when I returned to work. On March 11 came the news that Ban Me Thuot had fallen, and that the Central Highlands were open wide to the revolutionary flood tide. A few days later Kontum was abandoned and Pleiku, and as the tide swept on, it pushed a wave of refugees before it into Qui Nhon.

Striking contrasts stood out in the kaleidoscope of tension and activity the city had become. Many people were packing their belongings and searching desperately for transportation. Boat prices went through the roof; the roads were choked with cars and buses. Others simply went about their lives as if nothing unusual were happening.

At the bank, crisis followed crisis. Refugees from the northern cities of Hue, Da Nang, and Quang Ngai crowded the floor demanding money, screaming that managers in those cities had promised their accounts would be available in Qui Nhon. Mixed in with them were our regular customers, all of them cleaning out their savings. Seeing that we would soon run out of cash, I instituted a policy of allowing only limited withdrawals. The days were filled with screaming arguments, people crying and begging, demanding what was theirs. Every bank in Qui Nhon witnessed the same scene. "There's no money. Money will be available in Saigon. There's no money!" Over and over, endlessly, from mid-March right up to the end of the month.

By then there was no more business to be done and no more money either. From Saigon I received an order to move out, to close up the branch. With our last assets I paid as much salary as I could, then bought a large fishing boat (complete with pilot). Into the boat we loaded all the bank's records and whatever equipment was movable, including our air-conditioning units and big, old-fashioned IBM calculating machines. Then I made sure our employees who wanted to leave were aboard with their families and watched as the boat moved slowly away from the dock.

For myself, I had decided to stay. I was doing my best to believe there was nothing to fear. I didn't want to feel that I had to flee; certainly there was no fighting in the vicinity yet. And soon they would come here. Soon afterward they would come to Saigon. I thought, it might as well be here.

That's what I thought as I watched the boat disappear toward the south. But two days later I wasn't so sure. The city was dead, not that everyone had left. In fact, with the great exodus over it appeared that the majority of the population had elected to stay. But the place was quiet, enveloped by a strange, expectant stillness. With the bank closed I passed the time playing tennis and, like everyone else, waiting—watching for the columns of *bo dois* to materialize out of the west.

One day near the beginning of April, after spending several hours on the courts, I got into my car and drove down toward the center city airport to see what news I might pick up. As I neared the terminal I noticed an Air Vietnam plane making its landing approach. Inside I talked with a friend of mine, the Qui Nhon manager for Air Vietnam, who was one of my best sources for up-to-date information. This, he said, was the last plane out. As soon as it left they were closing down the airport. There was plenty of room, so why didn't I go? In that moment, my resolution deserted me. Wearing shorts and tennis shoes I walked out onto the runway and got in, leaving my car parked where it was.

12

Saigon

Back in Saigon, I reported to the bank and made arrangements to receive the boat and its cargo. The city amazed me. It seemed not to have changed at all, as if the military disaster were taking place on some far planet and was of no local concern. Housewives went to market, men to work, children to school. At night first-run Hollywood movies played to full houses.

No one believed that the end was near. Saigon was too big, too full of life to be anything other than what it had always been. Many thought the Vietcong were walking into a trap, that the revolutionaries had been suckered into an all-out frontal assault and would now be ripped to shreds, as they were during Tet and during the 1972 spring offensive. Even the worrywarts were sure they had at least a few months ahead of them. Most people simply went about their business as usual, too inured to exaggeration and rumor to panic . . . at least so long as no bullets were whistling past their ears. Anyway, what if the Vietcong did win? Where was the risk in that? The new leaders would be stricter no doubt, but honest. At least they would be honest! And the war—after thirty grim and bloody years the war would be over.

In all this the Front's propaganda worked like an anesthetic. Everyone, including the soldiers, listened to Radio Giai Phong as it broadcast its assurances. Only the puppet leaders and war profiteers would be punished. For the people, a future of "reconciliation without retribution," a nationwide celebration of unity and concord. Those who had been dragged against their will into this fratricidal conflict could expect understanding and forgiveness.

Should we have believed it or not? The Front's government, the PRG (Provisional Revolutionary Government), was liberally sprinkled with moderates. The Front's program was a beacon of hope. People wanted to believe it. What, they asked themselves, was the alternative?

In the third week of April 1975 the sky fell in on the complacent and hopeful capital. During that week the first tidal swell of refugees broke over the city, gathering itself into the empty spaces and spreading news of what had happened. Under the French, Saigon had numbered perhaps six hundred thousand. As the new refugees poured in, the already enlarged city swelled up like a tick. How many there were no one could tell. Two million? Three million? Somehow they found room in the shantytowns encircling the city. Then another wave hit, then a third, as the retreating southern army fell back on the outskirts.

In the Nam Do Bank headquarters where I was now working, pandemonium was the backdrop to tragedy. Here the last days in Qui Nhon repeated themselves on a grander scale. All the refugees who had kept their accounts in Nam Do branches made their way to us. Each had his tale of woe, and each demanded his money. It was my job to process the problems from all the northern branch accounts.

With no updates from these branches since March, it was an impossible labor. Typically, someone would claim to have

had five million piasters on deposit in Da Nang. The last update might even confirm this, but who knew what withdrawals
might have been made afterward? Meanwhile this poor man
and his family were living under a plastic canopy with no way
to put food in their mouths. There was one gut-wrenching
story after another: old people, impoverished peasants, all the
frightened survivors of ruined lives. And even if the claims
sounded reasonable and jibed with the last update, still I
couldn't pay what they wanted. There was simply not enough
cash to go around. The National Bank couldn't print it fast
enough.

To deal with the situation, I devised a rudimentary screen-
ing system. I'd tell claimants that there was nothing we could
do now, that they should come back the next day. The next
day it would be the same story. "Sorry, come back tomorrow."
If they showed up a third time, I took their persistence as a
sign of honesty, and gave them . . . not what they were asking
for, but enough so that they could survive temporarily. What
was one to do? The lines had no end, and the money just was
not there. It was a horror.

But going home after work brought no surcease from the
blood pounding in my ears or the racing of my heart. My father was missing. He had been visiting a coffee-and-tea planta-
tion that my brother had bought in Bao Loc, 125 miles
northeast of Saigon. He had not arrived with the river of refugees, and now the route was cut. At best he was trapped. At
worst . . . we tried to keep ourselves from thinking it. I had
never seen my mother so distraught.

As the real world darkened, people now became more attentive to rumors, to undisguised hopes attempting to pass themselves off as truth. The city clasped to its heart news that the
Americans were landing, that they had at last decided to save
Saigon and the delta. But the only actual American traffic was
going the other way, and when that straw was abandoned
others took its place. People spoke knowledgeably of a cease-
fire that would be followed by negotiations between "Big"
Minh and the Front under French sponsorship. It was said
that French president Giscard d'Estaing had been given assur-

ances by Hanoi that it favored a "government of reconciliation." It was known that French ambassador Jean-Marie Mer-
rilon was working feverishly with Giscard's personal
representative on the spot, Paul d'Ornano, to implement the
understanding.

And as rumor gave wing to hope, so it did to fear. "Up
there," the refugees said, "up there" in Da Nang, Pleiku, Kontum, and Hue, cities where the Communists had ruled for a
month, there was no "reconciliation." Influential people who
stayed were shot. Everybody who worked for the old regime,
even the most insignificant bureaucrats, had been arrested.
The soldiers had been rounded up and the businesses confiscated. "It's going to be a bloodbath," the rumors whispered,
"everybody get out while you can!"

Even with the route blocked, refugees kept arriving by way
of side roads and obscure trails. Among them one day appeared
my father, footsore and sick with fever. Surrounded in Bao
Loc, he had escaped through the jungle with a group of people
from the neighboring hamlets. But the old man could only
walk slowly, and his fellow refugees had abandoned him on the
path. With no sustenance except jungle bananas and ground-
water he had collapsed, waking up to find other refugees carrying him on a makeshift litter. Without their help, he said, he
would have died. He had been so worried about us, and about
our anxiety for him, he had not wanted to die. After a time, he
did not know how long, they arrived within the Saigon perimeter. From there he had taken a bus into town.

From his experiences in Bao Loc, my father had developed a
hatred for the Vietcong. "Liars," he said. "Young bastards!
Took anything they wanted, threatened everybody! Bragging,
insufferable bastards!" As he bit the words out, I had a fleeting
image of him two decades before, raising to the sky the hand of
the young village guerrilla who had shot down the airplane.
"Long live Brother Hai," he had shouted. "A great victory for
the revolution!" The next day my brother used his contacts to
find room for him in a hospital. Together we drove him there,
praying that he would get well.

By this time we all knew the decision was on us. I talked it

over at length with my old *Tu Quyet* friends, trying to build up
my courage. What is there, really, to fear? I asked. We have
fought against the regime, helped the Front. We have cam-
paigned for peace and self-determination. And now we are
going to have peace. As for self-determination, this was the
time to demand it, to impose it. The northerners couldn't simply transfer south what they'd created in the North. In fact,
they'd declared explicitly that they had no intention of doing
so. "The South," they'd said in their proclamations, "has different traditions, customs, and a different mentality. These
must be respected." Besides, even if the Communists made us
work hard to rebuild the country, to have true independence,
why not? A diet of discipline and moral rigor wouldn't hurt at
all, especially not after the sink of corruption we'd been swimming in.

Underneath my remarks, and those of others, ran the intui-
tive sense that a Vietnamese could not live outside of his land.
No one said it explicitly, but everyone thought it. How could
we take our families and leave? And go where the language
would not be ours, where the people would not be us, where
our children would not grow up Vietnamese? That might be
something the puppet collaborators could do, the profiteers,
and the luxury whores. But us? What could we possibly fear
that would be worse than that? Also unspoken was a sense of
shame about leaving, about running away with the Americans
and those Vietnamese we had despised for so long.

By the end of the session, we had all pledged ourselves to
stay. Within a few days some of us would begin to waver, myself included. It was that kind of time.

On the afternoon of April 21, Nguyen Van Thieu resigned.
On television he was crying and smiling at the same time,
loading each word with vitriol for the Americans. "They have
betrayed us, lied to us." Thieu waved a letter from Nixon
promising aid. "He lied to us, the president of a superpower
lied. They are inhumane, inhumane allies!" Though he was
now yielding power, hoping his sacrifice would enable negotiations, or last-minute aid, still he would stay in the country with

his soldiers. At the end, he handed over the government to Vice-President Tran Van Huong. Huong, a half-blind and ill old man, accepted the reigns and swore to resist "until all the soldiers are dead or the nation is lost."

Watching this scene, I could tell what Thieu was up to. I knew he had been under pressure to cede control to "Big" Minh instead of Huong, since many felt that Minh had a chance of bringing off negotiations with the northerners and the Front. But "Big" Minh's first act as president would very likely have been to arrest Nguyen Van Thieu for criminal negligence and also for use as a bargaining chip with the other side. Now, with Huong placed to fight a rearguard action against "Big" Minh's bid for power, the former president had time to arrange his escape. (In fact Thieu left the country for Taiwan on April 23, and Minh assumed the presidency on April 28.)

With panic in the city, I set about meeting with everyone I knew who might have some real insight into the course events would take. At the time, I thought of my odyssey through Saigon as simple prudence, an effort to understand the truth behind the intricate and rumor-shrouded events of those days. Ten years later, as I write this, my search takes on a different color. Caught in a historic upheaval, I was looking for guidance. Like everyone else in Saigon, the decisions I made at that moment would determine the future—for myself and for those I loved most.

Like many others, I became a news addict, monitoring television broadcasts, the BBC, the VOA, Radio Giai Phong, and every paper I could get my hands on. I stayed as close as I could to my old protector and fellow *Tu Quyet* board member, Tran Van Tuyen, the dean of National Assembly opposition. Tuyen had been a student with Pham Van Dong (North Vietnam's prime minister) and Vo Nguyen Giap (northern defense minister) in Hanoi during the thirties. In 1946 he served as vice-minister of foreign affairs in Ho Chi Minh's first government, but had broken with the Communists over their methods. He was a nationalist, yes, he had told them, but also a democrat. Settling in Saigon, he practiced law, won an Assembly seat, and became a determined enemy of the Diem and Thieu dictatorships, a man of clear and unshakable moral vision. Tuyen, if anybody, was a rock upon whom one could lean.

At Tuyen's house one day near the end I met the Korean ambassador. Tuyen's daughter had married a Korean diplomat, and the ambassador was urging the old democrat to leave under his protection. Tuyen refused. I sensed he had no illusions about his own likely fate. But he also seemed resigned. I knew he loathed the idea of sharing the lot of those he believed had destroyed the country.

After the ambassador left, Tuyen advised me and his son (my close friend) to stay in Vietnam. The Communists, he hoped, would be more moderate this time around. After all, now they would have to deal with the entire southern people. "In any case," he said wistfully, "I have decided to stay here. I'd rather die in Vietnam than run like a frightened dog."

Another old politician I spent time with was our next-door neighbor, Nguyen Van Huyen. He had been president of the Assembly senate and in a few days would be chosen by "Big" Minh as his vice-president. Huyen was an ascetic Catholic who lived like a monk in his sparsely furnished house, an emaciated old man who needed assistance to walk. But his voice was still firm and his lawyer's mind as lucid as ever. Huyen's pessimism was complete. Staring directly into my eyes as if trying to reinforce his words, he told me, "Toai, if you can get out, then do it. They are going to take power, and they will take it completely. If you haven't been completely with them, you've been against them. For myself I don't care. I'm too old to be afraid of anything. But you get out!"

I got a different point of view from the monk Tri Quang, whom I visited at the An Quang pagoda.* He had been a close ally from my student days, allowing us to use the pagoda for

---

* An Quang was the center of the Buddhist opposition movement, of which Tri Quang was the leader.

Tran Van Tuyen

rallies and coordinating Buddhist demonstrations to reinforce those of the students. I found him reading peacefully in his small bedroom-study, his eyes deep and solemn as ever (though when his eyes gleamed, they and his thick lips made him look more the gangster than the monk). In Tri Quang's opinion, the situation was not all that bad. Buddhism, he said, was strongly rooted in the people. It could not be exterminated. Moreover, Buddhism was a political force that the Communists would have to come to terms with. I got the impression from him, as he sat at his desk talking, that he believed American popular support for his movement was still an asset. In that simple room he seemed isolated from events, and unaware of his isolation.

From Tri Quang's room I stepped down the hall to visit the Buddhist movement's chief strategist, Thich Thien Minh. This monk had fought doggedly against the generals and had brilliantly used the Western television men and reporters to build the Buddhists' power and influence. For his troubles he was sentenced to ten years in prison by Thieu's courts (for "pro-Communist activities") but had been released as a result of international protests and out of fear that the bonzes would resort to their ultimate weapon, public self-immolation. Thien Minh was even more sanguine than Tri Quang. Like Tri Quang, he told me that Buddhism had deep roots, and that no regime could persecute Buddhists and long survive. He believed the Communists would not run that risk. He told me too that he had "always had good relations with the Front."

Two days before the fall, a loud knock sounded on my door. As I got up to answer it, the door swung open and Huynh Tan Mam burst into the room. The former student union president had just been released from jail by "Big" Minh, part of Minh's attempt to demonstrate his desire to reach an accommodation with the Front. Mam was excited. He hadn't been kept well informed in prison, and now he wanted "to do something," play some role in whatever kind of transition was going to happen. He seemed to have the idea that he could act as a bridge between the government and the revolutionaries.

Together we drove to see Ly Qui Chung, whom Minh had appointed minister of information. Like the rest of the Minh government, Chung was casting around desperately for some intermediary to whom the Front might listen. And like the rest of the government, he wasn't having any luck. To Chung, Mam was a straw at which he could grasp, and he immediately took the ex–medical student activist in tow. Before he even had time to prepare a statement, Mam found himself on live television thanking President Minh for releasing him and proclaiming that the hour of reconciliation had come.

Whatever the chances of reconciliation, my brother Trung had already decided to get out. And as the time grew short his pleas that I should go with him became louder and more urgent. Trung's basic argument was simple. He thought that if the new rulers proved humane and constructive, then they would welcome back people who fled, at least those who hadn't worked closely with the Americans. But if we stayed and found ourselves living in a police state, how could we ever leave? Untroubled by doubts about his duty, patriotism, and allegiance, he saw it all plainly. At this juncture his allegiance was to his wife, Mai, and their seven children. His duty was to protect them as well as he could. As for his patriotism, he was Vietnamese, and nothing could change that.

On the morning of April 29 I had wandered out to listen to some source or other. Meanwhile Trung had arranged passage on a boat through one of his business friends, and he and Mai were packing up. Sensing my state of mind, he had told Yvonne to get all our things ready and to prepare the three boys. By the time I got home, all the baggage that could fit was loaded into Trung's Scout, which was sitting in the middle of the narrow street between our houses. Trung's children were being mustered out to the car, and Yvonne was looking at me apprehensively as I walked quickly toward her and the boys. When I understood what was happening, I turned to Trung and said, "I'm not going, that's all there is to it!"

"Okay," he answered, obviously expecting me to say what I had, "then stay here. But let Yvonne and the kids come with me."

Mai started to cry, joining my mother and father, who had obviously been weeping since before I arrived, and half of the children, some of whom were in the car by this time, while others were holding onto their grandparents.

At this point, Yvonne's parents joined the crowd around the Scout, arguing with each other. My mother-in-law was saying loudly that she was going to go, she was afraid of them. But my father-in-law pooh-poohed the whole idea. He didn't care if she went, and what was there to be afraid of anyway? He was going to stay right here with the house, and that was that! All of this in front of a street full of neighbors, who I thought might have had their own problems to attend to.

Amid it all, Yvonne made her decision. Looking into my eyes, she said quietly, "We're staying. I'll follow you wherever you go." Then I went over to the Scout and pulled our bags out of the heap.

At this, Yvonne's mother changed her mind too. But if my parents were relieved by our decision, you couldn't tell it from their eyes.

That evening at 8:00 P.M. Minister of Information Ly Qui Chung read a communiqué over radio and television ordering the southern army to stop fighting. On the streets, overloaded cars carrying last-minute refugees drove southward toward the last open highway out of the city.

That night no one slept. Lying in bed we listened to the sounds: shots, explosions, the distant wham of rockets. Tomorrow "they" would arrive, and what would "they" do, what would "they" be like?

13

Ho Chi Minh City

From midday of April 30, Saigon's streets were filled with *bo dois* in green uniforms, column after column marching by, shouldering their Chinese-made AK-47s. The NLF fighters wore floppy bush hats; the northerners, colonial-style pith helmets. The bush bats were swamped in a sea of helmets.

T-54 tanks rolled in, flying the NLF flag, half red, half blue, a yellow star in the center: Vietnam's two halves, united in a single purpose. A young Saigon architect—a student activist during Diem's time—hitched a ride on the first tank, then rushed up to the roof of Doc Lap Palace to unfurl another Vietcong flag. The first revolutionary troops inside the palace, though, were northerners; the tanks were from the North's 203d armored brigade, the infantry sitting on top of them from the 116th regiment. With eighteen other divisions in and around the city, it was apparent that the entire northern army had come south.

Since General Duong Van Minh had ordered all southern

soldiers to lay down their arms, the revolution's army just walked into the city. A few ARVN paratroop units fought on briefly at Tan Son Nhut airport. Here and there, some snipers took pot shots at the marching *bo dois*. Other than that, the city was ominously quiet, clothed with apprehension. Most people locked themselves up inside. Watching furtively from their windows, they saw the last southern soldiers throw down their arms, then strip off their uniforms, leaving little piles of clothing on the sidewalks. They saw the last looters scurrying by with goods of every imaginable sort, "liberated" from American offices, warehouses, and villas.

There followed a period of surprised mutual inspection, the Saigonese eyeing the Communist soldiers, the *bo dois* gawking at the citizens and the city. The Saigonese were nonplussed, staring at these invincible jungle fighters. For years, competing propaganda had created myths about them. For some, they were ferocious monsters, for others, heroic liberators. For everyone, fearsome warriors. And now, here they were: tired, sallow-faced, thin young men, staring in bewilderment at the wonders around them.

If the Saigonese were surprised by what they saw, the *bo dois* were flabbergasted. Twenty-one years had passed since the country's division, and most of these victors had passed their entire lives on an exclusive diet of Marxist ideology and northern propaganda. Shaped by nineteenth-century doctrines of class struggle and imperialist oppression, they were incapable of comprehending the reaction of the society they had suddenly walked in on. After years of inhuman sacrifice, they had now triumphed over the crushing evil that was enslaving their southern brothers. Everything in their experience told them to expect the glory and honor due saviors. Saigon's streets should have been awash with joy and adulation. It should have been the Parisians pouring out their hearts to the Free French in August of 1944, or the Hanoi citizenry embracing Ho Chi Minh's guerrillas in August the year after.

Instead, they found themselves camping in nearly empty streets watched by apprehensive eyes. The Saigonese were reserved and wary, curious certainly, but also a bit contemptuous. The *bo dois* couldn't understand it.

Another thing they couldn't understand was the fairy-tale wealth of the place. All of them had grown up in the most desperate kind of Third World poverty, and many had been living for years like wolves in the forest. In Hanoi a watch or radio was a major purchase, bicycles were a luxury, a refrigerator or television an inaccessible dream. Now they found themselves in Ali Baba's cave. Saigon's shop windows and markets were choked with transistors, stereos, cameras, refrigerators, televisions—all the paraphernalia of a modern consumer society.

Although they had been warned about these seductions—"poison encased in sugar pills"—they walked the streets with their eyes popping, buying up everything in sight, preyed on by happy merchants and streetwise children who quickly learned to exploit their simplicity. They were especially fascinated by digital watches, the "one-pilot" kind that showed the date and the "two-pilot" model that showed the day also. Men who had never heard of flush toilets became the proud owners of the latest Western and Japanese technology.

The Saigonese observed all this with wonder, and at times hilarity. They watched as young *bo dois* chopped down city trees to make their cooking fires in streets and courtyards, and sometimes indoors, when they failed to grasp the principles of the electric or gas ranges. Hundreds of stories made the rounds about the deprived *bo dois'* encounters with the new and strange. Nothing was too improbable. Hot-water indoor showers were an amazement to them (as they were to me when I first encountered them), and a neighbor who had several adolescent soldiers quartered in her house described how one of them had gone into the shower and scalded himself—then jumped out, yelling in alarm, "My nguy!" (American puppet), sure that he had been booby-trapped. Another puppet booby trap was the toilet, a sparkling clean container of water evidently meant for washing vegetables (but why was it so low?). Then with a swirl and roar the precious greens were gone.

But though the stories may have been humorous, there was

a serious side to them as well. Many of the more thoughtful revolutionaries found themselves infected, not by decadence, but by disillusionment. Assaulted by the visible realities of southern life, the simplified Marxist caricatures that had informed their vision for two decades began to come undone. Nothing illustrated this disaffection better than my friend Hoang Van Liem's encounter with his father, a revolutionary cadre since the French war. It made Liem laugh and cry at the same time.

His father was one of those who had left for the North after Geneva, hoping to return in two years when elections reunified the country. As the years went by, he never lost hope that he would one day be reunited with his family. Meanwhile he had risen through the ranks and had even been sent to Moscow for advanced training. There he had bought a transistor radio and a watch, treasures that he would present to his son when the glorious day came.

During the same years Liem had been able to attend school and had become an electronics technician. He made a decent if modest living for himself working in the Con O battery factory. He had also gotten married, and had bought a small house not far from ours.

After liberation, his father had been sent to Saigon as a middle-level administrator. Immediately he began searching and before long had found Liem's address. With the Russian watch and transistor in his pocket, he located the house, but blanched when he saw that the address belonged to a private home. He couldn't believe his son lived in such a place. Finally he rang the doorbell and was greeted by a woman who assured him that it was indeed Liem's house and that she was Liem's wife. The answers she gave to his questions removed the father's lingering doubts, and he sat there in silence, refusing to touch the tea and oranges she served, waiting for his son to come home.

When Liem's father saw him pull up in front of the house in his Dalat (South Vietnam's version of a subcompact), his worst suspicions were confirmed. My friend's wife met her husband at the door and told him about this extraordinary visitor. As her words came out, Liem rushed into the living room, his arms opened to embrace the father he had not seen in twenty years and only vaguely remembered. But the man standing there shoved him back angrily. Taking the transistor and watch out of his pocket he threw them to the floor, breaking the radio into pieces. Then he spat out at Liem, "I've saved these for you for years, because I thought you were worthy of being my son. But I see you're a traitor to the country, and a CIA agent."

Astonished at what he was hearing, Liem managed to stammer out that he had never even worked for the Saigon government. What did his father mean about the CIA? But the older man was enraged, "You have a house, a television set, a car! . . . How could an honest person get such things?"

It took days for Liem to convince his father that in Saigon even a technician could afford such things. The revolutionary cadre had lived for twenty years with an absolute faith in what the party newspaper and radio broadcasts had told him. The reunion with his son and his observations of the city he was supposed to help administer were a shock from which he wouldn't recover. At Liem's house he immersed himself in books and back issues of newspapers and magazines. One day while I was visiting he murmured to me, "I've wasted twenty years of my life with those bastards." He was a broken man. They had stolen his life.

As soon as the Front's troops came into Saigon I went out looking for my friends from student days who had joined the underground. The first old friend I met, though, was Nguyen Van Thang, the "southernist." Thang was watching the *bo dois* gathering in front of the presidential palace, and together we drifted from one group to another, part of the curious crowd of Saigonese youths who were striking up conversations with their pale, exhausted-looking northern peers.

From the palace we walked down Thong Nhut Boulevard past the American embassy, still smoldering from the looters, smashed television sets and overturned filing cabinets littering the ground in front. A few blocks farther on we came to the radio station, guarded by a cluster of lounging *bo dois*. It occurred to us that something might be happening inside, that after Minh's formal surrender announcement (which had been broadcast just a little while earlier) the station might draw some opposition political leaders who wanted to make announcements, and perhaps some of the Front people we had known in the past.

To the relaxed guards I said that Thang and I were "with the Front." But they didn't seem to care one way or another, and we just walked in. The old elevator of course wasn't working (it rarely had), so we climbed the stairs up to the fourth-floor broadcasting studios.

But instead of a bevy of politicians, we found only the two technicians who had played the surrender tape and were now sitting around wondering what to do next. They seemed relieved that somebody had arrived to take charge, and were disappointed when I told them we weren't cadres and didn't have any authority to do anything. But as we waited to see who might show up, Thang and I began to think that perhaps we could do something ourselves.

Talking it over, we decided to draw up an announcement about the piles of guns and ammunition that had been strewn all over the streets by government soldiers anxious to shed their ARVN identities. M-16s, grenades, pistols, even machine guns were there for the taking by children, gangs, or any troubled person who might be moved to action. In a few minutes I had put together a draft statement (to give it weight we titled it "Directive Number One") calling on citizens to gather up the weapons in their neighborhoods and take them to designated collection locations: the palace, the student union, or the Buddhist university.

After it was broadcast, we called up Trinh Cong Son, the celebrated composer of peace music and lyrics, whose work had long been banned by the regime. Getting into the spirit of it, he came down to the station with his tapes, which the technicians were happy to play, lighthearted now that the responsi-

bility for the station was no longer theirs. Before long a variety
of third force people and religious and cultural leaders were
climbing the stairs with statements of support for the new regime to be read over the air.

As the studio was crowding up, four men in uniform arrived
to ask what was going on. I told them about the weapons statement and about Trinh Cong Son's music. The leader glanced
at Directive Number One and grunted his approval. As far as
Trinh Cong Son was concerned, none of them seemed to have
ever heard of him. The solidarity statements he would look at
later; now he just wanted to know how things worked around
here. Obviously he was taking me for a radio official, so I introduced him to the technicians and said that they would explain
the details. "Good," he grunted again, and began asking them
questions. Thang and I stood around awkwardly for a few minutes, then walked down the stairs to resume our tour.

Within a few hours I had met three friends from my activist
days who had disappeared into the jungle years ago. I saw one
among a milling group of bo dois and students near Duy Tan,
the old student center that had become a gathering place for
people who had been part of the movement. He was surprised
to see me. Stepping away from his buddies, he took me by the
arm and walked with me a few yards down the street.

"Toai," he asked softly, "what are you doing here? Why
haven't you left?"

I didn't know what to make of this. He was as aware of my
student activities as anyone. At first I thought he might be
testing me, trying to find out if I was still friendly to the cause.
But then he became more specific. "You didn't commit yourself completely. You should have gotten out when you could."
It occurred to me that he might be angry at the Front—from
the insignia on his uniform it was apparent he had only made it
to sergeant after five years in the jungle. But he wasn't interested in prolonging our discussion, and I was left to try and
figure out for myself what he meant.

The two others I ran into later in the evening made ominously similar remarks, talking quietly so as not to be overheard.

"Toai, you should have left." One of them, Phan Van Triet, was explicit: "It's going to get worse than before. These people are narrow-minded, dogmatic; you can't discuss anything with them. They're unbelievably ignorant!" If that was what Triet was saying, in his green uniform and floppy hat, there had to be some truth to it.

Over the next few days I found other friends and acquaintances from the old days. Some were more optimistic, believing that the Front would succeed in establishing its own government. Others were already bitter. "The Front's of no use to them anymore." "*They're* in control of the whole thing." "*They* don't trust anyone!" "You know how it goes: '*Vat Chanh Bo Vo*'—'squeeze the juice from the lemon; throw away the peel.'" There was no mystery about who "they" were. "They" were the Communists from the North.

What I was hearing troubled me deeply. I could feel my decisiveness melting away. What if my brother Truong had been right after all? The next day I decided to make a quiet trip down to Rach Gia on the coast, to explore the possibility of somehow getting passage out. At the bus terminal I rented a minivan and joined the flow of car and foot traffic heading south. It was a happy crowd, made up of peasants and provincial people heading back home after their refugee existence in Saigon. In Rach Gia I spent a couple of hours making discreet inquiries among local businessmen and boat owners. But it was not something that could be arranged easily, and in my undecided state, I was not ready to pursue the matter.

Driving back to Saigon, I tried to calm myself enough to take stock. It was true that the city's atmosphere was peaceful, and that the peasants were joyous about returning home to resume their lives. It occurred to me that an alternative I had not considered was the countryside. I could take Yvonne and the kids, my parents too, and go back to the land, somewhere around Vinh Long. I could go fishing and take the time to think, try to see things more clearly.

In Saigon events seemed to be moving in slow motion. The city's people were living in anticipation; there had been little violence, relatively little disruption. But what might the future hold? The new authorities seemed to be taking their time, moving slowly, very slowly . . . as if they were as unprepared for this as were the Saigonese themselves. Odd, after thirty years of war—you'd think they would have made their plans long ago. By now the city was being administered by the Military Management Committee, headed by Vietcong General Tran Van Tra. "Only the U.S. imperialists have been defeated," he declared at the committee's May 7 inauguration. "All Vietnamese are the victors! . . . The people of Saigon have become the complete masters of their city."

The public buildings were hung with red banners, their slogans rippling across the city: Nothing Is More Precious Than Independence and Liberty! Our Great President Ho Is Still Alive in Our Hearts! Long Live the People and the Army, United to Establish Socialism! Democracy, Reconciliation, and National Unity. Life, they were saying, would go on. More austere, of course, but peaceful and free from carnage, corruption, and foreign control. It all sounded encouraging. But of course nobody knew exactly what shape this new life might take, how things might be managed. So far it was just slogans.

In early May all the bank's employees were asked to report to our offices. In the week or so that Nam Do was closed to the public, the new authorities had been busy drawing up lists of names and inventories of equipment. Accounts were still frozen, safety deposit boxes sealed. When everybody arrived there was a meeting, called to give us directions. Now, at last I'd have a specific idea of how they were thinking about running the country's affairs. Policies would of course be the same for every bank, and bank policies determined so much else. Would we just keep on operating as we had been, or would there be different regulations, perhaps some confiscations?

The first announced change at Nam Do created such shock waves it was impossible to think beyond them. All those holding senior positions would now hold junior positions. Junior employees would now become the bosses. I shook my head in amazement. This was straight out of China's Great Cultural

Revolution. They couldn't possibly be serious! The junior employees, anyway, were alive with delight at the prospect of gigantic new salaries. A month later, at payday, their delight turned sour. The magnificent old executive salaries—150,000 to 200,000 piasters—had been leveled, as had the junior salaries. Now everyone was making between 10,000 and 23,000 a month. And as fast as liberation had brought down salaries, just so fast had it sent prices skyrocketing. By the end of June, a kilo of rice, which had cost eighty preliberation piasters, now cost five hundred postrevolution piasters. A quart of gasoline went from two hundred to sixteen hundred.

With the country's financial system tottering crazily, there was at least no doubt about whom the spoils belonged to. The banking system's new revolutionary directors lost no time in dividing up the villas and cars of the old bourgeois directors. The president's villa of Saigon's Chartered Bank was a special plum, a magnificent property set amid acres of gardens in the center of Saigon, near the archbishop's palace. But before the new owners could get comfortably settled, they in turn were dispossessed by even higher-ranking officials freshly arrived from Hanoi. The executive perks went from hand to hand, right up the ladder, as northern officials streamed into Saigon to carve out their empires. Nam Do's experience and that of the other banks was repeated wherever there was property to be claimed.

But though they had more authority, the newest set of Nam Do directors had no more idea of what to do with a bank than their predecessors had. Faced with a complex system with which they had no experience, they quickly reversed the decision that had made juniors seniors and seniors juniors. Middle managers like myself were lured back with salary incentives and asked to get things running again.

While these gyrations were going on at the bank, other elements of Saigon's life were receiving equally destructive attention. From day to day the newspapers disappeared from the street. First *Chinh Luan*, then *Hoa Binh*, then the entire vital and raucous gaggle of Saigon dailies. From now on the southern capital's omnivorous readers would have to be content with *Giai Phong* (*Liberation*), a carbon copy of Hanoi's *Nhan Dan*. A bit later a second daily appeared (*Tin Sang*) sponsored by the Patriotic Front, a newly minted mass organization purported to represent the spectrum of popular opinion. Needless to say, the opinions expressed didn't differ significantly from the "official" views of *Giai Phong*.

As its papers disappeared, so did Saigon's bookstores. First they were closed down and locked, then their inventories were confiscated by Vanguard Youth members sporting red armbands. Every book had to pass censorship, and to the revolution's cultural arbiters all books published under the old regime were decadent. The South's most renowned writers found themselves on the prohibited list, even those who had succeeded in publishing books critical of the generals. All foreign books were equally suspect: Dale Carnegie and Henry Miller right along with the prorevolutionary philosopher Jean-Paul Sartre.

Before long the cultural gestapo became bolder, more intimidating. Youth commandos led by northern *can bos* began raiding people's homes, rummaging through bookshelves and carting off private libraries. Raids by especially zealous commandos were capped off by impromptu book burnings in the streets, rare, religious, and historical works going up in the same blazes that consumed trashy romances.

Films and music fell under the same baleful attention. The Westerns and martial arts movies that had been so popular were replaced by edifying movies about revolutionary heroes, norm-surpassing workers, and life on model collective farms. The audiences for this new fare were not large, but those who came stayed; it was forbidden to leave before the end of a movie, since that would be a sign of contempt for the new culture.

Radio Saigon's stock of American-style pop and rock also faded into memory. But along with the junk went other Saigon favorites such as Joan Baez and Sylvie Vartan. The old repertoire was replaced by a steady diet of propaganda music praising Ho Chi Minh, socialism, and revolution. Perhaps fearing that listeners to the new music would be few, the city's management committee erected a vast network of street loudspeakers—one for every twenty houses or so—throughout the city. The noise went on at all hours, martial strains interspersed with announcements and directives. One could never claim ignorance of some new regulation, or of the most popular tunes in the People's Army. As the weeks passed, some of the "old" music was once more broadcast, but only instrumentals. Uncensored lyrics apparently posed an unacceptable danger.

Other blatant symbols of capitalist corruption received equally short shrift. Teams of Patriotic Youth commandos stationed themselves on streetcorners, stopping passersby whose clothes or hairstyles offended them. Armed with scissors, they cut down flared pant legs and sheared off men's overly long hair. People were commanded to button their shirts.

The irony was that while the southerners were getting their hair trimmed and their trouser legs narrowed to avoid trouble, the northerners were paying Saigon's tailors to make over their own nondescript pants into bell-bottoms. As the ordinary citizens' lives turned more austere, the *can bos* and *bo dois* were making a clean sweep of the cornucopia offered by shops and the famous thieves' market. They were like a giant vacuum cleaner, sucking up every loose camera, television, stereo, and motorcycle.

It wasn't just that the northerners found themselves defenseless against the sea of material temptations that poured over them. Not just, as one friend put it, that "they came to purify us, but we are corrupting them." It seemed clear to me that the hordes of liberators had been infected not simply by decadence, but by a burgeoning cynicism. The same inner rage that embittered my friend Liem's father was surfacing in the revolution's soldiery as a ravenous preoccupation with things.

Given the Skinner box society they had come from, it couldn't have been different. In twenty years the infusion of United States aid and money, and the seductive power of the American life-style, had transformed the South into a different world from what it had previously been. Personally, I regarded it as an insidious transformation. But insidious or not, it was a fact that life in the South and the North had diverged hugely over two decades. The South, especially its cities, had grown used to modern, consumer-oriented ways. At the same time, the traditional life in the North—always more rigorous than in the South—had also transformed itself. While Saigon's rulers were aping American norms, Hanoi's had turned their half of the country into a massive, half-starved corvée on the worst Russian model. Under these circumstances the suddenly transplanted northern soldiers couldn't have been anything but startled.

But these real differences were immensely magnified in the *bo dois'* minds by the false conditioning they had received all their lives. Most of them were simple country people who had firmly believed the crude whip-and-slave propaganda that had been their only information about conditions in the South. Now they saw not only that quite ordinary people had refrigerators and cars, but that the farmers used tractors and the fishermen motorboats. As these revelations sank in, you could see their zeal almost visibly crumbling. An epidemic of cynicism began to take hold, its most conspicuous symptom the uncontrollable hunger for goods.

Events in South Vietnam's economic and cultural life were disquieting, even scary. But from a larger perspective, it was possible to say that real chaos had been avoided. In Saigon we knew nothing factual about the liberation of Phnom Penh. If we had, perhaps the streetcorner youth squads would have seemed laughably benign. After all, despite ill omens, "reconciliation and concord" were still the watchwords.

By early June, the revolutionary government felt ready to apply the "reconciliation and concord" it had been proclaiming so persistently. Announcements were made over the radio loudspeakers, in the two newspapers, and on posters and notices that "reeducation" courses would shortly begin. Everyone who had been associated with the Saigon regime—with its government, its army, its police, or its political parties—would be expected to participate. Private soldiers and low-level civil servants would go to special classes for three days. Here they would learn about their mistakes, the culpability of the government, and the crimes of the imperialists. Middle-level people from the army, administration, and parties would attend a ten-day course devoted to these and related subjects. Officers, members of the national police, higher-level government personnel, and party functionaries were asked to bring food and clothing sufficient for a thirty-day retreat. Since their responsibility had been significantly greater, reeducation for them would be longer and more concentrated.

Waves of reassurance spread out from these announcements as if someone had dissolved tranquilizers in the public water supply. Almost every family in South Vietnam had at least one member in the army, the government, or in one of the other specified categories. And all of them had been living in a welter of apprehension about the future. It was an unspeakable relief to know at last that even those who had fought actively against the victors, even those who had led the fight . . . would be forgiven. Three days of study, or thirty days for that matter, was little enough penance to do. Even hardened ARVN paratroopers and rangers got ready to report to the reeducation centers—men who had been quite prepared to filter back into the jungles to resist violently.

After a month, not one of them would be back, nor after a year. But I wouldn't know that, since by then I too would have slipped unnoticed into the gulag that had been secretly prepared.

14

The Revolutionary
Finance Committee

Sometime in the middle of June I got a call from Huynh Tan
Mam, the former student union president. He said that he and
Duong Van Day, whom I had met in Chi Hoa Prison five
years before (and who was now chief of District One) would
like to get together with me and with Tran Ngoc Hien, the top
official of the Patriotic Intellectuals' Association. He proposed
that we all meet at my house the next evening.

It was an unsettling conversation. Tran Ngoc Hien was well
known for his espionage activities during the war, which came
to light after his arrest by Thieu's police. A ranking party
cadre, he had been badly tortured in prison, and it was said he
bore terrible scars from his experiences. What he might want
from me, I didn't know, but I wasn't looking forward to the
meeting.

The next evening, at eight on the button, two Toyotas
pulled up outside my house. Out of one came several body-
guards; out of the other Mam, Day, and Hien.

Hien turned out to be thin and pale, without a glimmer of humor or warmth. But though a committed Communist, I sensed he was no fanatic. As we talked, I noticed that he would allow for nuances of opinion, that he didn't display the overweening arrogance that was the trademark of Communist officialdom. That was probably why he had been put in charge of the Patriotic Intellectuals Association of the new South Vietnam.

Not far into our discussion I began to understand why I had been honored with this visit. Tran Ngoc Hien's first priority was recruiting southern intellectuals, and obviously he had been running into problems. A great many of the old opposition people were taking a wait-and-see attitude toward the revolutionary government. For years they had been fed on promises of southern independence and a careful, step-by-step approach to reunification. Solemn assurances of respect for the south's distinct economic, social, and political systems had been given by the party, and also by the Front and its sister revolutionary organizations. Such southern insurgent leaders as Nguyen Huu Tho, Trinh Dinh Thao, Pham Vung Cung, and Truong Nhu Tang were known to be moderates with the strongest nationalist sentiments. Their presence in the new government had given credence to the slogan, "The Socialist Revolution in the North; The National Democratic Revolution in the South." But now, what was happening? Everywhere you looked there were northern troops. Every important business and organization had its northern directors.

Given these developments, the southern intelligentsia were nervous. My old friend Tran Van Tuyen had shut himself up at home, as had Kieu Muong Thu, the Assembly militant. The activist priest Father Tranh Huu Thanh was also keeping quiet, while the Venerable Tri Quang and his assistant, Thien Minh, were staying close to their cells in the An Quang pagoda. It was a time to be wary, and not many of the southerners were responding enthusiastically to the call of the Patriotic Intellectuals. I was certainly no big fish for Comrade Hien. But, on the other hand, my name still drew some recognition, and I was likely to be friendly. Obviously I was worth a shot.

"Yes, we've been following your activities for a number of years," Hien was saying. "We're impressed by them . . . Comrades Mam and Day can attest to that. We feel it's time to ask for your active involvement." Hien sat erect in the chair of honor—stiff, formal. He hadn't touched the tea and cakes that Yvonne had placed in front of him. No wonder this guy can't generate any enthusiasm, I thought. He has all the personality of a mud turtle. Mam and Day just sat motionless on the sofa, apparently frozen by the occasion's solemnity. They looked like little boys. I had the impression I was taking an exam, which of course I was. A great deal would depend on the answers I gave Hien.

Since I myself had no clear understanding of the future, if ever there was a time for temporizing, it was now.

"I'm sure the revolution has overestimated my qualities," I said. "I'm far from being as capable as you suggest. But I'm ready to work in some way if you think I can be useful. What exactly do you think I might be able to do?"

"Well, Brother Toai, you knew a great many political people." (I could feel the probe coming—see exactly what Toai's attitudes are. If he'll inform, he'll do anything.) "You might, for example, point out to us some of them who were . . . uh, quietly . . . supporting the puppets." (As if they needed me to know who was working with the puppets!)

Speaking as deliberately and gravely as Hien, I replied, weighing each word. "Comrade Hien, the Americans and puppets left very suddenly. The archives are full of intact documents. I'm sure they have more precise information than anything I might remember. That's where the revolution can find out what it needs to know, much better than from me." (Deflecting the probe—not an informer, but maybe open to collaboration.)

Hien changed his approach.

"I know you've worked at the Nam Do Bank for a long time. . . . Yes, yes, I know you were in jail in Phan Rang and that you helped out in Qui Nhon. But what's interesting to us is that you know how banks operate, you know something about finance. This is a difficult period, a difficult transition for the revolution. I think your advice would be useful. Perhaps you could write us a report."

"What kind of report?"

"Well . . ."—he hesitated for a moment, as if the idea had just occurred to him—"first: What do you know about American goals concerning South Vietnam's economy? Second: What do you know about the traps they left in the South to sabotage the revolution? Third: What overall direction would you take to resolve the South's economic and financial problems?"

I blinked my eyes. This was the last thing on earth I expected. Why in the world was he asking these things of me, a former pharmacy student whose entire knowledge of finance had been gained managing two branch banks?

"Comrade Hien, may I ask why you don't go to the real experts for questions like these? National Bank people are still around, ministry people. A lot of them were even trained in the United States. I can't answer these kinds of questions well. I just don't know much about high finance or the national economy. I know how a bank works, but . . ."

Suddenly Hien's face was animated. "What do you mean, you don't know much about it? Didn't you write this? And this?" Out of his briefcase he pulled a number of issues of *Tu Quyet* (just like the Phan Rang province chief, I thought) and began reading underlined passages—decisive, authoritative statements about South Vietnam's businesses, her economic system, American manipulations of National Bank finances. I had indeed written them all, expressing opinions that were as comprehensive as my competence was limited. And now that the victorious revolution needed to dig up some friendly southern economics experts, they had remembered me. What a turn of events!

"I'll expect your report in four days," said Hien, getting up from the chair. For the first time he smiled a bit, a thin, forced smile that was both a promise and a threat.

In four days I had filled about thirty pages. The first question, about American economic goals in Vietnam, didn't present any great problem. I wrote that for the United States, Vietnam had been a place to unload surplus goods. They had created an exclusively consumer society of the most unrestrained sort, a wartime consumer economy. The millions of dollars of American aid had been used solely to buy American merchandise. No steps had been taken toward establishing foundations for Vietnam's own economic development.

The second question, on the "economic traps" the Americans had supposedly left behind, required more finesse. The Communists were convinced that they were tiptoeing through a minefield, that the Americans had set afoot a variety of Machiavellian schemes to sabotage the revolution. These fears were not to be ridiculed. But what might the "traps" be?

After a good deal of thought, I wrote that the chief trap was the pattern of consumption the Americans had instituted among the South Vietnamese. The economy had become dependent on foreign oil and oil-related products, on imported foodstuffs and other consumer items, and on war-related employment. South Vietnam was living far beyond its means, in an artificial prosperity created by an influx of dollars. A return to economic reality might well cause severe popular dissatisfaction and resentment toward the revolution. I noted that this problem would have been far less dangerous had victory come a few years later, when America's abandonment of Thieu would have caused massive bankruptcy and misery.

All in all I was satisfied with my answers to the first two questions. I felt I had given them what they wanted to hear, without straying too far from the truth. Whatever American economic goals might really have been, Vietnam had in fact become a receptacle for American production. And though the Communists were certifiably paranoid about United States "traps," still there was no doubt about the difficulties the Americans had left behind.

But I was not particularly proud of my response to the third question: my suggestions on financial policy. Here I said that my experience was not in high finance, but at the grass roots level, with the people. From their point of view, it seemed to me that strict measures were called for, large accounts frozen, assets over a certain amount confiscated, investment debts immediately called in. In other words, the better part of the revolutionary steamroller.

I didn't believe a word of it. Even my inexpert eyes could see that these steps would do nothing to promote a rebirth of economic activity. Quite the contrary. But I could also see the direction the revolution was taking. I had met the new Nam Do directors and other northern officials. Every sign shouted that whatever I might write, the general course had already been set. Under these circumstances, my primary concern was to protect myself and my family. I was not about to be classified as an enemy of the people, as a defender of capitalist ownership. I would give them exactly what they wanted to hear.

Now I was operating strictly from fear and from my instinct for survival. In my heart I felt I was degrading myself, and I tried not to think too much about motives. Care for my future, for my dependent family's future, argued strongly for exercising the utmost wit and prudence I was capable of. But . . . I had always been a militant! I had left the student movement and politics when I was convinced there was no viable path between the extremes. You could be a lackey of one side or the other, or you could fool yourself about a "third way." So I had left. But I had never been afraid to speak my mind. My failings had always been on the side of rashness and truculence, even as a bank manager. But the world was changing quickly, and I felt the shame of changing along with it.

A few days after submitting my report I received another visit from Tran Ngoc Hien. This time he was open and more relaxed, almost friendly. Obviously I had passed the examination. In a display of conviviality, he even ate and drank the refreshments we served. Between sips of tea he told me that the same three questions had been put to about forty economics specialists. My own answers had been particularly welcomed, even more so than those of several renowned experts such as Professor Nguyen Van Hao, former deputy minister of economics. Apparently I was one of "the few people whose intellects have not been contaminated by capitalism." "I congratulate you," said Hien. "Your suggestions are in accord with the correct policies, especially in regard to the confiscation of assets. Now we would like you to develop this project in a more detailed manner. Please think it over. I'll be back to see you in three days."

Three days later Hien was back, this time accompanied by Vuong Ky Hiep, who was temporarily filling in as minister of finance. Rather abruptly Hiep proposed that I join the Provisional Revolutionary Government's finance committee. I was expecting something of this kind, and had thought hard about my answer. It was no.

No—but of course no tempered with all the modesty and logic I could muster and with an inducement that might interest them. I cited my youth (just thirty), my complete lack of experience in national finance, and my utterly inadequate background in basic economic theory—I had not taken so much as a single course in the subject. The inducement I dangled before them was also my hope. I was, I told them, a man from the countryside, someone who found city living distasteful and difficult. My single ambition was to go back to my home village with my wife and children, and perhaps my parents. I was sure that the revolution needed educated cadres there, in the delta. And I was willing to discuss whatever position they thought might be appropriate.

My real reasons for rejecting the post were somewhat different. First, my experience with the bank directors and financial cadres they had brought down from Hanoi had been enough to demonstrate their utter incompetence. These people were going to do nothing with the South's economy except destroy it. Second, beyond their incompetence, they were impossible to get along with, the most bigoted, arrogant, and ignorant group I had ever come across. I could not comprehend how they could know so little and at the same time believe so firmly in their own omniscience. Finally, I was well on my way to seeing that other southerners and I would be little more than window dressing for the new power structure, useful as symbols of cooperation to help smooth over the very rough changes that were likely to come. This was not a prospect I thought I could stomach.

I had prepared my polite refusal as carefully as I could, hoping to find some way to distance myself from whatever was coming so I could evaluate the changes and make a rational decision either to stay and join the revolution wholeheartedly, or to pursue the unfinished business I had left in Rach Gia.

But I hadn't counted on Hiep's persistence. He played at length on my patriotism and my duty to help build the nation. But his real argument could be summed up in a phrase: "You are from the South!" Hiep and Hien, party members though they were, were looking hard for ways to bring young, acceptable southerners into the bureaucracy. Perhaps they saw the possibility, even at that early date, that the southern party leadership itself would before long find out who had really conquered whom. At any rate, they wanted me, and when I saw that this offer could not be refused, I accepted it. I would, I told them, take part—at least on a temporary basis.

My first experience of a finance committee meeting wasn't encouraging. The committee chairman was Tran Duong (at this writing head of the National Bank of Vietnam), who manifested exactly the same unlovely personal characteristics as the upper economic officials I had previously encountered. The burden of his song was the triumphal worldwide success of the Soviet Union and North Vietnam. Its melody was simple: Vietnam had defeated the Chinese, the Japanese, the French, and the Americans. Surely we could overcome whatever economic problems we faced. In practical terms, we had to draw up as swiftly as possible a detailed plan to nationalize and collectivize the South. "We must proceed quickly toward socialism, in line with the party's decision."

Some of those sitting there, like Professor Hung, seemed to suck in their breath at what they were hearing. But there was no argument and little discussion. Everyone was clear about what was happening and about what role they were expected to play. I had as clear a sense of that as the rest did, but inside I was beginning to boil.

My initial approach to these meetings was simply to listen and to go along. But Chairman Duong's directives caught me up short. Not only was I appalled by their ramifications, but they did not even correspond with my understanding of what the party itself was saying. Xuan Thuy, the northern Central Committee member who had served as Le Duc Tho's nominal superior at Paris, had written publicly, not once but many times, that in the South there would be five separate economic categories in which the private sector would play a role. *Nhan Dan*, the party daily, had reiterated the same assurances. I had heard similar statements from Hiep, the finance minister. All in all it was enough to encourage me to take the matter up with Chairman Duong personally.

My idea was to present my thoughts in a constructive way. I would not be an angry young man looking for an argument; I simply wanted to clarify my understanding, so that I could work more effectively. In private, perhaps Duong would let down the mask of scorn that was his invariable public face.

When we met in his office, I told Duong that my interpretation of the Front platform and various party directives was that the South should have relative economic autonomy for a period of time. I understood that to mean that we should take things slowly, allow the factories and businesses to reestablish themselves as viable enterprises—under government supervision of course—and then carefully enter onto a course of socialization. Immediate nationalization would destroy the incentive to work and would needlessly sacrifice the managerial expertise that we had.

His answer, as angry and loud as any I had heard during our meetings, was that what I had suggested was "dangerous revisionism," that it was "not according to the policy!" It was as clear an example of bourgeois thinking as he had ever encountered. "*Anh khong biet gi ca!* [You don't know anything!]" he yelled, dismissing me.

I left, but not happily. Burning with resentment, I went to

see Finance Minister Hiep with the story of what had taken place. He tried to calm me, telling me that of course there would be a lot of fighting, but that in the end the North would not simply impose policies, that the South had its friends in the world. "But I don't think it will come to that," he said. Party leaders had given precise assurances on these matters.

Less than half convinced, I asked Hiep to give me a few days to consider what I would do—by then I would know whether I could continue to work with the committee or if I wanted to retire to Vinh Long Province. Then I walked out. The next evening's National Orchestra concert would help me relax, and think.

15

The Vietnamese Gulag

The door is set into a blind wall. Above it is a red signboard. In bright yellow letters on this signboard are the words *Khong Gi Quy Hon Duc Lap Tu Do* (Nothing Is More Precious Than Independence and Liberty). Of all the slogans Ho Chi Minh used to exhort his people, this is the most famous. So embedded are these words in the nation's subconscious that signs like this are invisible. Perhaps that is why they have been chosen to mark the entrances of all liberated Vietnam's prisons and re-education camps. Or perhaps some high official with a taste for irony ordered it. Having read that the Nazis marked their death camps *"Arbeit Macht Frei,"* he started looking around for some Vietnamese equivalent—and there it was: *"Khong Gi Quy Hon Duc Lap Tu Do."*

Until 1975, few Saigonese had ever heard of Le Van Duyet Prison, even though it had been sitting right there in the pleasant Giadinh suburb for thirty years. The reason was that Le Van Duyet was small potatoes. Even at the height of the

Thieu repression, it had sheltered only some two hundred souls. Chi Hoa, Saigon's central prison, sometimes bulged with as many as eight thousand. If some relative or colleague disappeared, you went to Chi Hoa to search, not to some place like Le Van Duyet.

When I entered Le Van Duyet on September 6, 1975, two thousand prisoners—ten times the former number—inhabited its cells. (You could not say they "lived" in them.) After I had been there for a while, my job enabled me to count them. At the same date, Chi Hoa housed forty thousand—only five times the previous high.

Underneath the red-and-yellow sign two sentries lolled. Otherwise there was nothing to set Le Van Duyet off from the neighborhood bustle. On one side the prison shared a wall with the Ho Ngoc Can High School. On the other it abutted Giadinh's City Hall. Each day, directly in front of the prison door the Chi Lang Boulevard market came alive with the haggling of vendors and housewives. Across the boulevard stood the Le Van Duyet memorial, erected to honor the nineteenth-century Vietnamese hero whom the prison commemorated. Legend insisted that Le Van Duyet's bravery was such that upon seeing him tigers would flee for their lives. By the old regime's last years, the Giadinh temple built in the hero's honor had become the center of a cult. Officers' wives would go there to prostrate themselves and pray for their husbands' protection or promotion. Newly engaged couples would swear fidelity under the hero's aegis. ("If you betray me, may Duyet kill you.")

Collective cell number two, which I share with my friend Nguyen Van Hien and sixty others, is located in what is now called Zone A. In former times Zone A was Le Van Duyet's only cellblock. It contains nine collective cells and ten individual cells. The collective cells hold approximately sixty prisoners each. In what had originally been Le Van Duyet's large courtyard, the new regime has erected two new cellblocks, Zones B and C. Zone B contains five collective and twenty individual cells; Zone C, sixteen collective and fifty individual. With only the remnants of a courtyard, there's no place for prisoners to walk or exercise. Life in Le Van Duyet is a permanent lockup. In the twenty-two months I will spend here, various jobs and tasks get me out of my cell from time to time. Other prisoners are not so fortunate.

A large number of Le Van Duyet's inmates are former Communists or Front members who went over to the Thieu side under the *Chieu Hoi* (Open Arms) program. The old regime had announced that over 250,000 guerrillas turned themselves in during the years following the Tet defeat. Captured, disillusioned, or just sick to death of fighting, they had responded to Saigon's standing offer of amnesty and resettlement. After April 30, those who hadn't left the country faced an especially grim future. In the rush of events since liberation I hadn't thought much about the fate of these *hoi chanh* (ralliers). Now I was sharing it.

Nguyen Dich Nha, cell two's leader, was a *hoi chanh*. Ten years before he had been captured during a commando raid against an American facility in Saigon. First he was condemned to death, then pardoned and sent to Con Son Island—which was scarcely better than death. Unable to deal with the horrors of that place, he saved himself by recanting his allegiance and going over to the government. After his release, he had married and opened a little shop in the capital. Now he is here, among the first to be arrested after Saigon's fall.

Nha has been made head of cell two because he lives in a state of perpetual terror and so is useful to the *bo dois*. Not only does he have a guilty conscience about having betrayed the revolution to save his skin, he is also keenly aware of the "blood debt" he owes his former comrades, who might collect it at any time. To the other prisoners he is irritable and nasty. In front of the *bo dois* (to whom he tells everything) he trembles obsequiously. Both groups despise him.

As in all the cells, number two's prisoners are divided into groups of between ten and fifteen individuals. Each of these is called a *to*, and each *to* chooses its own representative. The representative is responsible for everything that happens among the *to*'s members. He watches over their behavior, apportions their food, and represents them to the cell leader, who in turn is the only one authorized to talk to the guards.

The object of this system—and often the result—is to divide the prisoners by creating jealousies, rivalries, and quarrels among the various *tos*. With sixty-two of us jammed together, nothing could be easier. Irritable, tense, and excruciatingly idle, the inmates are ready to fight about nothing, and often do. Inducing arguments over food, water, or sleeping privileges is child's play. In this way solidarity among the cell's prisoners is undercut, and the authority of the head prisoner/informer and the guards is reinforced. The Romans knew the approach as "divide and conquer." In Le Van Duyet it is called "training a dog to bite other dogs."

Among ourselves we often talked about the contrast between prisoners' behavior now and what it had been in earlier times. There were hundreds of examples of how militant prisoners in Thieu's jails had made life hard for their keepers, who often wouldn't even dare enter their cells. One of my *to* comrades, formerly an inmate at Phu Quoc (a prison island near the Cambodian coastline), told me about how his collective cell had literally torn an informer to pieces and hung his remains from the ceiling. The guards had been forced to use vomiting gas to storm the cell and get the body out. In the six months it took before the administration gave up the investigation, not a single prisoner had talked.

Of course I had never received anything like the full treatment in Thieu's prisons, but regardless, I was inclined to think that the new regime's methods were simply smarter than those of the old prison masters. I had gotten a foretaste of one of the favorite ploys back in isolation at Tran Hung Dao, when they threw old Professor Thong into my cell. The full-blown procedure was more elaborate. As a way of gathering information and sowing distrust among the prisoners it was brilliant; you could never even tell whether they were using it or not.

It would start with a piece of information gleaned from a stoolie, something about one of two close friends in the cell.

Perhaps the stoolie has overheard some compromising fact that one friend had told the other during one of those endless, intimate talks with which friends filled their days. (With everyone squatting or sitting cheek by jowl, a determined eavesdropper could pick up anything.) Now the *can bo* checks the information against the prisoner's interrogation report, including his one or more autobiographies. If it is truly new and incriminating, say an act against the state that the prisoner had not confessed to, the *can bo* then sits on the information for ten days or two weeks. At the end of that time, he calls the prisoner's friend in for interrogation, discussing with him some entirely different subject. Two days later, the prisoner himself is called, and the *can bo* accuses him of his former crime. ("We know that during May 1975 you spread slanders about the state!") The prisoner wonders how they found out. The only person he's told has been his friend—and now he recalls vividly that two days earlier the friend was here with this very *can bo*.

If the prisoner is not really close to his friend, chances are good he will denounce him on the spot in a desperate attempt to ward off the consequences of his crime. Even if the two have been faithful intimates, a seed of suspicion has been planted. Two days later, a *bo doi* will come into the cell and announce loudly that Prisoner X (the friend) should prepare for a visit from his wife. Now the whole cell suspects X has said something he shouldn't have during his recent interrogation, and that this is the payoff. The subject of the ploy is not only sure of that, he is convinced he knows exactly what information his former friend, the Judas, has sold.

But it isn't just the dog-eat-dog techniques that undermine prisoner solidarity and morale. In my own experience, I tell the others, formerly everyone was proud to be a prisoner. We had such contempt for the puppets, and we idealized the revolution. Being arrested then was a badge of honor. Now, no one has any ideals left; how could they? But we can't completely erase the "idea" of the revolution from what is, or what might even yet be. So in spite of ourselves, we wonder if in some way we aren't guilty. Because to acknowledge once and for all the inhumanity of the revolution is to admit that our ideals are as dead as dust and that our past struggles, whatever their purity and courage, were (even as we fought) being compounded with shit by those we honored. No, it's easier to hope in some corner of our minds that maybe we really are guilty.

To the hard-bitten Phu Quoc prisoner there is a more prosaic explanation: isolation. Under Thieu, the prisoners had hope—hope in their comrades, their families, their lawyers perhaps, the opposition, the newspapers, international agencies; hope for negotiations, hope for victory. Maybe most of these hopes were illusory, but they still gave the prisoners something to hold on to, something to nourish the spirit of resistance. "At Phu Quoc I even saw International Red Cross representatives once." He says it softly, with a touch of awe—like a man who has once witnessed a miracle and knows it won't come again. "Of course, they weren't shown everything; but it boosted the hell out of our morale just to know they were around."

Of course he's right. Even the Con Son tiger cages had been discovered by a visiting delegation—of Americans, no less. They created such an international furor that Thieu and his cronies had been forced to exercise some restraint and caution. Now there's no International Red Cross and no world opinion. Our families don't even know where we are, or if we're dead or alive. We are lost men. We have already disappeared from the face of the earth.

"Dai Dollars," one of the cell's bona fide criminals, confirms the Phu Quoc veteran's analysis. "Dai Dollars" is a hardcore thug, a hired killer from Cholon who told us he had been arrested fifteen times during the Thieu years. Each time he had managed to get out, thanks to the protection and bribes of his friends. In those days "Dai Dollars" had had nothing but scorn for the guards, people who were meaningless, or who at worst could always be paid off. The legal system had worked for him. Lawyers and judges could be bought or intimidated by the crime lords who employed him; investigations could get sidetracked, evidence lost, witnesses might refuse to come forward. So when he was inside, he ruled the roost. It was said that he had even strangled one of his cellmates in Chi Hoa.

Whatever he might have done in Thieu's Chi Hoa, "Dai Dollars" with his elaborate tattoos is as meek as a lamb in the new Le Van Duyet. One of his gangster friends, "Nam Heo" (Number Five Swine), had met an untimely end shortly before Hien and I arrived. He had beaten up a "political" who had insulted him, and subsequently had been hauled off to an isolation cell. For two days he screamed out his defiance. On the third day there was silence, and that was the last anybody had seen of him. "Nam Heo's" passing was no great loss to anyone, but it had made "Dai Dollars" thoughtful. With no legal system to exploit, he knew he was as defenseless in this place as the simplest delta peasant boy.

Under cell leader Nha's gimlet stare, the atmosphere in number two is tense and heavy. Nha stays in a corner by himself, observing everyone's activities—not that there's much to observe. We wake up at six in the morning and go to sleep at ten at night. We are not allowed to read, write, or lie down. Napping is prohibited, as is talking in groups. What Nha sees mostly is quiet conversations between individuals and a lot of glazed-over expressions, whose owners have retreated into the worlds of daydream and memory.

The only periods of "relaxation" are mealtimes, when it is permitted to talk freely. So in spite of the constant, gnawing hunger, we make the miserable bowlful of red rice last as long as possible, relishing whatever discussion or entertainment we can provide each other. In this regard, cell two is fortunate to number among its residents Thanh Viet, one of the South's best-known comic actors. Any audience will do for him, even one as motley as this, and his joking and good humor are infectious.

It was his joking that landed him in here in the first place. When the female lead in one of his stage farces was being seduced by a sweet-talking gigolo, Viet had yelled at her, "Don't listen to what he says. Look at what he's doing!" The audience had laughed uproariously. "Don't listen to what they say. Look at what they do" was the single slogan that Nguyen Van Thieu bequeathed to posterity. By "they," of course, the dictator had meant the Communists. At least one theatergoer, however, found Viet's use of the phrase distasteful. Now he was in jail for "spreading counterrevolutionary slogans inspired by American puppets."

My regard for golden-toothed Hien has only deepened. We are together all the time, and with nothing to do but talk, our friendship has flowered into the richest I've ever shared. We have long, soul-to-soul discussions. Hien's natural authority commands the respect of all the prisoners. Even the guards show their deference in little ways. The situation has aggravated the misanthropic Nha into a silent rage. But he doesn't dare attack Hien directly. God only knows what protectors the former official might still have on the outside. So by default I become the object of Nha's ill temper. Any occasion at all will do. If I talk too loudly, I'm admonished; if I stand in the wrong place, I get a reprimand. Despite my irritation, I keep quiet, doing my best to avoid or ignore the cell leader's yelping voice.

One morning toward the end of October, two *bo dois* shuffle into the cell bearing stacks of new, green pajamas. For the first time in four months I can change clothes. Since my arrest I have been wearing the same shirt, pants, and underwear, which I wash as often as possible and which are now miserably frayed. Putting on the brand-new prisoner's uniform gives me a distinct physical pleasure. What luxury there is in the feel of new, clean cotton!

For a few minutes number two becomes a giant, packed dressing room as the prisoners strip down and lovingly get into their new outfits, amazed at their luck. In the hallway we can hear *bo dois* bustling around and calling out to each other. Several times the door opens and one of them sticks his head in to see how the dressing is getting on and to yell orders about making sure the cell is clean. Also to remind us curtly of the rules: "Everybody in his place! No talking!"

No mistake about it, inspection's in the air. A fever of excitement comes over the cell. Hopes leap.

"What if it's the Red Cross?"

"If it's the Red Cross we'll tell them we're starving!"

"We can't write to our families!"

"Where are our lawyers?"

"Are we going to have trials?"

"If it's the Red Cross, I'm going to tell them everything. The hell with it! What's to lose?"

"Shut up!" screeches Nha, watching anxiously out the partially opened door. "Everybody up!"

The door swings in, the inspectors appear. Shit . . . they're all Vietnamese. For a moment a barely audible groan ripples the air.

"Attention!" Nha shouts. "Cell number two, sixty-two men present!" We straighten our shoulders in a military parody, sticking out our shrunken chests. Worse than monkeys in a zoo, I think. At least monkeys could show them their asses!

The head inspector is Tu Tuan, the prison warden. He's wearing a uniform with four stars underlined with double gold bars, showing he's a colonel in the North Vietnamese Army. Behind him there's another officer and four civilians. They all squeeze into the cell. Suddenly one of the civilians looks at Hien. "What?" he says, "you here?"

"For five months," Hien replies calmly.

The civilian inspector is visibly shaken, but he recovers quickly. He doesn't ask Hien why he's behind bars—better not get into that. Instead he says, "Do you know your father died?"

The familiarity of the tone says that these two aren't just passing acquaintances.

"I know," answers Hien, his face expressionless.

"Do you want me to write your mother?"

In a low voice, trying to make this exquisitely public conversation as private as possible, Hien says, "She probably knows already. If not, it's better you don't tell her anything."

"All right." The inspector's voice takes on a tone of forced breeziness. "Okay, if you need anything, you'll let me know, huh?"

That's it. A few more moments of looking around, and the door pulls shut behind them. Everyone sits down, silent and depressed. Also a bit awed at the interchange between Hien and the inspector. Hien just folds his hands in his lap and stares down at them. When after a few minutes talk in the cell starts up again, I say, "Hien?"

He looks at me, his wrinkled face showing a kind of bitter satisfaction. "There," he says. "There you have a true *can bo*. No untoward curiosity, no compromising intervention, friend or no friend. But you know, he's one of the most courageous. Some of them wouldn't recognize their own fathers if they met them in prison—especially their own fathers!"

With this, Hien falls silent, losing himself in thought. A bit later he says, "I should know. When I went on inspection tours at Hoa Lo [Hanoi's central prison] I didn't have the slightest doubt that everybody there was guilty. A true revolutionary has to have absolute trust in the party, right?" The gleam is back in his eye. "And the party's infallible, right?" A flash of gold. Hien the ironic, once more in complete control.

◊   ◊   ◊

Every morning, one prisoner from each *to* gets to go outside and hang up whatever laundry his colleagues have done. It's a prize job, since there's no other way to get out of the cell. On laundry detail you can at least breathe the outside air for fifteen minutes or so while you do the most leisurely hanging job you're capable of. Everybody in the cell eagerly awaits his rotation, which comes every ten to fifteen days, depending on the number in the *to*. One morning Hien gives me his turn, saying, "You're young. You need the exercise more."

On my return Nha stops me and snarls, "Toai, that's a serious offense!" Since the inspection, his dislike for me has surged in direct proportion to Hien's prestige.

"Why, what have I done?"

"You left the cell without authorization!"

At this my temper snaps. The arrogant little prick has been picking on me unmercifully for the last few days. It's been all I could do to contain myself, and now I can't hold it in.

"Authorized? By whom? By you? You're nothing but a prisoner—like me and everybody else. You try to suck up to the guards by giving it to us. But the guards think you're a piece of shit, just like the rest of us do."

Nha is stung. He's not used to hearing this kind of thing. "You!" he snaps back, "you're against the cell leader who's been appointed by the revolution. That means you're against the revolution!" At this, I burst out laughing. Others in the cell are laughing too. If they're not laughing outright, they're snickering.

"Revolution! That's a fine word for a little stool pigeon like you!"

Nha looks around, aware of the general hostility. Suddenly he doesn't feel so safe. He's not sure if he should pursue this confrontation or back off and wait for a better opportunity. He chooses to back off, ignoring my insult.

"Fine, fine," he says, pretending a laugh. "It's true, we're all prisoners here. It's better for us to avoid silly arguments with each other."

As quickly as the fight started, it dissolves. But Nha has lost face, and now his authority is diminished. I know he's going to plot his vengeance and that I'll have to be on guard. But I feel as if I have the upper hand. That momentary threat in the air when the others started snickering was something that neither of us expected. He's got to feel intimidated, in here with sixty very unhappy people who just maybe haven't been entirely transformed into sheep. I've enjoyed our little confrontation, and I'm enjoying the battle of wits that has already started in both our minds. At least it's something to do.

Nha is a pain in the neck, but his presence just adds to the pressure cell life exerts on everyone. One constant problem is water. When the new regime tripled the number of cells in Le Van Duyet, it neglected to enlarge the prison's water supply. Or maybe it wasn't neglect. At any rate, the same pipe that once watered two hundred prisoners now has to supply two thousand.

Most often the single faucet in number two furnishes only a trickle. If you want to wash yourself, you better get up at four in the morning. The same for doing your laundry. As far as the toilet goes, the one hole in the floor, used by sixty-two prisoners, is a horror. Do what we might, we can't keep it clear. All too often it gets clogged, and filth overflows onto the floor, spreading slowly through the cell. When this happens, the only way of dealing with it is to get the prison administration to call the pumper and clear the line connecting cell two's holding tank with the central tank underneath the courtyard. Of course no one can hold himself in indefinitely (though everyone tries) and so while we wait for the pumper, the mounds of excrement grow higher. Everyone who can fit moves onto the sleeping bench. The others stand around in it, exactly like pigs in shit. We all breathe through our mouths.

Several days after the laundry incident, the cell is awash in muck from another one of these overflows. It's disgusting beyond words. Everybody pesters Nha to protest, to make demands, to do something! But the same motives that make him report every infraction to the *bo dois* also frighten him away from making even the most reasonable and necessary demands. For six days we live in a cesspool. Finally I can't take it any more and I begin a tirade.

"Why don't you do something? What the hell are you afraid of? We've been living in shit for a week . . . But maybe you like it, huh?"

Now is the chance he's been waiting for. He's not going to back away from this one.

"Toai, you shut up! Ever since you came into the cell you've been inciting people and giving me trouble!"

"Nha, I don't give a damn about you! You're just a little son of a bitch! But I'm fed up, and so is everyone else. You better do something about this. If you don't, I'm going to talk to them myself."

When the *bo doi* brings in the rice, Nha asks to speak to the *can bo.* Soon another *bo doi* returns to fetch Nha to the office. Half an hour later the cell leader is back. With him are a lieutenant and two *bo dois* with submachine guns.

The lieutenant is Nguyen Van Kieu, whom we've seen once or twice before this—a tall, thin, supercilious individual who affects civilian clothes. As he enters the cell, it's all he can do to pretend he doesn't notice the stench, which must be bowling him over. The two machine-gun-carrying *bo dois* are practically vomiting.

"Criticism session for this cell," Kieu proclaims curtly.

That's the signal for Nha to start talking. "As representative of collective cell number two, I must point out to the *can bo* that this cell has always maintained perfect order. But the last few days, prisoner Toai has upset the discipline of the cell. He refuses to acknowledge the cell leader's authority, and he does not obey the prison's internal regulations."

Kieu looks us over and say, "Which one is Toai?"

"I'm Toai," I say, standing up.

Kieu motions for me to sit down, then nods at Nha, who continues with the indictment.

"The other day Toai left the cell to hang laundry without authorization. This morning he impugned the cell leader's position. . . . He called me a 'son of a bitch.' "

At this there's a kind of stifled glee from the residents. I raise my hand, and Kieu nods at me.

"I went out because another prisoner gave me his turn. I didn't break any rules. But it's true I called Mr. Nha a son of a bitch. It's because we've been living like this for a week already" (pointing at the mess on the floor, which Kieu has carefully avoided stepping in). "It's unfit for human beings. And he hasn't said anything to anybody about it."

I'm expecting the worst. But what can they do, throw me in isolation? I'd give anything to get out of the stench and the press of bodies for a while. But Lieutenant Kieu isn't as interested in my insubordination as he might have been. It's obvious that he doesn't think much of Nha. Besides, he wants to get out of this stinkhole as fast as appearances will let him. So

222 ◊ THE VIETNAMESE GULAG

he contents himself with a severe warning for me to watch myself. Then he turns on his heel and leaves, followed by the two choking machine gunners.

The next day I am transferred to collective cell number five, a few yards down the hall. Hien shakes my hand and holds onto it for a moment, saying, "You were right to do what you did. But be careful, they don't like that kind of thing. And you're young. You have to stay alive, so you can tell our story one day. It's over for me. . . . All I can do is try to keep my dignity." Then, with a last flash of teeth, Hien left my life.

16

The Party's Way

Those who have sampled some of the new regime's other prisons and camps are unanimous in their praise for Le Van Duyet. "A paradise among prisons," one of cell five's residents calls it. I don't know if he's being ironic or just exaggerating. Whatever the case, of Le Van Duet's three cellblocks, Zone A is by far the most livable. And in Zone A, cell five is privileged.

My old cell, number two (and every other cell so far as I know), is subjected to regular thorough searches. Every eight to ten days four or five *bo dois* burst in and order everyone to strip to their undershorts and move outside. Then they comb every inch of the cell, feeling each article of clothing and tapping every conceivable place that might accommodate a hidden pencil, scrap of paper, or smuggled razor blade. Even the walls are scanned for new inscriptions, and if any are discovered the inhabitants can look forward to long hours of grilling while the *bo dois* try to identify the culprit.

Cell five, though, is never searched. Cell five also furnishes the fifteen-plus prisoners who work in the kitchen, the most coveted privilege of all. And control of the kitchen of course means food; that is, it means everything: precious extra dollops of rice in the cell's food pan.

Prior to April 30, 1975, free South Vietnamese city dwellers ate about five hundred grams of rice a day, peasants about seven hundred. In those days, rice diets were supplemented by vegetables, fruit, meat, and fish from the South's varied larder. In contrast, our ration in Le Van Duyet during the first rainy season of the new era was three hundred grams of rice a day, on top of which was ladled a spoonful or so of *nuoc mam* fish sauce. Twice a day the kitchen orderlies would carry in the cell's pan, whose red rice contents would then be scooped into our individual bowls by the cell's "apportioner," using his own bowl as a combination measuring device and serving ladle. From the little tin bucket the orderlies also delivered, a bowlful of *nuoc mam* would be ladled, one to each *to*.

While the food was being distributed, the "apportioner" found himself the object of universal suspicion and hawklike scrutiny. A thumb placed too far into a bowl would deprive its owner of the offending digit's volume of rice. A bowl that left the server's hand a little too mounded or a little hollow in the middle screamed favoritism and corruption. But in cell five there are fewer problems of this sort, and a little more rice to spread around.

Number five's kitchen connection and its freedom from searches are due solely to the character of the cell leader, Huynh Cu, a tall, strapping northerner with a loud voice who talks to the *bo dois* as if they were his own soldiers. Cu is in fact used to command and conducts himself with dignity and an impressive authority. Up until 1967 he was an officer in the North Vietnamese Army. Then, disillusioned by North Vietnam's political policies, he defected.

Joining the Saigon government, he took a position with the Ministry of Information, but quit in 1971 in a fit of contempt toward his superiors there, particularly Hoang Duc Nha. This Nha was a favored young relative of Nguyen Van Thieu's.

Educated in the United States and fluent in English, he tried to imitate the Americans in everything, while at the same time he held them in the deepest contempt. Nha had been appointed minister of information, then special adviser to his dictator cousin. "An incompetent," Cu rumbled. "The only things he cared about were making money and sleeping with women. As much money as possible, and as many women as possible."

As disgusted with Saigon's brand of politics as he had been with Hanoi's, Cu resigned his position and opened a small restaurant in the capital's Thi Nghe suburbs. It was there that the *bo dois* found him a few days after victory. Cu's strength of character demands respect from us, while his magical ability to arrange preferential treatment is enough to induce devotion.

Cu's popularity with number five is enhanced by his attitude toward informers. His short, standard speech on the subject goes like this: "If there is ever a stool pigeon in this cell, I want to give him fair warning. First, he'll be wasting his time; they won't accord him any thanks or let him go one day earlier. Second, if I find out, I'll kill him with my own hands. I've got nothing to lose. I've already betrayed the party, so I'm here for life anyway." Not a person in the cell doubts his word.

◊   ◊   ◊

Somewhere in the distance I hear a voice: "Toai! Hey Toai! Get up so we can open the door!" I'm sleeping on the floor next to the cell door, blocking it. I open my eyes and find Cu shaking me, swearing: "Shit! Another batch of new guys. It's the goddamn middle of the night!"

"New prisoners? Where?" Slowly I begin to get my bearings. "What new prisoners?"

"Listen, don't you hear them opening the doors? They're handing out another batch."

Yes, now I can hear them, a group of people walking toward the cell. The key turns in the lock of cell number four (next to us), then in ours. The door swings open, and a *bo doi* removes the blindfolds from the eyes of two young men, then pushes them into the cell. Checking the list in his hand, the *bo doi* looks at Cu and says, "Two new ones for you. How many is that all told?"

Cu objects: "Listen, that'll bring it up to seventy-two. We don't have room to sleep as it is. The guys who work in the kitchen have got to be able to rest."

"Look," says the *bo doi*, "don't complain so much. Number four has eighty-one." He gestures to the group waiting in the hall. "We didn't have to give you only two of them." As the door swings shut, I catch a glimpse of about twelve more newcomers, all blindfolded.

The two who have been pushed into the cell are standing stock-still, blinking their eyes and wondering where they've landed. They're only youngsters, like the few others we've taken in most recently. Cu looks at them and snorts derisively—"Hhmmh! More jokers from Phuc Quoc, I'll bet!" The two young men avert their eyes and bow their heads.

For some time now, a steady trickle of adolescents has been flowing into Le Van Duyet, and no doubt into the other prisons as well. They're all from a new resistance movement calling itself Phuc Quoc—Restore the Nation. When these poor kids come into the cells it makes the NLF and party old-timers laugh. Phuc Quoc not only seems to limit itself to adolescent recruits, it even gives out membership cards certifying that so-and-so is a member in good standing; that is to say, these people carry around with them certificates of opposition to the regime. Only the very young are capable of such naiveté.

Cell leader Cu holds firmly to the opinion that Phuc Quoc is actually a trap laid by the regime to catch young people who have enough guts to oppose the new ideology. Whether he's right I don't know; it's certainly the kind of scheme they could think up. As it turns out, our two newcomers do belong to the movement. Chau Van Ha is eighteen, and his buddy, Le Van Sang, is sixteen; they were caught shortly after they joined.

"Come on," says Cu, tossing two pairs of green pajamas at them. "Put these on and try to squeeze yourselves in somewhere."

Cu's theory about entrapment sounds reasonable. But personally, I don't think it's necessary to explain the childlike ways of the movement. The previous Phuc Quoc member to come into number five told me how he'd been captured. His story was credulity itself.

A bit older than most of the other Phuc Quoc, he had been in the army. When April 30 came he decided not to surrender but to become a guerrilla. Somehow the Phuc Quoc had put him together with a group of other army people who were forming themselves into a small resistance unit. During a skirmish with People's Army troops, he had unfurled a flag and started waving it at the enemy. "How could you do that?" I asked. "They'd know exactly where you were." "Oh, no," came the answer, "you don't understand, the flag had a 'Kill Communists' spell on it. It would kill them!" I neglected to ask how successful the spell might have been. Perhaps I assumed the answer was self-evident, considering the venue of our discussion.*

At mealtimes in cell five, groups gather to talk, just as they do in all the cells. Cu attracts to himself the former party members, Front people, and sympathizers, in which group I qualify. Mealtime is confidence-sharing time, and confidences are not shared with just anybody. Our dinner circle includes a former Front lieutenant whose name is Nguyen Thanh Hai. Hai had been in charge of the commissariat at "R," the Front's wartime headquarters on the Cambodian border. While supervising a supply transfer he had been knocked down and run over by a runaway cart, and had never healed properly. As a result he suffered severe pain in his lower back and walked around in a peculiar, twisted fashion. Like almost all the long-

* Of course the story indicated the simplicity of the Phuc Quoc. But it also suggests the extent to which spirits and magic live just below the surface for many Vietnamese. The story was told that in Go Cong Province during the Tet offensive, a martial statue of the ancient hero Tran Hung Dao came to life and drove back the attacking Vietcong, thus saving the provincial capital. Many highly placed people at least half-believed this story, though they might not have said so in public. Of course many South Vietnamese were sure that the United States would intervene to save them, even after the Communists had won. It was an opinion I heard right up until the time I left the country in 1978.

term jungle dwellers he also was subject to recurrent bouts of malaria that would send him into days of shaking delirium followed by prostrate exhaustion.

Hai was one of the new Le Van Duyet's first occupants, transferred directly from a Front prison, where he was being held for attacking an upper-echelon officer. According to Hai, he had been muttering invocations to Buddha about his pain one day and was reproached for it by this officer, who didn't believe God had a place in Communist prayers. In the ensuing discussion Hai had upbraided the officer for his callousness. "He knew my wife and children had been killed in an American bombing, and that I was suffering miserably. And still he had the gall to criticize me for complaining." Insulted, the officer had responded in kind to Hai's anger.

In the end, Hai lost his temper and attempted to throttle his tormentor, landing in jail for his efforts. Victory had brought no amnesty, though after the jungle prison he considered Le Van Duyet a salvation of sorts. Here at least he could complain about his aching back as much as he wished, and nobody noticed to whom he was addressing the complaints. Hai was one of the first post-victory residents of number five, a group that numbered thirty-six in all. With our last Phuc Quocers, we've just doubled that.

Another transferee from wartime Front jails was Nguyen Van Tang, a grizzled fighter known in the underground as Hai Tang. As he talked, the understanding came over me for the first time that I was turning into something of a repository for personal histories. Almost from the beginning of my imprisonment I had determined that whatever time I was going to spend in jail would not be wasted. I would not allow these people to take a portion of my life from me. My strategy, my defense, would be to observe, to store up every experience against the day of my release . . . then to write it down. How long (I thought) could they keep me? Ten years? Twenty years? If they kept me twenty years, I'd still be only fifty when I got out, with plenty of time and energy left to tell it all.

Listening to the old warrior Hai Tang, I am suddenly aware

that in these cells, the experiences that are mine to record . . . are not my own. In these universes of suspended animation, where the shifting grip of a prehensile thumb on a rice bowl engrosses the attention of seventy human beings, a man lives, if he lives at all, through others—through the intersecting of his life with theirs. To resign oneself to the interior world of memory and recrimination: that is death—a fate I can see in the brain-dead stares of those who sit hunched motionless among their neighbors. The ones who live are those who can derive sustenance from others. For these lucky ones, curiosity means existence. They are the fish in water. They are the survivors. And the recorders.

The veteran Tang is one of my links with history. Through his story I feel I'm beginning to understand the past, not just marvel at it. In his person the jails of the revolution militant lock arms with those of the revolution triumphant.

In 1972 Tang headed the Front's administrative section in the Binh Chan region, just south of Saigon. At one point, circumstantial evidence suggested to his superiors that Tang was working as a double agent. Despite indignant denials, he was thrown into a maquis prison, "so terrible," he says, "that I feel good here." (He's the one who calls Le Van Duyet "a paradise.") The "prison" was a trench about five feet deep covered with branches. Since both guerrillas and prisoners were on the move all the time, nothing more permanent could be arranged. At night the prisoners would be manacled by the feet to an iron bar. There was no way to get up. "If you couldn't wait you had to relieve yourself right there, like an animal." The diet was primarily manioc. Though they helped cultivate rice from time to time, there was never any of it to eat. The great thing was to catch an occasional small frog in the rice fields and gulp it down raw. "We were so hungry," says Tang, "that we ate roots and bark, anything we thought might be edible."* Disci-

---

* American army lieutenants Nicholas Rowe and Dan Pfizer lived for years in "prisons" very much like this. Rowe's captivity is described in his memoir *Five Years to Freedom*. Pfizer tells his story in Al Santoli's *To Bear Any Burden*. They were the only survivors from their group of POWs, several of whom starved to death—Ed.

pline in the trench prisons was ferocious. The guards simply would not tolerate any kind of quarrel or protest, and a quick execution was the standard punishment. Living so close to the edge of death themselves, they had no incentive to make life reasonable for their prisoners.

After the fall of Saigon, documents from Thieu's police files proved that it was Tang's assistant who had been the spy. About Tang himself there was nothing. Of course that, as his interrogators told him, was no proof that he hadn't known what was going on. So he stayed in, although his standard of living had now been raised considerably.

These are the first details I have ever heard about the Front's wartime prisons, and Tang's description helps me better understand the conditions under which we live in Le Van Duyet. I now see that Duyet is not a "prison" in the usual sense of the word, no more than was the trench Tang previously lived in. An ordinary prison is part of a system of justice; it exists for punishment, or correction, or rehabilitation. Each of these rationales accords the prisoner a certain dignity. He is a human being who is worth punishment or correction or rehabilitation.

But Duyet, where seventy people sleep pressed together on their sides in a space built for twenty, cedes nothing to its inmates. Like the jungle trench, it is simply a storehouse, a place where inconvenient bodies can be stacked for an indeterminate duration. These bodies, of course, might simply be disposed of outright, as they were in the Nazi death camps (or as they were at that very moment in the Khmer Rouge prisons). But in its wisdom the Vietnamese revolution had decided that, all in all, storage would be less troublesome than murder. It was a decision I was sure they had made carefully, on the basis of the most objective considerations.

Hai Tang himself could not see it that way. When we first started talking he was still looking for justice: exoneration and an apology. But as the months passed he grew less hopeful. After all, the party had discovered its "mistake" in May and still had made no move toward releasing him.

But even after Tang gave over his hopes for some kind of

personal vindication, his faith in the party remained firm. The nobility of its goals (toward which he had devoted his life) was what counted. Next to these, whatever treatment he or any other individual experienced was insignificant. "The party's methods," he would admit, "are brutal and unreasonable, that's true. But apart from the Communist party, which party can you trust? None is more honest, more intransigent. Even if it is sometimes unfair, there is no other way but the party's way."

I tried to argue with him. During the war against the French and Americans, what he was saying might have been believable, that a struggle against ruthless foes required ruthless methods. But now we were no longer at war, and the party's methods hadn't changed. At this stage one could see clearly that methods and goals had become one and the same. If the revolution's goals were truly noble, then its means must conform to that nobility. What was needed now in the South was socialism with a human face, the kind of socialism the Czechs had wanted in 1968.

Hearing these arguments Hai Tang would shake his head and smile: "Toai, I know your intentions are good, but you are almost as naive as the poor Phuc Quocers. On what doctrine do you base your new kind of revolution, your brand of socialism? There is capitalism, there is colonialism, and only one force can counter them, in spite of its errors. That's the Communist party. Tell me the name of one leader, just one, who has been able to create your wonderful humanistic socialism. Name me one country where the Communist party has changed itself after taking power."

Hai Tang, I thought, was putting on airs. Here he was, stacked in with the rest of the cordwood, and he felt proud to be a party member—because the party at least was strong!

As time passed, though, Tang became less and less communicative. Whatever strength he derived from his love for the party was not enough to sustain his vitality. When he did enter our political discussions, it would be to defend the party, but increasingly now, also to deprecate himself. He was old, he would say, and had seen too many people die. The Vietnamese people have suffered so terribly; now they needed a long period of peace. Only the party could give them that. Maybe he didn't understand very well the objective conditions that led the party to do certain things, but they must be necessary for the preservation of the revolution.

Little by little, Tang had grown used to the idea that he was the revolution's necessary victim. Why, he didn't know, but he was sure there was a reason. By the time I left Le Van Duyet he was practically mute. He wouldn't even answer questions. By then he was a man broken in spirit and health, but he was still faithful. He had found that he could serve the party until the very end . . . as a prisoner.

◊　　　　◊　　　　◊

Tet comes in February. We prick up our ears at the distant crackle of firecrackers in the street. It is a lugubrious sound, stirring memories of other Tets. Though no one says it, we are all aware that this is the first time firecrackers have been allowed since 1968. That year, the pop of fireworks had masked the offensive's opening shots. Afterward they were banned.

So this is the first Tet of freedom. I had often dreamed of what I would do during the Tet vacations after peace came. I had promised myself a tour of the country—visits with my family to all the places I wanted to see. We would go to Dalat, where the air is fresh and perfumed by pine trees, to Sa Huynh beach, where the clear water stays shallow a long way out, and multicolored fish dart among the bather's legs. Yvonne and I would go to Hue and take walks in the romantic parks where the emperors' tombs lay. I would also travel to Hanoi, the national capital, a hostile foreign city for so many years.

But if travel wasn't in my immediate future, neither was I expecting the gift that was bestowed on us a week before the holiday. We would be allowed to write home, the first time since my arrest, eight months ago. In announcing this unbelievable news, the *can bo* said, "You can write whatever you want. But I think it would be best to give your families news about your health and to send them your good wishes. Of course you may ask them to send you a package—but only candy, cigarettes, or clothing, the whole thing weighing not more than one kilo."

Everyone took the hint. Write about something other than what the *can bo* suggested and the letter would never be forwarded. But that hardly mattered. We were too overjoyed at the chance to let families know we were alive. The cell became unnaturally quiet, as the inmates began composing letters in their heads. No rough drafts would be allowed. Each of us was given a quarter of a sheet of paper, one side of which we were allowed to cover with our most lovingly prepared phrases. Then a *bo doi* collected them, and they were launched.

No replies or packages were ever received. Eight months later when my wife was allowed to visit she told me she had never received anything in the mail. I was sure then that none of the other two thousand letters was ever sent either. It's likely they went straight into the prisoners' dossiers, helping the *can bos* decide which prisoners needed special attention.

This Tet, party secretariat Xuan Thuy sends greetings to the South Vietnamese people on behalf of the party. In his message he wishes "courage to the women and children of the former regime's soldiers and civil servants who are still separated from their husbands and fathers." "In future Tets," he says, "all families will once again be united."

As cynical as most of us are, it's impossible not to notice the expectation that this speech insinuates into our minds. On the first day of Tet this trace of hope swells to unexpected size, when an army captain and three prison officials make a lecture tour of the collective cells. The captain's optimistic little speech goes something like this: "As representative of the revolution, the party, and the government, I wish you a new year filled with good luck and good health. Do your best to be released as soon as possible. I do not want to see you in here next Tet."

Such is man's need for hope that all the prisoners laugh and applaud. Huynh Cu, the cell leader, gives the officials best wishes for the new year on the cell's behalf.

Then the captain starts speaking again: "I have some good

news to announce. Since it's Tet, you will get some meat with your rice. Not much. I know there was more of it under the puppet governments—I was a prisoner then myself. But those regimes lived like whores of the Americans. Today we are poor, but we are independent. We don't owe anybody a thing, and we share what we have." With that ringing proclamation, the four of them leave to spread the good news to the next cell.

In order to heighten the euphoria of the occasion, the captain orders the cell doors to be left open. Naturally, it is forbidden to wander out, and armed guards watch the halls. But the open door is a symbol, a promise. And we can call out to each other from cell to cell. Getting into the mood, we start to sing, revolutionary songs, of course. Nobody quite has the guts to quaver out some popular tune from the days of decadence. But if you listen closely enough, you can hear certain individual variations on the accepted lyrics. As we chime in with "At Night I Dream I See Uncle Ho," I realize that several voices in the choir are changing "I see" to "I kill." No doubt the new version corresponds more closely to the reality of their dreams.

With it all, an unaccustomed atmosphere of happiness pervades the cell. A new year has come, and new hope. People talk enthusiastically about the captain's speech: "A lot of people are going to be released this year, you can count on it! The captain said he didn't want to see us here next Tet. He couldn't say any more, but his meaning's clear as day."

As for the meat, the cooks received a pig weighing one hundred and thirty pounds—for the entire prison. When they work out the figures it comes to less than an ounce and a half apiece. But with that meager supply they work wonders. On the first day of Tet, they serve the broth in which they cooked the meat, and it is drunk voluptuously. On the second day the menu is the same. But though the stock has become quite thin, it still has an exquisite delicacy. On the third day comes the apotheosis: each of us receives a morsel of meat. It is a meal we will talk about for weeks. Perhaps never before has one pig occupied the minds of so many men for so long a time.

17

Inside the Cells

Not too long after Tet there is a vacancy in the kitchen, and Huynh Cu offers me the job. This is an opportunity that cannot be passed up; it means getting out of the packed cell, walking around, killing time during the endless days. Most of all it means the chance for something extra to eat.

The kitchen is located across the way from Zone A. On its four large brick fireplaces seventeen or eighteen cooks and assistants prepare food for the entire prison. For the eleven o'clock feeding, we start work at eight in the morning, cleaning up and getting the fires going. Since I am the new boy, I find myself running all over the place: "Toai, sweep this up will you? Toai, bring that pot over here."

Each morning some of the assistants go to the storeroom for the day's rice allotment. There we certify the prisoner head count for the storage master, and he measures out the proper number of kilos, depending on the current daily ration. (In 1976 it was three hundred grams of rice per head. Later, farina was mixed in with the rice.) Back in the kitchen the cooks pour the rice into gigantic cook pots, each holding up to forty kilos. Then they add the water while we stoke the fires to bring it all to a low boil. As each batch is done we transfer the mixture into the garbage cans that are used as containers—one for each cell, with the cell number painted on the sides—then scrape the baked-on rice from the sides and bottom of the pots. This we save for later, most often using it as extras for cell five, but sometimes making a soup out of it for our own enjoyment.

I work at my new job with such zeal that within a couple of weeks I am promoted to food carrier. At eleven in the morning and four in the afternoon I help deliver the garbage cans to the cells in Zone A and Zone C. Zone B, wedged in between the original jail and the courtyard wall, is off limits. The few dozen rations for this zone have to be left out front with the guard. Zone B is always quiet. There's a mystery about it. We notice that *bo dois* who enter the zone have to show an identity card to the guard at the entrance. Nghe, my coworker, thinks it might be a special section reserved for important prisoners they are keeping in solitary confinement. Others believe it's probably just offices where they keep prison records. But if so, then why the rice deliveries? Certainly not for the *bo dois* or *can bos*.

In Zone A and Zone C we bring the garbage cans right up to the cell doors, which often allows us to exchange a few words with the people inside. While the Zone A cells are faced with a barred grille, in Zone C they have regular doors, each one with its peephole—the same as in Tran Hung Dao. When the *bo doi* opens the door we get a glance at murky interiors filled with a jumble of bodies. An indescribable smell wafts out, as if the cells have no ventilation.

Zone C is clearly a good block to avoid. But it's B that really has our attention . . . and our curiosity. After a week or so of observation, Nghe and I devise a little scenario that we think will enable us to learn more. We've noticed that exactly at noon the *bo doi* guarding the block leaves his post and walks over to the main section of the jail, probably to report and go for lunch in the guards' mess. There's always a couple of minutes' delay before his replacement arrives.

In collusion with the cooks, one day we contrive to "accidentally" shortchange one of the Zone C cells on its ration. We only discover this unfortunate oversight at cleanup time, after all the deliveries have been made—that is, just before twelve o'clock. Now Nghe and I are forced to make an unscheduled second delivery to C, carrying the container right past several of the Zone B doors, where there is at this moment . . . no guard. In my haste, I stumble, not more than two yards from a peephole door that we think might belong to a cell. Nghe does his best to hold the can upright, but can't keep some of the steaming rice from spilling onto the ground.

Angry, Nghe begins to chew me out: "Idiot! You spilled the rice! Do you want to get us into trouble?"

"So what?" I answer. "We're already in jail, what more can they do to us? Besides, nobody's seen anything. The guard's not here."

All this is in easy earshot of the door. If there's someone in there, he must have heard us. Meanwhile, we are picking the rice up from the ground with our hands, with a great show of haste, but actually as little at a time as possible.

"What do you think these buildings are anyway?" says Nghe. "Do you think any of the guys are in there?"

"Don't know. I've never seen anybody."

Suddenly a low moan reaches out from behind the door. It sounds something like "Oh, my friends . . . ," but we can't quite make out the words.

Nghe and I stare at each other, momentarily forgetting the rice. "Oh . . . my friends . . . ," it moans out at us again.

Busy again cupping the rice up from the ground, I speak toward the door without lifting my head. "Who are you? Are you a prisoner?"

"Nguyen Van Tai," comes the hoarse answer, "from Go Vap. They've beaten me. I'm so thirsty . . . so thirsty."

He sounds as though he's dying.

"How long have you been there?"

238 ◊ THE VIETNAMESE GULAG

Suddenly an urgent hiss from Nghe, "Watch out!" The relief guard is walking toward us very quickly. He looks furious. "What the hell are you two doing here?"

With my hand I gesture apologetically towards the rice that's still on the ground. "I stumbled, Comrade ... the rice ..."

"Get the hell out of here! Fast!" He's shooing us away with angry waves of his arms, scared to death himself that someone else might see us there.

Our discovery causes a sensation in cell five, which quickly spreads to the other cells. "There's torture in Zone B!" All the prisoners keep their ears open, trying to find out as much as they can.

A few days later we hear through one of the other food carriers that Nguyen Van Tai spent several days in one of the Zone C cells. The news comes from a prisoner in that cell, who had taken several days to put "the tortured man in Zone B" together with the quiet transient who had slept next to him for a short while. Tai was apparently a hairdresser from Saigon who had been accused of "armed conspiracy" for having kept a gun in his house after the new regime ordered all weapons to be surrendered.

Once the identification was made, other prisoners contributed their own bits and pieces of information, which eventually made their way to the kitchen newsmarket. Apparently, Tai had made so little impression on anyone that when the *bo doi* said, "Prisoner Tai, take all your belongings and follow me," everybody had assumed he was being released. What else could they be doing with someone so innocuous, especially since transfers to other jails or camps were always made in groups? Tai tortured? Those who remembered him couldn't believe it.

After that, every isolated departure took on ominous significance. Zone B was a major discovery, and with nothing else to do, a good number of the prisoners began to search their memories for other isolated departures. Eventually we were able to identify several other prisoners whom people thought had been released or transferred, but who had in fact gone only a few yards away into Zone B. Watching the rice ration carefully, we could tell when someone was moved there: Zone C, cell four would have one fewer ration, Zone B one more. If there had been no convoys, no deaths, we knew that "poor so-and-so must be in Ba Dinh Palace." (Having been Ho Chi Minh's residence in Hanoi, "Ba Dinh Palace" automatically offered itself as a nickname for Zone B.)

◇   ◇   ◇

The chief cook is a jovial former party member with a flair for doing the best with what he has and also for keeping his people in good humor. Of course all the kitchen workers know they are among the blessed, so they tend to be in good humor anyway. They have work, fresh air, extra food, and access to information about everything going on in Le Van Duyet. Work is always accompanied by jokes and the latest gossip. A number of *bo dois* have even taken to hanging around on their time off.

One of these is a northerner named Nam Luu. He sports a gold "two-pilot" Seiko watch and talks incessantly about his Honda motorcycle, its engine, its gears, and the various conquests it's taken him on. He has even had trousers made for himself, cut from a good-quality fabric in the latest Saigon fashion—widely flared legs. The signs are unmistakable. Nam Luu is one of those northerners who has been unable to resist the South's "poison encased in sugar pills," its material seductions. He's been bitten by the consumer bug.

The idea has been forming in my head that I might be able to use this jaunty person in the same way I had used the *bo doi* Tha back in Tran Hung Dao—as a messenger. Except for that one smuggled letter seven months ago, and the Tet letter (to which I have not yet received an answer) there's been no way for me to contact my family.

With these things in mind I begin to strike up a casual acquaintance with him. I learn that his family had lived in Thailand and had returned to North Vietnam to get involved with the revolution. When I asked what his initial impression was of Hanoi, he answered, "Not much," a response that moves my pulse rate up a notch. That "not much" is a pretty good indication that Nam Luu's allegiance is less than burning. Together with his materialistic ways, it indicates that I'm safe in moving this dangerous game to the next level.

"Listen," I say to him a few days later, "how much does a *bo doi* make nowadays?"

"Only twenty-five dong," he answers. (I note the "only.")

Let's see; twenty-five dong is about 12,500 former piasters. A Honda like the one he's been talking about used to cost in the neighborhood of 400,000 piasters. Over three months' salary for him. Probably much more, since I'm sure motorcycle prices have gone up crazily, like everything else. That's not bad for nine months' work since the revolution. Casually I ask him, "Do you have a pair of those special sunglasses that let you look directly at the sun without burning your eyes?"

"What, there are sunglasses like that?"

"Sure, I've got two pair at home. After I'm released I'll give you one."

There's no subtlety about this guy, and none of the scruples the *bo doi* Tha had to overcome either. He rises straight to the bait. "How much were they before?" he asks.

"Oh, maybe ten thousand piasters, about twenty dong."

Nam Luu doesn't blink an eye at the outrageous price. Sunglasses this special have got to cost a lot of money. "And you'd give me a pair?"

"Sure, I don't need two." Now for the clincher. "Especially not while I'm in here."

"I guess not, ha ha." Sharing a little joke with me. "Where are they, at your house? Is that far?" He's dying to get his hands on them this very instant.

"No, actually it's quite close. If you like, you could go and get them. I would just have to write a few words to my wife to tell her to give them to you."

Nam Luu has obviously done this kind of thing before. Without missing a beat, he pulls a three-quarters-empty pack of cigarettes out of his pocket, saying, "Here, Toai, take a few cigarettes for yourself." The cigarettes will make my cellmates happy—and on the inside of the pack I can write a few words to let my wife know where I am, and to tell her to give my sunglasses . . . to the bearer.

Two days later, Nam Luu gives me another mostly empty pack. Inside is a letter from my wife, who has been trying desperately to locate me. At Tran Hung Dao they had told her that Doan Van Toai was "not on the list of prisoners," and that "his whereabouts are not known." She had knocked on the doors of every prison in Saigon, except Le Van Duyet, which she had never heard of. "Maybe," she was told one time, "he has been transferred to the North." She, my parents, and my sister have been in despair. I can imagine their feeling of gratitude toward Nam Luu. And he seemed quite pleased with the sunglasses.

Unfortunately, the ease with which this transaction went off makes me overconfident, and that leads straight to disaster.

One of my cellmates is named Le Van Bao, an ordinary, stolid character who has one remarkable achievement to his credit. Somehow he has managed to hide his watch from the searchers who examine every prisoner on arrival at Le Van Duyet. Seeing that I am on some kind of terms with Nam Luu, Bao asks me to inquire if Luu would sell his watch for him. Bao impresses me as a trustworthy individual, so I agree. But shortly after Luu took the watch, a bo doi comes into the cell to summon me "to work." Of course I had worried continuously about my connection with Nam Luu, and this order makes my heart stop.

As we walk toward the interrogation rooms my mind is racing. There are two possible punishments for suborning a guard, and it would be difficult to choose which was worse. Caning wasn't used often, but when it was, it was ghastly. Administered by a professional torturer whose very name gave prisoners the shakes, twenty or twenty-five slashes would leave the recipient in agony and very nearly dead. The other punishment was imprisonment in one of the isolation boxes. Older prisoners who were subjected to it often died, if not in the cell, then shortly afterward. Of course it was always possible they would cane you first and then throw you in isolation.

As soon as I get into the interrogation room, the *can bo* begins shouting at me, accusing me of attempting to corrupt a guard. In the course of his tongue-lashing, I come to understand that it wasn't Le Van Bao who informed, but someone who had wanted to denounce him. I just happened to be in the way, not that that helped. There is no denying the truth of the *can bo's* accusation, so I simply admit it. Afterward he marches me back to cell five and announces my crime and sentence in front of the entire group. The shame is harder to bear than any punishment would have been, not that they are going to be satisfied with shame. The sentence is twenty days in isolation.

The isolation cell is a tall box, six feet long by three feet wide by six feet high. The rear two-thirds of the floor area are covered by a cement platform raised about a foot above the ground. At night a single bulb shines weakly from its recessed socket in the ceiling; during the day a funnel of daylight peeks in through the open vent above the light. With my right hand cuffed to my left ankle and my left hand to my right ankle, I sit on the platform, staring into the murk. Occasionally I vary the position, lying on my back with my legs and arms folded above me. In that posture sleep is also possible. After a while I get used to the discomfort, though it certainly doesn't disappear. There's not a great deal of pain involved, but after a couple of days I develop a kind of internal trembling that won't go away. The rice ration—half of the prison norm—is brought in twice a day, and I am unlocked for a time, to eat and to relieve myself in the helmet that serves as a toilet.

I am not sure how many days I stay lucid; ten or twelve, I think. I remember noticing the symptoms of beriberi: my legs seem to be asleep or partially paralyzed, and I am afraid I will never be able to move again. At first hallucinations come sporadically, Ho Chi Minh appears, then my mother, then gray-skinned, long-haired ghosts. At some point I begin to feel a fever coming on. Then the hallucinations become more frequent. I know I am going unconscious for periods of time. I vaguely remember being unlocked and propped up in a standing position, my legs buckling under me. Though I can't seem to see, I know I am being carried across someone's shoulders. Then a familiar, nauseating smell overwhelms me, and just before I lapse into darkness I remember where I smelled it before. It's the smell that wafts out of the Zone C cells when you open the door to hand in their pail of rice.

For two weeks my new cellmates nurse me selflessly, helping to wash my face and collecting a little extra rice for my bowl. Naturally no doctor comes, and no nurse; and no one has ever seen medicine in the cells, although beriberi can be cured with shots of Vitamin B. But medicine or not, slowly I begin to feel better; I begin to come back to life.

The life I come back to is one that makes me sick for the comforts of my old cell in the French-constructed Zone A. Zone C, like Zone B, has been designed and built by the new regime. Zone C's collective cells cannot be made to contain quite as many souls as Zone A's; they do not have as large an overall floor area. But the biggest difference is that the Zone A cells have tremendously high ceilings and a grilled front wall, which allows complete air circulation. Though the bodies are cramped in together, at least you can breathe. The Zone C cells, by contrast, have eight- or nine-foot ceilings and a solid door. The food port in this door remains open all the time; it is the cell's only source of ventilation. Because of this, the air in the cell never changes; it is thick and rank with the odor of sixty bodies. It literally takes your breath away.

In this cell, where I have reentered the world of the living, there is an endless rotation of prisoners waiting in line for a turn to breathe at the open port. Each prisoner is given one minute, except for the old and sick, who get two. Since nobody has a watch, those who wait count up to one hundred—or two hundred—to measure their predecessor's turn. This human clock method is a regular source of friction. "Hey, so-and-so is counting too fast!" or "Listen to that count, the guy's counting for his buddy!" Once you've had a turn, it will be more than an hour until your next.

The second necessary element, water, is rationed as strictly as the air. Those who once lived in Zone A talk nostalgically about the trickle of water that flowed day and night from the faucet, allowing the prisoners to drink whenever they wished, and even to wash themselves and their clothes if they could get up early enough. But the new regime's prison architects had decided against the expense of running a pipe through the new cells. Instead, water is distributed for fifteen minutes or so a day by means of a rubber hose poked through the peephole into a water tub that sits next to the door.

Water discipline is all the more necessary because one of the two prisoners in charge of sticking the hose through the port has become mad with power. A former party member from the North, he was arrested in 1973 on suspicion of planning to defect. The three years he has spent in jail have made him an insane sadist. He seems to believe that he has been reinstated into party membership and that he has been given the responsibility of disciplining Le Van Duyet's counterrevolutionaries. It is frightening the way his insanity—if that's what it is—meshes with the reality of his position. When it is his turn to bring the hose around, the quarter hour often shrinks to ten minutes, or even less, according to the practiced time-counters in the cell.

When this happens there is a loud chorus of protests from the cell, answered through the food port by a stream of insults.

"You are nothing but dogs, you reactionary bastards! Men like you don't deserve water!"

"And what about you? Aren't you a prisoner, the same as us?"

"No, not the same as you, you dogs. I'm not your kind!"

But fighting with him of course only exacerbates his rage. Eventually two talented ethnic Chinese merchants find a simple way to manage his volatile temper—bribes. One offers this former party member the expensive shirt he had been wearing when he was arrested (and which he has managed to keep rela-

tively fresh). The other comes up with a few piasters. After that the hose stays on for the full quarter hour and sometimes more, as the glibbest inmates vie with each other to see who can keep the water bearer occupied longest with flattery through the food port. In fifteen minutes the tub fills with about twelve gallons of water, or something under a quart a day for each of us.

Under such conditions, the young and strong can survive. Weaker individuals decline into sickness, and on occasion death—though the official policy is to minimize the number that actually expire in prison. As soon as an inmate is deemed terminal, the release process is begun, and families are notified to present themselves at the prison. It is not unusual, though, for the papers to arrive too late. Even the dying are not exempt from the regime's bureaucracy. Relatives who come to the prison expecting to welcome home a father or husband who disappeared into the gulag a year or two before often receive instead his body, released "through the clemency of the government and the party."

Such is the case of Do Duc Vu, who was my cellmate in cell C-seven and who was the first prisoner I actually saw die.

Vu was a man of sixty who had made his living as a trucker prior to his arrest (and that of his wife, son, and daughters) for "intending to leave the country." A family man and a hard worker, he seemed to have no political feelings at all. He had not cared much for the old regime, but they had let him carry on his life without bothering him, and he was grateful for that. He was perfectly willing to acquiesce to the new one on the same terms, and was in fact doing so when someone denounced him falsely, perhaps someone who wanted his truck.

From the moment he arrived it was clear to me that Vu would not survive. Unlike the former soldiers and partisans whose combative spirits had been honed by years of struggle, he was a gentle and passive man who was profoundly traumatized by what was happening to him. Plunged into the stinking, jammed cell, he seemed to be in a state of shock. He didn't stand in line for a turn at the food port, and he ate almost nothing. When I or others tried to engage him in conversation, he would quietly say, "I am going to die."

Already in a state of spiritual collapse, Vu's physical collapse advanced rapidly. Dehydrated, his skin became dry and cracked. After a week or so he developed a fever and drifted into a state of semi-consciousness. He was, as he had said, dying.

In vain the cell leader appealed to the *bo dois* for help, but their response was predictable: "What can we do about it? We don't have any drugs either."

"Then release him, instead of letting him die here."

"It's not up to you to decide who can be released."

"But at least you can tell the *can bos* that people in here are dying. It would be better if they just executed him instead of leaving him in agony like this."

"Listen, there are a lot of problems to deal with, not just yours."

That was the stock answer, the one that came almost automatically whenever there was an immediate problem that they didn't want to address. There were always "other problems."

Meanwhile lying next to me in the cell, Vu was near the end. Occasionally his eyes would open part way, showing white in the dull fluorescent glare that lit number seven at night. Now and then he would whisper faintly, "*Troi oi, Troi oi.*" Then, as several of us watched, he closed his eyes for the last time and just slipped away, making as little trouble in his passage to the next world as he had in this. Near the door, the prisoners began yelling: "*Bo doi, bo doi,* someone's died in here!" It was a cry that we heard almost daily echoing in the Zone C hallway, especially at night: "Hey, *bo doi,* there's someone dead here! Hey, *bo doi!*"

◊   ◊   ◊

Do Duc Vu's death gives a different focus to my own struggle to live. Up till now I had strengthened my will with the vow that I would record everything. On one level I knew my vow was really a strategy for mental health. But on another, it gave me a goal I could believe in. Most important, it worked. My interest in events and people remained sharp and active. I could sense my memory growing stronger and more capacious as each day I set myself to review at least a portion of what I had seen in the past.

And as I worked to compose in my mind the words I would someday write, new dimensions of the effort opened up to me. As time passed I started to think of myself as a historian, an oral historian at least, thrust by fate into the dead center of the crucible in which the essence of Vietnam's revolution was distilling itself. At the same time I found myself reflecting more deeply than ever on my own life, which since my birth had been entwined with the course of that revolution.

I saw that after the student movement collapsed and my brief hope for a political career died, I had allowed myself to be driven by circumstances: my marriage, children, my need for a job. But even as I accepted the dictates of fate, I had railed against them. I was a banker, yes, but a Front contact too. I had welcomed the revolution, yet I feared it as well. Before the overmastering complexity of events I had remained indecisive. "Wait," I had told myself. "Buy time, and eventually the situation will clarify itself, will reduce itself to terms that a human being can understand." Most of all, I had wanted the revolution to justify my indecisiveness—to reveal itself finally as complex and ambivalent, but in essence good and constructive. A revolution that would understand my hesitance and forgive it, that would welcome me into the task of rebuilding the nation.

That it had not done. But the revolution had offered me another gift, not the gift of vindication, but the gift of understanding. Through isolation, through life in C-seven, through Do Duc Vu's quiet dying, the revolution had laid for me a path into the simplicity of its innermost heart. It had allowed me not just to understand, but to take up residence at its very core, a shadowy cave where the flame of existence flickered, deprived of the sun, water, and air it needed to live.

◇   ◇   ◇

Vu's death marked a turning point for me. It made me realize that though the revolution had finally revealed what it truly was, I did not yet know why it was. The great question (I began to think of it as The Question) that now loomed up was: Why had the revolution, whose fighters had struggled so heroically to rid the nation of bloody oppression, become in its own turn drenched in blood and oppression?

The answer, I thought, could be found, if anywhere, among the Communists themselves, the *bo dois* and *can bos* who, having liberated the people, had now been set as wardens over the people they had liberated.

But I soon realized that these individuals did not hold the key to the secret. For the most part they were just ordinary human beings. Some were vicious, some not. And the more you studied their viciousness, the more it seemed that it was mostly due to indoctrination. Conditioned to regard their prisoners as wicked enemies, they simply believed any brutality was justified.

The intelligent ones, the ones who had resisted the conditioning, were more interesting. Although they knew we were innocent victims, they too found it impossible to treat us with sympathy. In order to protect themselves, they had to do what was expected of them, so that they too could survive. We were hostages, but they were hostages no less than we. And so, of course, were those above them. The system was a vast network of surveillance, which differed at each level only in the degree of scrutiny.

At the bottom level, air, water, and food were restricted, while informers and *bo dois* monitored every thought and action. Outside, the apparatus of control was still as tight as possible (given the number of people to be watched), with watchers set over groups of families, blocks, neighborhoods, and districts. Within the party itself, the monitoring was constant (though one former Communist described having party membership to me as a little like having political asylum; it provided a measure of safety unavailable to others).

At every level, fear was the motivator. It was fear that separated the *bo dois* and *can bos* from their essential humanity. And it was the same fear that during the war had given the revolution its internal steel. The revolution had never changed. To achieve its goals it had molded a machine of unearthly strength. And in the course of time it had simply become what it was doing.

18

Soup Day

In the aftermath of Vu's death, discussion in the cell takes a medical turn. Would some analgesic have brought down his fever and saved him? Or was he a goner anyway, because of his emotional state? If the *bo dois* had reported it, would a doctor have come? Or would no doctor have come in any case, because of course it was policy never to treat prisoners?

In the course of these discussions, I make an amazing discovery. One of the prisoners has heard that the doctor at Le Van Duyet is a young man named Nguyen Van Quang. I am pretty sure I know him. If he is the Quang I'm thinking of, he was one of Huynh Tan Mam's good friends at medical school during the student movement days.

The next day, as the water hose is being poked into the cell, I am the one at the food port flattering the water bearer. I ask about his party experiences, about how many men he had been in charge of, about the victories he had won—any subject at all that gives him a chance to preen. After fifteen minutes of this he is swelled up like a peacock. It hardly ruffles a feather when I ask if he wouldn't just tell Dr. Quang that his old friend Doan Van Toai is in C seven.

Two days later I am summoned by Lieutenant Ban, the supervisor in charge of Zone C. "Dr. Quang," he tells me in his formal way, "needs competent aides, and it seems you were a pharmacy student. It also seems that you have cooperated with the revolution in the past, and that your case is not too serious. In light of these facts, I have decided to trust you and give you an opportunity to make yourself useful. From eight to five tomorrow you will be at Dr. Quang's disposal. If he is pleased, the situation may continue. If you do your work well, that will be taken into account, and you will get your freedom back sooner."

This last is a ritual utterance that caps off any sort of appeal for cooperation. The more amenable you are, they tell you, the shorter your stay will be. It's a lie, but who cares when your heart is light because starting tomorrow you will be able to breathe the clean, fresh air for nine hours a day!

The next morning at eight I am led to the prison infirmary. It is indeed Nguyen Van Quang. We had not known each other well at the university, and now he does a superb job of pretending not to know me at all. In his most official tone, he describes my duties and answers my questions. Then he leaves.

The infirmary consists of an outer room and a small examination room off of it. At first, my whole duty is to keep the place clean and make sure everything is in proper order. It turns out that Quang and his associate, Dr. Tam, are not at Le Van Duyet all the time, but are part of the medical administration for Saigon's prisons. That is to say, they and a few others are responsible for the care of *can bos* and *bo dois* who serve on the prison staffs. There is no medical administration responsible for the prisoners. Nevertheless, a prisoner may in fact receive treatment. As rare as that is, it has been heard of. But any eccentricity of that kind is due solely to the humanitarian instincts of a particular doctor.

Dr. Quang is no humanitarian, though he impresses me as a

competent doctor. His colleague, Dr. Tam, is not even competent. Dr. Tam in fact is hardly a real doctor at all. She is a graduate of Hanoi University Medical School, where she apparently specialized in politics. Now she practices as the political head of the Ho Chi Minh City prison medical administration.

Dr. Tam is a true-blue Communist militant, though irreproachable in her own way. Her conception of the West features millions of starving strikers battling hordes of Fascist mercenaries. After I get to know her a bit, I dare to ask why the prisoners have no right to medical care. She answers matter-of-factly that she is responsible for officials. She does not know what might be done for prisoners since that is not her function.

Quang is less honest about it. When I tell him that there are prisoners in Le Van Duyet who at that very moment need emergency attention, without which they will die, he replies that these people must have been sick before their arrests and that they would have died anyway.

But though Quang and Tam are both cold fish, neither is utterly devoid of compassion. On several occasions when I describe some especially urgent case to Dr. Tam, she gives me medicine to administer: analgesics and once or twice vitamins (antibiotics are strictly reserved for officials). As for Quang, I once actually get him to make a call to Zone C.

It takes all the persistence I am capable of, and I wouldn't have done it at all except that the patient is the former monk Nguyen Huu Hieu. Though still a young man, this Hieu was something of a phenomenon in South Vietnamese literary and philosophical circles. While serving as a dean at Van Hanh Buddhist University, he had translated an amazing number of Western philosophers and authors, among them Nietzsche, Schopenhauer, Rimbaud, Baudelaire, and Henry Miller. All of his favorites, it goes without saying, were now found to be decadent, and so Hieu had disappeared into the maw along with most of the South's other leading literary figures.

The maw in his case was Le Van Duyet, Zone C. Now Hieu had developed a gigantic abscess on his right hip and was in

SOUP DAY ◊ 253

severe pain. As I would walk by his cell on my way to the infirmary, his cellmates would shout through the food port at me, "Tell the doctor! Tell the doctor!" In the end, I make such a pain in the ass of myself that Quang relents and grudgingly agrees to visit the cell. Out of the medical cabinet he picks an immense syringe, so big it looks like a stage prop. I can imagine a veterinarian using such a thing on a pig, but the idea that Quang might stick it into the monk makes me blanch.

I go first, to tell Hieu and his cellmates that the doctor is coming. By the time I arrive, I have gotten over the shock of the syringe and have begun to feel inordinately proud of myself. It is, after all, my doing that the doctor was coming. Who before in the history of Zone C had ever managed to get a doctor into the cells?

When Quang arrives we climb over the bodies to get to the monk, who looks serene and relaxed, despite the excitement this occasion has aroused in everyone else. Examining the abscess, Quang says, "That's not so terrible, I'll just draw out the blood and pus." Then he takes out the pig sticker and tells four of the prisoners to hold the monk, two on his arms, two on his legs. Up to this point Hieu has not noticed Quang's terrifying machine. Now he's nervous. When the four prisoners grab his extremities, his lidded gaze turns into a wild-eyed stare. He can't believe that Quang is really going to do it.

Neither can I. Not only is the syringe monstrous, but the abscess, as big and angry as it is, doesn't look ripe to me. I say as much to Quang, but he is intent on the patient and doesn't even respond. Then he just sticks it in, drawing a half-stifled cry from the monk and a spasmodic jerk that is controlled by the prisoners at his extremities. Slowly Quang pulls back the plunger and extracts . . . nothing. Like an idiot, I blurt out, "*Thày chưa!* [See!]"

Quang pretends not to notice, but now he is in danger of losing face in front of the assembled prisoners. Again he jabs the syringe home, at which the last shreds of Hieu's monkish serenity disappear, and he begins to scream.

As Quang draws out the syringe, blood begins to seep from

the abscess, and keeps seeping. Satisfied that the job is done, Quang grunts, gets up, and walks out. I run after him and return as fast as I can with cotton and alcohol.

A week later, I hear that the abscess has healed completely. It truly is, I think, one of Gautama Buddha's greatest miracles.

◊   ◊   ◊

At first there is not much to do in the tiny infirmary. Most often the work takes only a few minutes, and with Quang and Tam away most of the time, I simply sit and rest, thankful for the chance to take a sip of water whenever I want and to breathe. In time I begin to feel the strength coming back into my legs, which had felt partially asleep ever since my experience in isolation.

But once the doctors feel comfortable with me, they start giving me simple pharmaceutical tasks. It becomes my job to mix batches of iodine from powdered chemicals and water, and cough syrup from essence of menthol and sugar. Before long I am dispensing medicines to the *bo dois*: quinine for their malaria, coramine for their heart difficulties, and vitas carbol as a general stimulant.

By and large they are an unhealthy lot. The pallid, fatigued faces that greeted Saigon on April 30 were not simply the result of hard fighting and lack of sleep. A great many of the *bo dois* are suffering from malaria and chronic vitamin deficiencies. They are plagued by liver problems and by the inability to sleep well. Most of all they want vitamins. From our supplies of powdered thiamine and ascorbic acid, I measure out doses and mix them with farina. Then, since we have no pill-making machine, I fold the doses into little paper packets that can be handed out to the *bo dois*. At intervals we receive supplies of injectable vitamins, and I quickly recover my knack with a hypodermic syringe.

In the infirmary I also learn that the death rate is higher than I had thought. Even with the standing policy of releasing terminally ill prisoners to their families, almost every day one or two bodies are carted out of the sinister Zone C. Under the conditions in those cells, almost all the older prisoners who fall sick know they are condemned to death. The only thing they don't know is where they will die, and that depends on the glacial movement of the bureaucracy.

In time I feel at home enough in the infirmary to begin sneaking medicine out to the ill prisoners in number seven. Not much; a few aspirins here, a vitamin packet or two there, items I know will not be missed by Dr. Quang, whose inventory control is lackadaisical at best. For the most part the medicines serve a psychological rather than a therapeutic purpose. But I feel I can't risk stealing larger quantities; I simply find the prospect of another round in isolation unbearable.

But despite my caution, one day I am summoned into an angry Lieutenant Ban's office to hear the riot act read. One of cell seven's inmates had died the previous evening, and a search of his clothes had turned up an aspirin tablet. Where else could he have gotten it but from me? I have stolen drugs reserved for officials, I am deceitful, I have betrayed Lieutenant Ban's trust, I am a chronic malcontent working underhandedly against the revolution and the class struggle.

Ban threatens me with solitary, but in the end he does no more than terminate my job. Allowing me to continue my criminal activities in the infirmary is simply out of the question. So once more I have to accustom myself to living twenty-four hours a day in the putrid atmosphere of number seven. But my narrow escape from solitary gives me solace, as does the thought that the last few months have given me the opportunity to rest and rebuild my health. As I walk back to the cell with my escort, I know I will be needing all the resources I can muster.

Inside, as I squat down with some of my friends to tell them what has happened, a ritual is taking place at the cell door. One of the prisoners has buttonholed the *bo doi* and is doing his best to get a conversation going—the object being to keep the door open for as long as possible. The procedure never changes. First, one must ask the *bo doi* for permission to speak: *"Thua ong, can bo, toi muon* . . . [Excuse me, Mr. Official, I would like to ask . . .]." The tone of voice and vocabulary are those traditionally used by a young man who wishes to convey the expected deference to an older and more experienced man. Except that in jail the relationship is reversed. Here, graybeards speak this way to adolescent soldiers whose education consists only of a few memorized slogans and whose only experience is in handling an automatic Kalishnikov.

That's what is happening at the door now, as one of the cell elders goes through the usual routine with the sixteen-year-old *bo doi* who escorted me in: "Excuse me, Mr. Official. . . ." With a nod, the *bo doi* gives him permission to speak. Though I can't hear the words, I know exactly what's being said. The graybeard is asking about some topic, though what topic it might be makes not the slightest difference. If the cell gets lucky, the *bo doi* will be flattered by the attention he's receiving from someone who might be his grandfather, and will begin to hold forth. More often, such interchanges last only a minute or two. The answer to the question is unexpectedly simple, or the request cannot be granted, period, because it is against regulations or because "the revolution has other problems to deal with," or because the *bo doi* must consult with the *can bo*. In any case, it's a rare *bo doi* who wants to stand in the doorway enduring the aroma any longer than necessary.

This interview, like most, ends in fairly short order, the prisoner thanking the *bo doi* for his response. What under other circumstances would be a humiliating comedy, here has become an art form of sorts, sanctified by the general interest. Each *bo doi* has his weaknesses, just as the insane water bearer does, and there's a sharp competition among the cell's bullshitters to see who is cleverest at identifying and exploiting them.

These encounters at the cell door bring a momentary diversion to the prisoners, but unfortunately contribute nothing substantial to their health. Better food would make a difference, but the quality is going down, not up. Sometimes the food pail contains the usual red rice. But more and more often now we get a kind of cooked paste made of a flour-and-rice combination. "Black rice" has also made its appearance on the menu, the rice used by the Montagnard highlanders for animal feed.

As the standard fare deteriorates, our delight in the once-a-week "Le Van Duyet soup" intensifies. We remember its flavor from week to week, although to tell the truth, the soup is nothing but a thin stock in which a few green leaves can be found floating. Since the number of leaves is always far fewer than the number of prisoners, it has been agreed that these precious vegetable bits will be reserved solely for the sick and elderly.

What remains after the leaves are divided up and eaten would seem to a well-fed person not much better than tepid water. But the thought of it makes C-seven's residents salivate in anticipation. "Oh, the day after tomorrow, it's soup day!"; "Hey, tomorrow we're having soup!" On a perpetual rice-and-flour diet, the body lacks so much that it seizes almost with animal pleasure on the few vitamins and proteins diluted in this miserable broth. And when, as occasionally happens, there is no soup on soup day, the cell's morale sinks to zero. But before long the prisoners start hoping again: "Maybe next week we'll have it twice!" And that too has been known to happen.

Food, I am coming to see, is a drug. Cut it down sufficiently, and people often react like addicts in withdrawal. Even those with the best backgrounds and training can do irrational things for a handful of rice. In our cell a former minister of the Diem government and dean at Saigon University dishonored himself by trying to steal a spoonful of *nuoc mam* fish sauce from another prisoner. He was thoroughly beaten up for his trouble. Not too long afterward, the engineer Lam Truong Thi was caught taking someone else's share of rice. He too was beaten up, then thrown into isolation by the *bo dois* who came to investigate the commotion. There, during the night of July 14, 1976, he committed suicide out of shame, somehow managing to slash his wrists.

Both of these attempts were irrational. Nothing is watched more jealously than the rice, from pail to bowl to mouth. The "apportioner" might use a subtle trick or two to help a friend get a trifle more, but outright stealing is impossible. Only those who are being driven insane by their hunger would even try.

Starvation also leads to the death of Tran Tien Tai, a twenty-five-year-old student. Apparently, the last time we had soup, Tai's good friend, a mathematics professor named Linh, gave Tai his share, and now it is time for Linh to have two portions. But Tai turns a deaf ear to Linh's remonstrations and brings the bowl up toward his mouth. Seeing this, Linh tries to grab it, and in the scuffle Tai's lip is cut. Furious, he throws the bowl at Linh, and the two are at each other's throats.

In the few seconds before their neighbors can intervene, the damage is done. A guard passing the cell hears the brief uproar, and in a minute the door swings open and four *bo dois* are standing there pointing their guns at us. Linh and Tai are still enraged, and when one of the *bo dois* barks out, "Who started the fight?" they fall to accusing each other. Without trying to determine who is lying, the *bo dois* handcuff them both and lead them away.

The next morning a *bo doi* comes into the cell and orders us to get dressed; that means putting our green pajamas on over the underpants that are the only clothing most of us ordinarily wear. We are only told to do this prior to one of the rare visits from an official. A little later Lieutenant Ban makes his entrance, accompanied by two armed *bo dois*. In his high-pitched, officious voice he proclaims the verdict: "Prisoner Nguyen Van Linh, a reactionary criminal, and Tran Tien Tai, who attempted to leave the country illegally, have violated prison discipline. According to the regulations, the penalty imposed is two months' solitary confinement on one-half food rations. In addition, Tai will receive thirty blows with the cane."

Isolation I know can kill you. But the prospect of thirty blows with the cane makes us all cringe. For this punishment—a rare one—is administered by a specialist in torture by the name of Tu Cao.

This Tu Cao is a tall, lean, horse-faced individual of about fifty who the prisoners think has "the face of a killer." He is said to have been a torturer in the French jails twenty-five years ago. And some of the Le Van Duyet inmates have personally experienced his ministrations as prisoners under Diem and Thieu. Arrested shortly after the Communists entered Saigon, Tu Cao had soon resumed his profession . . . talents such as his do not lie fallow long. Anyone who survives his caning is at best half-alive. Tu Cao boasts of having caned more than two thousand prisoners in the course of his career, and of having killed one hundred of them.

Under the *bo dois'* close watch, cell seven's forty-five-plus prisoners line up in the oppressive stillness of the courtyard. Tran Tien Tai is brought out, stripped to his underpants. He is ordered to lie on the ground, face down.

With a vile smirk on his face, Tu Cao checks the flexibility of his instrument, a rattan cane about four feet long and a half inch in diameter. He bends over and feels Tai's shrunken hips and thighs, no doubt to gauge their resistance so he can administer his blows most effectively. Tai is not to be beaten to death.

As Tai feels the touch of Cao's fingers, his eyes widen in fear. He is lying with his right cheek on the ground, staring at us as if in mute appeal. I feel my heart turn to water, but it is forbidden to look away. This lesson is meant for us as much as it is for him.

After an eternity, the *can bo* snaps his wrist in a quick downward movement and says: "Begin!"

Tu Cao raises his arm and strikes, once . . . twice . . . three times. Between each blow he pauses for what must be a half a minute. The anguish in those thirty seconds is palpable. The whole world seems to hold its breath waiting for the next blow.

At the fifth, Tai can't hold it in anymore. As the rattan cracks down onto his upper thigh he screams, *"Troi oi! Chua oi!"*

The *can bo* stretches out his arm toward Tu Cao: "Stop!"

I feel my tensed-up muscles suddenly relax. Around me I am aware that my cellmates are breathing convulsive little sighs of gratitude. The *can bo* is going to be satisfied with five!

Then, in a dead cold voice, he says, "The regulations specify that the prisoner shall not cry out during physical punishment. The first five blows do not count. We'll start over."

I have the feeling my blood is congealing. Thirty-five of those blows, the whistling cane slashing down through the heat, the smack as it cuts into Tai's skin and bones. Tu Cao looks at him and says, "You heard that? No shouting!" Then he begins. "One!" Thirty seconds. "Two!" Thirty seconds. "Three!" Thirty seconds.

Tai has closed his eyes and clenched his jaw tight. Not a sound comes out of him. Every thirty seconds the blows slash down on his buttocks and thighs. I want to scream, "Faster! Faster! Get it over with!" But the animal knows his job. The *can bo* watches, his face impassive, his eyes flicking from one of us to another. Tai seems unconscious. He's probably fainted—so much the better for him.

"Twenty-nine!" "Thirty!"

"Get up!" orders the *can bo*. But Tai remains motionless. A little stream of blood is trickling down his lips into the sand.

The *can bo* raises his voice a pitch: "You refuse to obey?"

Suddenly Tu Cao is down on his knees holding Tai's wrist. Now it's the horse face that shows panic. "It's unbelievable," he stammers. "Unbelievable."

Still holding the limp wrist, he puts his ear next to Tai's nose and mouth. "I think . . . I think he's dead, sir." He seems frozen with fright. He was not supposed to kill this prisoner.

I feel the relief of exhaustion. At least Tai's ordeal is over. After that beating I feel sure he wouldn't have survived more than a day or two in the isolation cell.

Tu Cao has now turned the body over in the dust. He pries Tai's mouth open and stares into it. "Sir," he exclaims to the *can bo*. "He committed suicide! He bit his tongue and swallowed it. That's why his mouth is bloody!"

The *can bo* walks over and squats down while Tu Cao keeps the mouth open. Then he stands up facing us. "Prisoner Tai died voluntarily," he says. "It was not the revolution that killed him. The revolution does not wish to kill, but to reeducate.

We do not torture prisoners as the puppets did. If we must punish them, it is like a father punishing a son, to educate him. We do this publicly, as you can see. If Tran Tien Tai is dead, it's because he decided to kill himself, as you all witnessed."

But the *can bo* feels very uncomfortable about this. Shortly after we return to number seven, a *bo doi* brings in a prepared statement for the cell leader to sign. "I, Nguyen Hau Nghi, representative of cell seven, am witness to the fact that prisoner Tran Tien Tai committed suicide by swallowing his tongue."

19

Perhaps It's Not Too Late

After Tran Tien Tai's death the atmosphere in the cell grows sullen and depressed. People talk quietly, about more personal things, as if the incident has forced them into the kind of pessimistic introspection that it is an object of their daily existence to avoid.

As time passes, though, the gregariousness that is the southerners' natural defense against life's bleakness reasserts itself. The rounds of raucous gossip and storytelling assume their normal place in the prisoners' endless battle against ennui and madness. The "oral newspaper" takes up where it left off.

In the period after liberation, the prison system is choked with the cream of South Vietnam's intelligentsia. All the "decadent" writers, artists, and scholars who showed signs of persisting in their independent ways have been swept up. As a result, cell seven (and all the other cells) has a strong ratio of inmates versed in every variety of knowledge and experience— and all of them love to talk.

This talk is our sustenance: food for our starving minds and water for our arid souls. Despite my own background as a university student and political journalist, never before have I encountered such a concentration of talented talkers. Something about life in prison has sharpened their perceptions and enabled their tongues. In the cells, newspapermen who on the outside might have been journeymen writers take fire as contemporary historians. Professors whose lectures before might have put hundreds of students to sleep at a time find in their cellmates a fascinated and avid audience, and it energizes them.

People talk about what they know, and the subjects range from archeology to jazz. But despite the variety, there is no doubt which topics draw the widest attention and give the greatest pleasure. Most of all, the inmates love to talk about politics and sex. Judging from their popularity in cell seven, an outsider might have concluded that politics was the national pastime and sex the national preoccupation.

The stories are, literally, endless. People describe in loving detail the nightclubs they have been to and tell ribald tales about their adventures and exploits. Those who had traveled talk authoritatively about the exotic sexual habits they have encountered in Japan or the United States. Often these stories are stretched out from one episode to the next, like a serialized novel. "Tune in tomorrow," the storyteller says, "for the next installment." The more artistic and inventive the embellishment, the louder the audience's appreciation. Often we hear the same teller adorn the same story with new characters and additional action. "Hey," someone will shout out, "I heard that one differently last time!" To which the teller answers, "Last time? Listen my friend, this is the fourth edition, and each revision gets better."

And it is not just the made-up characters that keep the inmates' attention. Cell seven also has its real characters, those who live their own strange and fanciful lives right in our midst.

One of these is the "King of Champa," an ethnic Cham from the Phan Rang region with the dark skin and small black eyes of his people. His name is Chau May (a Cham name), and he is in his mid-fifties. Tall, thin and angular, his frail physique belies a strong voice and a commanding tone. But though his voice demands attention, the fact that he hasn't a single tooth in his head undermines the sense of authority he tries so hard to project.

At the time of liberation Chau May knew, as did everybody else, that one of the Front's well-publicized objectives has been to create semiautonomous national minority zones. Ibih Aleo, a racial Montagnard, is even vice-chairman of the NLF Central Committee. To Chau May it seems obvious that one of these zones will of course be for the Cham. Since he himself is of Cham royalty (a claim that may be true for all anyone can tell; the last recorded Cham king died in 1390), who better to set up and administer the autonomous zone than Chau May?

Accordingly, right after the revolutionary victory, Chau May presented himself at the Provisional Revolutionary Government's Interior Ministry to claim his people's inheritance. He demanded of the no doubt startled Front officials that they honor their pledge of autonomy (Point seven, Article one of the *NLF Manifesto*—he knew it well) and hand over power. Chau May would never describe exactly what happened at the Interior Ministry, but the result was clear enough.

But just because the Front did not honor its word (what else is new?), that does not mean Chau May is going to forgo his just claims. He insists that people call him "king" and complains bitterly that he isn't being shown sufficient respect. He is especially sensitive about other people's touching him (apparently the Champa royalty, like the British, claim the prerogative of bodily inviolability), which is unfortunate, given the sardine-can intimacy the prisoners share. It is at night that he really gets annoyed about this, since when one person shifts position in his sleep, everybody around him shifts as well. But even asleep, we have gotten used to his angry growls of "Don't touch me, I'm the king!"

While he demands that everyone else address him as "king," he himself addresses everyone else as inferiors. The *bo dois,* whom we are all supposed to call "Mr. Official," he calls instead *thang* (guy). "Hey you, guy, come over here." The first few times this happened they hauled him off to isolation for breach of revolutionary discipline. But afterward they left him alone.

He seems to like it when some of the youngsters in the cell mockingly salute him with his royal titles, and he promises more than one of them a Cham beauty in marriage. He claims too that his royal blood gives him magical powers, and threatens to put a spell on those who anger him. He did, he tells us, put a spell on Nguyen Van Thieu, also a Phan Rang native, and look what had happened to him. Whenever word gets around that someone has died in the zone, Chau May attributes it to one of his spells. There are even a few in the cell who believe him.

Eventually they let Chau May go. One day Lieutenant Ban comes into the cell and reads off the proclamation releasing him and ordering him back to Phan Rang, out of which province he is not in the future to set foot. It is the only time anybody has ever heard of a release being publicly announced. It makes some of the inmates wonder how Chau May has managed it.

A character who elicits a good deal more belief than Chau May—though to my mind he is every bit as loony—is Prime Minister Phuong, formerly known as "Kerosene" Phuong. This Phuong was a wealthy businessman who earned considerable notoriety in the Diem period over some sort of giant kerosene import scandal, from which he derived his nickname. He spent some time in jail then, and now he is in jail again, though this time his crime is political, not economic.

The story of his most recent arrest illustrates as well as anything I had ever heard the credulity of many Vietnamese, and the ability of the revolutionaries to exploit it.

Toward the very end of the war, Phuong received a letter from an American friend of his, an army major, promising to assist him in any way he could. Most likely, the major was offering to help get Phuong out of the country before the Communists arrived. But in the end Phuong decided not to leave. Instead he used the major's promise of assistance (American support) to gather around him a group of nonpolitical businessmen who called themselves "The Three Force Coalition Government."*

Phuong's idea was that with the war over the Communists would now establish the tripartite coalition that had been stipulated in the Paris peace agreement. They had, after all, agreed to that, as witnessed by many nations. More important, the United States had promised at Paris to "contribute to healing the wounds of war and to postwar reconstruction," and informed people were saying that the promised "contribution" would be in the neighborhood of three billion dollars.

Phuong's businessman's mind told him that the Communists would do anything to get hold of that three billion, and certainly the United States was not about to hand the money over to a Communist government that had been established through the wholesale violation of the agreement. On the other hand, the Communists would obviously not deal with anyone associated with the old Saigon regime, as they had demonstrated so clearly when they sent the last president, "Big" Minh, packing.

The solution to this conundrum, the solution that met everyone's criteria, was to set up a true coalition government that was completely independent of the defeated southern puppets, the kind of government, for example, that Phuong himself— with his promise of American support—might head.

With his plans laid out, at the beginning of May 1975 Phuong went down to the Saigon central post office. There he sent off a carefully composed telegram to Pham Van Dong, prime minister of the Democratic Republic of Vietnam (the North). The message invited Dong to come to Saigon for talks between the North and the Three Force Coalition Government, according to the guidelines established by the Paris agreement.

---

* Phuong's ruse wasn't at all crazy. In 1945, Ho Chi Minh had used a personally autographed picture of U.S. General Claire Chennault as proof of American backing for his leadership.

What Prime Minister Dong said upon receiving this invitation from his southern "counterpart" has unfortunately not been recorded. But he did not do what he might have been expected to do, namely have the Saigon security forces grab Phuong posthaste and make him disappear. Instead, Phuong received a formal reply—not, admittedly, from Pham Van Dong himself (Phuong regretted that), but from Colonel General Tran Van Tra, former commander of Vietcong main forces and currently chairman of the Military Management Committee, the de facto, pro tem government of South Vietnam. In his most proper protocolese, Colonel General Tra invited Phuong to meet with him for an "exchange of views."

And that was how, in early June, Phuong and Tra came to sit down together in the offices of the Military Management Committee. The wonder was that at the conclusion of this meeting, Tra did not have Phuong hauled off kicking and screaming. On the contrary, the general was cordial and polite. He discussed various matters that Phuong put on the table, and indicated by word and manner that he respected the businessman's positions.

If Phuong had managed to convert a letter from some unknown American major into political capital, his "exchange of messages" with Pham Van Dong and his "review of the situation" with Tran Van Tra were dynamite. After all, the only reasonable explanation for these things (and the only possible reason Phuong wasn't immured in a dungeon) was that he did indeed have some real leverage, as unapparent as that might be to the casual observer. It was even conceivable that the Ford administration and the politburo, unable to discuss matters directly in the immediate aftermath of the Great Spring Victory, had chosen him as a private go-between.

Subsequent to the Tra meeting, this opinion began to carry the day with quite a number of Saigonese personalities who had themselves not given up hope of dealing with the revolutionaries. These people, including the president of the Da Nang Bar, Mr. Vu Dang Dung, gathered around Phuong, cheered by the thought of participating in whatever negotiations might be in the works.

It was only after a sufficient number of them had volunteered their services that the guillotine fell and the Three
Force Coalition Government and all its cohorts were swept
away to the four corners. The corner reserved for the Three
Force prime minister was Le Van Duyet's Zone C, cell seven.

The strange thing was that Phuong's sudden fall from power
did not necessarily affect his ability to persuade. If you looked
at it in the right way, it did sound reasonable that the North
would want to establish a coalition that could deal with the
Americans. After all, now that they had won, they had everything to gain and nothing to lose by making friends with the
imperialists. And it was certainly plausible that the Americans,
tender from their recent humiliation, would not want to meet
formally with the northern treaty breakers, but nevertheless
might see some diplomatic advantages for themselves in beginning to forge a relationship with the new Vietnam.

Besides, the fact was that you could (and did) meet anyone
in prison. If former ministers, full professors, famous artists,
and legendary heroes were not exactly a dime a dozen, neither
were they at all rare. And there was no question that Phuong
believed thoroughly in himself. As far as he was concerned, he
was the coalition prime minister. He'd yell at the *bo dois* that
he had negotiated with their boss, General Tra, and that just
because he was temporarily incarcerated didn't mean he was
going to take this kind of treatment. They could be sure that as
soon as he got out he'd report it personally to Tra. With some
of the prisoners he discussed appointments in his government,
and he went on at length about American aid and about the
famous three billion the Communists would never get except
through the coalition.

On the other hand, there were plenty of reasons for believing Phuong was suffering from schizophrenic delusions. Why
in the world would the Americans have chosen "Kerosene"
Phuong to make their overtures for them? And if they had,
why was he in jail? And why did he keep talking about the
ARVN division (that no one else had ever heard of) that was
still intact near the Cambodian border and had vowed to support him?

All in all, the case seemed unclear. Maybe he was both crazy and being used as an emissary. So many people in the cell believed at least part way in Phuong that sometimes I thought maybe I was the crazy one. That uncomfortable feeling did not diminish when Phuong appointed a former ARVN major in the cell to be the province chief of Chuong Thien. The major, one of Phuong's believers, got permission to write his wife, telling her not to worry because he would soon take on his new position. The letter, of course, went right to the *can bos*—who had the major thrown into isolation . . . for having accepted the appointment.

◊   ◊   ◊

One morning in July of 1976, a *bo doi* comes into the cell and calls my name.

"Doan Van Toai?"

"I am Toai."

"Prisoner Toai, get dressed for work!"

"Work!" They are going to resume my interrogation. Some of my friends look at me anxiously. One or two others mumble, "Released! You're going to be released!" Released or condemned, I think, anything's better than rotting in here. "Toai," someone whispers, "not so fast, take it slower." Lost in thought about what this new interrogation might mean, I'm putting the pajamas on over my underpants too quickly. Whenever people are called to go out, they get dressed as slowly as possible, so that the door can stay open a few moments longer. I begin fumbling at my shirt buttons.

The *can bo* sitting behind the metal desk is about fifty years old. Sitting off to the side is a younger man, probably an inquisitor in training. As I come in the *can bo* smiles and greets me: "Brother," he calls me. "Brother Toai, how is your health? Are you being well treated? Do you have any complaints? Would you . . . like to see your family again?"

I can't remember the last time an official called me "brother." I'm not used to such politeness. Of course it could be pure hypocrisy . . . most likely there's a trap here someplace. "Do I have any complaints?" I'm not that crazy. But on the other hand, not complaining is just as clumsy, like announcing to them outright that you're a liar. And what does he mean about my family?

I weigh my words carefully: "Mr. Official, when you're a prisoner of course it's impossible to say that everything is perfect. Of course I miss my family very much. Above all I would like to know why I was arrested. Let me know what my mistakes are so that I can think about them and correct them."

Without answering directly, or saying anything more about my family, the *can bo* tells me that there are some points that are still unclear. He would especially like to know about my contacts with the Front and about my trips abroad. With that, he gives me a pencil and several sheets of paper, and tells the *bo doi* to take me into the next room.

I'm not surprised about having to resume the story that was left in midsentence in Tran Hung Dao. These people are truly obsessed with autobiographies; they feed on them. From all the recent prisoners, we hear that every single adult individual has got to write his autobiography at least several times: for the neighborhood administration, for the place of employment, the women's movement, the union . . . each organization to which one belongs wants its own. Needless to say, all these autobiographies end up in the hands of the police, whose thousands of administrative workers scrutinize them, collate them, and compare them with the autobiographies of friends, relatives, and coworkers.

Naturally, those who played a role in the official life of the former regime get special attention, as do prisoners. Prisoners in particular. The *can bos* seem to delight in finding pretexts to make prisoners rewrite their stories. And woe be to him whose autobiographies contradict each other in some way, or who "forgets" an event that the police discover in someone else's report.

With these thoughts in mind I go about writing down my contacts with the Front and my trips to France and the United States. Though couched in the most progressive language I can generate, every word is the truth. It had better be, otherwise I'm likely to find myself caught lying somewhere down the road. By lunchtime I'm finished, and the same *bo doi* takes me back to the cell.

"Toai, you're back! How did it go?" Every time someone returns from interrogation, everyone else wants to know how it went. What they really want to hear is that you're going to be released. After all, if they release you, that's a sure sign they'll be releasing others, maybe them. Hope springs eternal, even though aside from the terminal cases and the King of Champa, none of us can remember more than a couple of individuals who have actually been freed.

That night I can't get to sleep. In my mind I go over and over the descriptions I wrote. Every detail is a potential booby trap. Are there any facts they can use against me? Do they know something from somewhere else that I've omitted to describe?

My sleeping neighbors for some time have been Dang Giao, the journalist, and old Dong, a Vung Tau fisherman who was accused of wanting to leave the country. (Like Vung, the trucker who died, he had never thought about leaving. Also like Vung, he owned a valuable piece of property: his boat.) Dong realizes that I'm awake and whispers, "Toai, it's no use thinking about these things. Try to empty your mind. Worrying only weakens your resistance."

"Yes," I whisper back, "but they asked if I want to see my family. I know my mother and my wife—they must be dead with worry. I'm sure my children wouldn't even recognize me."

Giao, the journalist, isn't sleeping either, and now he joins the conversation: "Listen, Toai, I've thought of a fantastic scenario for a movie I'll make when I get out of here. How does this sound? A man spends ten years in a labor camp in the jungle, and then he's released. By this time, he's got long white hair and limps along on a cane. Meanwhile, his wife has married a *bo doi*. One day she sees this old man hesitating in front of her house, and she says to her new husband: 'Look, there's a beggar.' So she sends her oldest son out to give the beggar a bowl of rice, and of course it's his own father. What do you think of that?"

I told Giao I didn't find it soothing.

The next morning I'm summoned back. It seems that the various trips I took at the end of 1970 have caught the *can bo*'s attention.

"Brother Toai, I've heard that you went to Hong Kong and Manila to participate in a meeting of anti-Communist students?"

Without stopping to think where this might be leading, I find myself responding angrily: "Anti-Communists? I was the foreign relations representative from the student union! The conferences were for the Asian Students Association and the International Student Movement, associated with UNESCO. In Hong Kong I personally proposed that delegations from North Vietnam and China be invited. I was cheered for that proposal. I've never had anything to do with anti-Communist students." I tell him how I was mistaken for Ngo Vuong Toai when I was arrested. "But I thought that was all clear to everybody."

The *can bo* seems attentive, if not convinced. "UNESCO, he says, "that's a capitalist creation. And the Asian countries in this ASA, they're capitalist countries controlled by the CIA. But what interests me more is your American trip." He looks at his notes. "You say you spoke at the universities of Berkeley, Redlands, and Stanford, and that you attacked American imperialism and the puppet regime? At American universities?"

"Exactly," I reply. "The students and professors there didn't even think I went far enough."

This is a bit much for the *can bo*. No doubt he had read in the party's newspapers that "each day the brave American people rise up in ever greater anger against the evil war of their imperialist government." But he also knew how to interpret these papers, and perhaps he was skeptical about the reports of American sentiments. The whole idea of a Vietnamese student denouncing America inside the United States without at least encountering problems with the police must have boggled his imagination. How could it possibly be true? He knows what would have happened in North Vietnam, and his mental universe does not extend beyond seeing his enemies as anything but a reverse image of himself.

"Who can verify your tales?" he asks. "Maybe you'd like us to call the CIA as a witness?"

This is so discouraging. If I have to prove that I was an adversary of the Saigon government while I was abroad, as well as while I was home, I'll be here forever. So I tell him that revolutionary cadres like Huynh Tan Mam and Duong Van Day knew all about my speeches overseas. "If you can show me the slightest proof that I engaged in any anti-Communist activities, I agree to be imprisoned for life!" I can't say any more. I've exhausted all my arguments.

But does he really think that I've been connected with the other side? He knows that like all the student leaders I was approached from time to time by Thieu's cops, but he also knows that I always rebuffed them. He knows too all about my pro-Front activity. I can understand his puzzlement about what happened in the United States. To him my description of the American campuses must have sounded fantastical—and there is no way of conveying my memories of the long-haired students and their Ho Chi Minh pins. But if he doesn't completely believe me, he doesn't have any other information either. I conclude that he must just be fishing.

As if to confirm my conclusion, the *can bo* finishes up his questioning with a little sermon that tells me clearly what I've suspected for a long time about why I'm in jail. "Patriotic action," he says, "must always be controlled by the party. Otherwise it is inefficient and worthless." According to the *can bo*, I have always acted like an individualist, without submitting to collective discipline. Don't I know that there is no such thing as solitary patriotism? Real patriots must assemble under the party's leadership and be guided by the correct policy. The party had contacted me during the war, but I was unwilling to accept its authority. If I had understood the objective conditions of the struggle against imperialism, I would have agreed to submit to the party's direction then. Again, after liberation, I was invited to cooperate with the revolution, and again I had hesitated. Why was that? Because I did not believe in the party's policy? That would be incomprehensible, since without the party the Americans and their puppets would still be here!

As this exposition goes on, the *can bo*'s voice has been rising. Then, abruptly, he stops and puts his hands on the table, as if waiting for my approval. But what can I say? He starts leafing through the file in front of him: "Besides," he smiles at me, "we know you are aware that we are right about you! Look at this, for example." He pulls out a sheet of paper. "Something you wrote yourself, an article called 'Reform or Revolution in Education.' " And then he reads back to me my own words, words I had written over six years ago in *Tu Quyet*. " 'With the puppet leaders, a revolution in education is not possible. Those leaders must be struck down, for they are serving foreign interests. They must be replaced by true revolutionary leaders.' "

I'm getting a sick feeling in the pit of my stomach while he's reading this. It's unbelievable how my articles have come back to haunt me. It seems as if every time I turn around some angry official is quoting my own words to my face. "You also wrote," says the *can bo*, rummaging through the papers and waving another one around, "you also wrote, 'One must struggle first of all against American aggression, because it is foreign. The revolution is of our own people, and with them we can talk.' Unfortunately"—his smile has turned into a smirk— "you added: 'If experience shows that the Communists are worse than the present leaders, we will go back into opposition.'

"So now," he looks straight at me, "tell me, are the Communists worse than the American puppets?"

Just try answering that one. You can't say they're worse, but how can you say they're better, after you've been dying slowly in prison for the last fifteen months. "Mr. Official, I can't say anything about it. I was arrested a month and a half after liberation and I've been in jail ever since." A little too smart-alecky, but at least not a blatant lie.

Not very satisfied with the answer, the *can bo* dismisses me with words that are half one thing, half another: "If you had recognized the necessity of being united with the party, you would not be here. The party's watchword is 'Dictatorship for our enemies, tolerance for our friends.' You, Brother Toai, are not an enemy, but neither are you a friend. And under the present conditions, those who are not our friends cannot be trusted. It is unfortunate you did not understand that earlier. . . . But perhaps it is not too late."

20

Going to
"the Country"

The *can bo*'s words preyed on my mind: "Perhaps it is not too
late." Am I by some chance reeducatable? If I am, what do I
have to do? How can I prove I've reformed?—if that's what
they want. It's remarkable, this system I'm caught in. Not a
single person I've met in fifteen months of prison has either
had a trial or been given a sentence. We are here at their pleasure, for as long as they want to keep us. The result is that you
find yourself looking for signs, omens of release. A word here,
an unexpected politeness there, might mean that your case "is
not too serious." You would like to ingratiate yourself with
them, if only you knew how. The whole thing is repulsive. Everyone feels it, this slithering instinct that sneaks up on you
and makes your mind search the horizon for signs of imminent
absolution. Worse, that makes you poke around for something
you might do to hasten that blessed event.

There's no real defense against this instinct of the mind's to
turn traitor, despite the fact that reason tells you they won't let

276

you out a moment sooner no matter what you do. Huynh Cu, my old cell leader back in Zone A, used to drum that lesson into our heads: No matter how you comport yourself, you will be here for just as long as you are needed. And that, my friend, depends upon the politburo gods on their thrones, not upon whatever sniveling little accommodations you find it possible to make with your keepers.

Yet how do you calm your racing mind when they ask you if you'd like to see your family, and when they tell you your case is not, perhaps, hopeless?

Not too long after my visit with the *can bo*, the signs and omens start to multiply. Real signs and omens, not just a fever induced by some ambiguous remark. A new supervisor has taken over Zone C, a southerner by the name of Sau Cau. Sau Cau was in the Front as well as the party. He was also a guest in Thieu's jails for seven years before his exchange following the Paris agreement.* "I have been in prison," he tells us. "I understand how it is." And he orders the cell doors to remain open all day long. Of course it's strictly forbidden to step outside, but at least the air is better. And the open door—isn't that somehow a sign of things to come?

Moreover, Sau Cau has a list drawn up of all the prisoners (the huge majority) who have not yet been interrogated since their arrest. "The government," he says, "has not had time to examine each of your cases. But that will be done before the end of the year."

The sense of Sau Cau's remarks seems to be that the government now intends to bring order and "legality" to the mass confusion of arrest and imprisonment that followed liberation. In fact, we know that since April a police powers ordinance has been in effect (the "3/76 Law") that defines jailable offenses and requires formal charges to be filed. Although the police still have full power over what may be done with prisoners, at least things are regularized to a degree. No one is particularly impressed by this law, but it does give a certain background

---

* The Paris accords called for a mutual release of prisoners.

credibility to Sau Cau's declaration that our cases will be heard.

The reason no one in cell seven is impressed by the "3/76 Law" is that Dang Giao, the journalist who sleeps next to me, was one of the first to be arrested under its provisions. Giao had been editor of the Saigon daily *Song Than* (*The Tidal Wave*), a newspaper so critical of the Thieu regime that it had been closed down for good in 1974. Even though he was no friend of the Communists either, Giao had refused to leave the country in April 1975, saying that he'd "rather die in Vietnam than live anywhere else."

He has told his story in great detail both to me personally and in the group discussions. "I was one of the law's first beneficiaries," he says. "Up till me they did things arbitrarily without a warrant. Now they do them arbitrarily with a warrant."

Giao was arrested, along with his wife and fifteen-day-old baby, one night at the end of April by a *can bo* and a troop of *bo dois* who pulled up in front of his house in an old American army bus. The *can bo* planted himself in front of Giao and read off a formal declaration of arrest (something no one else in the cell had ever heard of before): "Given the security requirements of the nation, upon the people's denunciation, the central security office of Ho Chi Minh City hereby orders: 1) The search of the house of Tran Duy Cat (pen name: Dang Giao) and the confiscation of all property belonging to Tran Duy Cat and his wife Chu Vi Thuy, daughter of the notorious reactionary Chu Tu; 2) the arrests of these two persons for their many activities against the people as journalists on the cultural front; 3) the sentencing of these two persons under the law of 3/76."

Then the *can bo* put the warrant on the table and turned the house over to the troop of youngsters he had brought along. These separated themselves into groups and began searching the house. They climbed on the furniture and knocked out parts of the ceiling where it looked as though it might have been patched. They pulled out the wood paneling in the sitting room and slashed open the sofa and chair cushions. They ransacked the family pictures and mementos, which made Giao's wife wince and close her eyes.

From time to time the *bo dois* would bring the *can bo* suspicious items to inspect, including the family album, back issues of newspapers, and love letters Giao had written to his wife before they were married. One of these suspicious items was a notebook that immediately caught the *can bo*'s attention. Inside he read entries marked "1 A.M.," "4:30 A.M." and so on. One of them said: "The night is already advanced. It is cold and windy outside. The planes are coming back to the base one after the other. Their noise keeps me awake. Oh, how I miss you and wish you were here." A later entry that night stated: "Fell into a deep sleep, but suddenly awoke when the telephone rang. A flash of happiness, but it was not you, just someone dialing the wrong number."

Holding the notebook up to Giao's face, the *can bo* asked, "What's this?"

"What do you mean?" answered Giao, "You've read it. It's my wife's diary from ten years ago, before we were married. That's her private life."

At first Giao thought that the *can bo* was asking just for the sake of asking, but he was wrong. In fact the security officer was sure he had come across a coded book of signals. Why else would the actual times be noted, like 1 A.M. or 4:30 A.M.? Why would the times be associated with reports of incoming plane flights or telephone calls? Here was at least part of the proof of Giao's conspiratorial activities they had been looking for.

By now Giao understood completely his own situation and what lay in store for him. But he found that he was having a hard time controlling himself in front of this incredibly obtuse *can bo* who was destroying his home. Nevertheless, he managed to calm himself enough to try to make a deal. "Have it your own way," he told the *can bo*. "You can charge me with anything. I only ask you to leave the baby and his mother at home for a while. You have me. They're not going anywhere. You can arrest them later on."

But the *can bo* was immovable. Northern women had given

birth and then gone out to shoot at American planes before fifteen days had passed. Besides, the state would take good care of wife and baby. The only thing Giao had to concern himself with was following orders and reforming his thought. Then the *can bo* paused for a moment and asked, "What's the baby's name?" Infuriated, Dang Giao blurted out, "*Giai Phong* [Liberation]!" The *can bo* couldn't believe his ears. "What?"

Dang Giao repeated it, but his wife stepped in quickly. "He's only a few days old, we haven't had time to name him."

At this, the *can bo* sat down with the arrest warrant and began to write. While he was busy, one of the young *bo dois* came up to Giao's wife carrying three thick volumes in his arms. "What kind of books are these?" he asked.

"Dictionaries."

"I asked you what kind of books."

"And I said, dictionaries."

Another *bo doi* standing nearby came to his friend's assistance: "What he means is, what does it say in them?"

Giao's wife laughed. "Oh, they're books that give you the meaning of French words in Vietnamese, or that translate French words into English."

"Really?" said the *bo doi*. He had made a discovery and seemed fascinated by it. "Really?"

By now the *can bo* had finished writing. Standing up, he barked out a command: "Silence!" Then he read the amended warrant: "Given the security requirements of the nation, upon the people's denunciation, the central security office of Ho Chi Minh City hereby orders . . . the arrests of Tran Duy Cat (pen name: Dang Giao), his wife, Chu Vi Thuy, daughter of the notorious reactionary Chu Tu, and the unnamed child of the aforesaid Tran Duy Cat and Chu Vi Thuy."

The need for a legal arrest warrant for the baby was thus taken care of. "And that's how," Dang Giao tells us, "my two-week-old son had the honor of being the youngest prisoner in Tran Hung Dao, where he came on April 26, 1976, in the arms of his mother. Neither of them were handcuffed. But I was handcuffed. We left behind our six- and eight-year-olds, whom

I told to call their grandmother to come and get them. So much for the 3/76 Law," he says.

◊   ◊   ◊

But regardless of Giao's experience, hopes are once again rising. Almost everyone thinks in the back of his mind that if procedures are regularized, we will soon be on our way out of here. And it's true that more interrogations are taking place. It's also true that this Sau Cau is a marvel of humaneness compared to his predecessor.

Not only is Sau Cau personally more humane, but a certain excitement seems to be gripping the prison, an excitement triggered by the Fourth Communist Party Congress that will be coming up toward the end of 1976.

Periodically, the approach of a historic date raises a great stir throughout the country. It might be the anniversary of the Democratic Republic, or Uncle Ho's birthday, or an especially important meeting of the party. After my release, I was amazed by the nature of these celebrations. In the weeks preceding, it seems as if everyone has received an electric shock. Factories, offices, communes, and villages take sacred vows to "reach and surpass production goals." Individuals and work units compete to see who can "contribute" the most overtime, work through the most days off, beat the most production records. Party fanatics work themselves into a frenzy on such occasions, and who can afford to seem laggard?

Finally the glorious day itself arrives amid a starburst of triumphant communiqués and victorious slogans. Work Heroes and Production Heroes are praised; 105 percent of the norm has been met, or 125 percent, or 150 percent! And afterward . . . afterward everything is precisely as it was before. If some benefit has been realized, the Work Heroes don't see it, nor do the Norm-Surpassing Production units. Life returns to normal, normal work days, normal Sundays off, the normal struggle survive . . . until three months later a new and even more glorious campaign is launched.

Nor are the prisons exempt. Though largely unaware of the

consequences these celebratory campaigns have on life outside, we know they affect the guards with unusual zeal and sometimes bring a surprise to us as well. And the Fourth Party Congress is going to be a leviathan of a celebration. Le Van Duyet Prison was caught up in a wave of "agitprop." We hear long harangues on national reconciliation, and we are asked to follow the regulations more closely and to cooperate better with the comrade guards and investigators for the sake of our reeducation. We are even urged to put in writing our suggestions, our proposals, our wishes. So I do. I write a letter to the prison administration asking first to be brought to trial; second, to be allowed to see my family.

Two days later I am summoned to Sau Cau's office, one of a steady stream of prisoners who are being called in to be interrogated or advised about the status of their cases. In his office, Sau Cau tells me that he has read over my dossier. There are still details to be clarified, but he feels strongly that I will be liberated one day, in accord with the party's policy of reconciliation.

Other cell seven residents recently have been given the same kind of "near promises." It's all too much. Even the stoniest cynics wonder if something isn't really going to happen.

"Did you hear? Half of all prisoners will be released this year," says one.

"Half?" says another. "Much more than half! The *can bo* told me that only the ones who committed war crimes will be kept in jail. Others might have to spend some time in a work camp, but most will just be released." Talk in the cell turns to enthusiastic planning for the future. Men who yesterday believed in nothing now believe in everything. People compete to find in Sau Cau's words reasons for justifying the most improbable optimism. And many who used to complain bitterly about injustice now seem to have forgotten all their grievances.

One day Sau Cau himself comes into the cell to see me. Giving me a pencil and paper, he says, "Write your family's address down, and draw a sketch of the streets so we can find it easily." I do, and Sau Cau leaves without any further explanation.

What does it mean? Maybe they are really going to allow them to come. Or maybe it means nothing at all. In the Fourth Party Congress craziness that's come over the prison, a lot of strange things are going on. *Bo dois* and *can bos* are constantly bustling around. Sometimes one of them will come into the cell with a list and ask, "Is Prisoner So-and-so here?"

"Yes," answers So-and-so.

"Good," says the *can bo*, who then turns on his heel and leaves. For days So-and-so will wonder what to make of the visit, since there hasn't been either any explanation or any follow-up.

My case, however, is different. I am about to get a huge surprise. Summoned one day to Sau Cau's office for what I believe is more interrogation, I walk in to find my wife and children standing on the far side of the room. Yvonne's cheeks are covered with tears. She is holding our youngest in her arms, while the other two cling to her legs and look with frightened eyes at this speechless bag of bones whom they have been told is their father, and who is now crying just as hard as their mother is.

Sitting at his desk, Sau Cau gives us permission to talk. Choking back her tears, Yvonne starts speaking quickly, telling me the news. "Your father and mother are in fairly good health, but your mother has been quite worried. My parents have gone 'to live in the country.'" She says this last with a slight modulation of voice that the *can bo* doesn't notice, but that I find extraordinarily significant, and extraordinarily encouraging.

My wife's parents, and my wife herself, are among the thousands of Vietnamese who have French citizenship. My wife's grandfather was in fact a Frenchman, a colonial administrator who married a Vietnamese woman. His chief legacy has been the citizenship he bestowed on his children and grandchildren. Given the way my wife has said her parents have gone "to live in *the country*," I am sure she means that they are now in France.

I answer, "You must try to join them. Life in the country will be much better for the children." There's no question that

Yvonne understands I'm telling her to get to France if she possibly can, though to Sau Cau it sounds as though I'm advising her to leave the city for farm life. This he thinks is splendid advice, since the party is trying desperately to move people out of the cities and onto the land—even setting up "New Economic Zones," uncultivated regions to which they are shipping large numbers of the unemployed and undesirable.

But Yvonne looks at me anxiously: "But I want to wait for you!"

I'm absolutely insistent, though. At least as insistent as I can be with Sau Cau sitting a few feet away. "You must leave Saigon and join your parents in the country as soon as you can. You've got to think of the children first, not about me. I can't tell when I might be released."

With this, Yvonne starts crying again and Sau Cau interrupts, "Okay now, it's time to go." But he gives me permission to kiss the children, and while I'm leaning over Huy, who's still in Yvonne's arms, I whisper to her: "Go!"

After they walk out, Sau Cau gives me a moment to compose myself, then treats me to a little propaganda. I can see, he tells me, that the party is treating me well. I've even been allowed to meet with my family, a privilege granted to very few prisoners. Now it's time for me to show my appreciation by "cooperating" a bit more. I'm reasonable, intelligent, my revolutionary ideas haven't changed. I could be of help, and also work toward my release so that I could be with my wife and children again and help comfort my mother. All he wants is for me to tell him from time to time what the mood is in the cell, and what the prisoners think about the revolution. Prisoners such as the Venerable Thien Hue, for example.

So that's the price for this family visit. I evade it as best I can. I'm not very close to the other inmates, I tell him. Some of the cell seven prisoners are true Communists and would like nothing better than the chance to serve the party. They would certainly be much more effective than I. But Sau Cau is skillful. "Toai," he says kindly, "I've spent many more years in prison than you have. I know exactly what you're thinking. You don't want to be an informer, and you're right. I myself have contempt for informers. That's why I never use them. I am not asking you to denounce your comrades, only to help me know them a little better, so that I can apply the policy of reconciliation, as I have been trying to do up to now."

These people are unbelievable. I wonder if Sau Cau has ever read Orwell ("war is peace," "freedom is slavery," "ignorance is strength"), but I decide not to ask. At any rate, for him, informing is fraternity.

I can understand, though, why he wants to keep tabs on the bonze Thien Hue and what effect he might be having on the cell. Thien Hue is about the most dangerous character they have in there. The problem is that he simply can't be frightened; he is beyond whatever they might do to him.

Hue never joins the various groups in the cell and rarely speaks, preferring silence and meditation. He eats his rice by himself and has never been heard to complain about anything or to confide in anyone. We know how he was arrested, but only because he was brought into Le Van Duyet with others. He himself doesn't speak about that any more than about other subjects.

The story was that in mid-April, government forces had made a sweep through the Song Vinh region on the road to Vung Tau, a seacoast area about seventy miles from Saigon. Their intention had been to trap a band of former Saigon soldiers who were operating in the area as guerrillas, occasionally stopping cars and buses and executing Communist officials.

But the government forces found these new-style guerrillas as difficult to track down as the old government had found the Vietcong when the roles were reversed. As a result, they ended up making a clean sweep of everyone who happened to be in the area; after all, you could never tell who might be an enemy. Among their catch was Vo Van Hai, who had been private secretary to the first president, Ngo Dinh Diem, and Tu Luu Dan, alias "Grenade," who previously had been a well-known NLF activist. Both of them had been planning to flee the country, and it was their bad luck to get caught as consolation prizes in this abortive operation.

It was also bad luck for 280 others, including the Venerable

Thien Hue, who was on his way to the Song Vinh pagoda. So instead of enjoying his cell in the pagoda, Hue eventually found himself in a cell at Le Van Duyet. But from the silent dignity with which he bears his fate, you can't tell if it has made any difference to him. And since he isn't amenable to the usual pressures, Hue has proved a great annoyance to the *bo doi*.

It is the bonze's habit to take his exercise twice a day, the same "prison yoga" routine that many of the inmates practice. Ordinarily he does his second session just before we are supposed to go to sleep. But one evening he is late. So while the rest of the cell is squeezing together for the night, he remains upright, pressing his toes into the floor, breathing rhythmically through his nose, and swinging his arms.

In the middle of this, a *bo doi* opens the door to give the cell a final check—and finds himself face to face with the exercising bonze. "Ha!" he says, probably more out of surprise than anything else. But then he sees who it is and begins an angry attack. "Why aren't you lying down? A bonze, huh, a reactionary with a bald dome!"

Thien Hue stops his exercise and looks calmly at the *bo doi*. "Are you talking to me?" he asks quietly. "I'm not disturbing anybody, and I'm not making any noise. But you are shouting and violating the rule. Have respect for the ones who are asleep."

Hue's tone is exactly the one he would have used in the pagoda to give instruction to some acolyte. It infuriates the *bo doi*, who begins shouting, "What is your name?"

"Thich Thien Hue, born in 1924 at Go Cong. But that is in your files," answers the bonze, resuming his exercises.

Not having been trained to handle situations like this, the *bo doi* flees the cell in a confused rage. Of course the moment he is gone, everyone else bursts into laughter and congratulations. "Bravo, Master, bravo! You certainly shut him up." But Hue doesn't pay any more attention to our sudden adulation than he did to the *bo doi*'s rudeness.

Before we have a chance to quiet down, the door swings

open again to admit the angry *bo doi*, four armed guards, and Lieutenant Ban—who orders Hue out of the cell. In the hallway, Ban speaks to him, trying to keep his voice under control: "You didn't lie down at curfew, you insulted the guard, you refuse to follow prison discipline! Why? Are you against the revolution?"

"I would like to be," says Hue, "but in prison I can't do anything. The only thing I can do is some exercises to try and maintain health. That does not disturb anybody. But this very young man came in and made a lot of noise, waking up the cell . . ."

"You have no right to speak with such insolence here," says Ban, starting to lose control. "You are a prisoner. You have no civil rights. You are here to reform your thinking, not to insult the revolution!"

"I am a monk," says Hue as imperturbably as ever. "I do nothing against the government. I live in silence and I pray. I have been in prison for two hundred days now, for no reason that I can tell. But it does not matter to me. Buddha is my only judge. If you want, bring me a gallon of gasoline, and I will burn myself right here. Dying twenty years from now or dying now is all the same to me. Or have your soldiers kill me, or let me die of starvation. It is all the same. I am not afraid of your threats. One day when you are a more serious man you will understand what I mean."

This is more than we have heard the bonze say in months and months of living with him. And it is a lot more than Lieutenant Ban wants to hear. Screaming now, he cuts Hue off, "Silence! Silence! What do you think this is, a pagoda? Any more of this kind of stuff, and I'll throw you in solitary!"

Ban must realize how ridiculous that reflex threat is the moment it is out of his mouth. Thich Thien Hue is a man for whom death is but a passage. Already detached from the world, force or detainment mean nothing to him.

That night we get to sleep late, with a kind of jubilation in our hearts. It has been a great victory for us, no matter what the bonze thinks of it. Yet the incident is also a reminder of how far the rest of us are from Hue's plane of freedom. Unlike him, we all have our attachments. And so we care about ourselves . . . and so we fear our keepers.

That night is my 479th in prison. Soon it will be Christmas, then Tet again. Another Tet in prison. Yvonne is probably trying to get to France with the children. Perhaps she is already there. I hope so. Despite the goings-on over the last couple of months, I see no way out for myself.

21

The Declaration of Human Rights

At the end of November 1976 I am transferred out of cell seven into cell four, still in Zone C. It is not a punishment (conditions in four are identical to those in seven), just simple precaution on the part of Sau Cau, the zone chief. I had let Cau know that I wouldn't watch the bonze Hue for him, and that I hoped he could find someone else for the job. That same day I am moved, something they do to everyone who refuses to inform, in an effort to keep their plans and fears away from the ears of potential targets.

The leader of my new cell is Tran Doan, a veteran party member who despite his imprisonment is still a devoted Communist. The one thing that makes life in cell four more trying than it was in seven is Doan's daily public reading of *Nhan Dan* (*The Party Daily News*). The paper is provided at the cell leader's request, and he reads news items and commentaries from it—which the rest of us are supposed to listen to and then discuss. The prisoners would gladly do without this routine, though occasionally we learn some worthwhile tidbit of outside news from it. (One such tidbit is a *Nhan Dan* report that American President Jimmy Carter's hobby is sleeping with women other than his wife. Nobody in the cell doubts the report's veracity; apparently Carter boasted about it in a published interview. But while nobody thinks Carter's hobby is especially unusual, we can't understand why he would admit such a thing in public. Years later in the United States I was surprised to learn that Carter had only said he "lusted in his heart." Even then I had to have the phrase explained for me.)

But as annoying as Doan's orthodoxy can be, he is a man of great personal rectitude. It takes a while, though, before I realize this; at first I couldn't have been more suspicious of him, and for good reason.

On my arrival in cell four, the *bo doi* escorting me pointed out the spot where I would sleep, and when night came I found that I was nestled right next to Tran Doan himself. That the *bo doi* would assign me a place was unusual in itself and set off all my warning sensors. And when Doan went out of his way to be friendly over the next few days, even a much less suspicious person than I would have smelled a rat.

Doan quite clearly wanted to get to know me, especially to know the evolution of my political ideas. With all the questions, I was sure he was a stoolie, and that Zone Chief Sau Cau had sent me to him for special observation. Still, I felt able to discuss my life with Doan (I hadn't much choice), though of course I was careful not to mention anything about the change in my thinking since "liberation."

Eventually our discussions turned less one-sided, and we found that we were even developing a liking for each other. Little by little Doan became convinced that I was not a threat to the party, and he finally "confessed" that he had been asked to watch me and to find out as much as he could. In fact, the cell leader was no stoolie in the usual sense. He acted only in the party's interest, and not out of any desire for personal gain. He had been told: "This Toai is dangerous," and so he conscientiously went about trying to discover what sort of danger I might be. Convinced of my sincerity, he told me, "I'm sure you're not an enemy of the revolution, and I'll say so to them."

Once we had established a mutual trust, I found out almost as much about Doan as he did about me. He was a southerner who had followed the Vietminh north after Geneva. At the University of Hanoi he had studied chemistry, then had gone on to China and Czechoslovakia for advanced training. Returning to Vietnam, he became a high-level technical administrator for the Democratic Republic's Economics Ministry, and was sent south after the victory. A month after his arrival one of his superiors accused him of stealing four hundred liters of gasoline, and here he was in Le Van Duyet.

When Doan confided this to me his voice choked and tears welled into his eyes: "Me, steal four hundred liters of gasoline! I didn't give thirty years of my life to the party to fall so low. In the position I had, people don't steal four hundred liters, they steal ten thousand liters. But I didn't steal anything! The truth was that my superior denounced me because he wanted to replace me with his own man, and that was the easiest way to do it."

Like many others, Doan remained faithful to the party, even after it had disgraced him. But the injustice and infamy of it made him sick at heart.

◊   ◊   ◊

In the spring of 1977 Le Van Duyet's barber is released, a man I had talked to briefly the few times I had my hair cut. Though I wasn't aware of this event when it happened, the barber's luck turns out to be mine too. A few days later, Lieutenant Ban walks into cell four and asks if there is anyone who knows how to cut hair. He hasn't even finished the question before I jump up and sing out brightly, "I do!"

My cellmates are no doubt surprised to hear this. I myself couldn't have told it to them a moment earlier. But the instant Ban opens his mouth I know this is a chance to get out of the cell, so I grab it. How hard could barbering be anyway?

I am not to waste any time finding out. As soon as I volun-

teer, Ban and a *bo doi* lead me out of the cell down the walkway through Zone C. We stop in front of one of the holding
cells, from behind whose door comes the loudest chorus of
mother curses I have ever heard. It's like a gaggle of monkeys
screeching away at the top of their lungs: "Fuck your mother!
Fuck you! Your mother's cunt! Your father's cunt!"

When Ban opens the door, the racket dies down quickly,
and I find myself looking at a jumble of filthy, grimacing grotesquely tattooed street thugs. My first impression is that each
one of them has at least shoulder-length hair. Some of them
have tied it back under bandanas or sweatbands, some have
knotted it into single or double braids, some just let it hang
loose and greasy around their faces. All of them look as if they
would murder their mothers for nothing. Thoughts about what
they might do to a barber are spinning through my head too
fast for me to keep up with them.

While I am standing there trying to smile, a *bo doi* puts a
little stool down in the hall and gives me scissors, a comb, and
a pair of sheep clippers. Ban yells out, "Haircut time!" and
disappears, but not before telling me, "Cut it as short as you
can!"

Out they come, one at a time, to sit down on the stool in
front of me while I work them over with the sheep clippers.
Despite their ferocious looks, they turn out to be docile in
front of the *bo dois* and almost reverential toward the barber.
But they did not want their hair short. "Oh, Master," says the
first, looking at me with real fear, "please don't cut it short,
Master!"

At first I cut very gingerly, a snip at a time. Then I get used
to it. The *bo dois*, with the northern style, are my model: clip
close up the sides, leave the top alone. Each one was the same,
straight up the sides, nothing off the top. The thugs don't like
it, but they don't complain much either, except for the sporadic exclamations of pain when the clippers find some knot or
tangle that I haven't combed out. They were just brought in by
convoy from the Dai Loi Hotel, which had been converted
into a prison to help handle the overflow of prisoners. Once

they have stopped cursing they seem rather cowed, apprehensive about what they might find in Le Van Duyet. The haircut is just the first unpleasantness they will encounter.

By the end of the first day my right hand is in a continuous spasm. The next morning, though, it is feeling all right, and I begin my first full day as barber for the prison's two thousand souls.

This job is a godsend—as are almost all the prison's few jobs to those who have them. Best, of course, is that it gets me out of the cell. But it also puts me in contact with every single prisoner in Le Van Duyet, except for those in Zone B's "Ba Dinh Palace." As barber I am at the very hub of the prison's clandestine communications system, hearing stories, news, exchanging messages and bits of information from prisoner to prisoner, keeping friends and relatives in touch with each other. It seems to me that I am becoming the repository for the secret history of Le Van Duyet.

From inmates on Zone C's second corridor I learn the details of the famous hunger strike Nhu Phong had undertaken the previous year. Phong was a widely read poet and political commentator who used to be known as "the voice of the BBC" for his reports on that network. He had fought with the Vietminh during the anti-French war and had been arrested successively by the French, by Diem and his successors, and now by the revolution. Swept up in the mass arrest of artists that also engulfed my old cellmate Dang Giao, Phong asserted his defiance in a strike that had been the main topic of prison conversation for several months.

Hunger strikes were nothing new to Nhu Phong; he had maintained some lengthy ones in previous prisons. This one was a pure battle of wills with the Le Van Duyet wardens, and it was fierce. The *can bos* had thrown him into solitary for his refusal to eat, telling him that "with us, iron becomes pliant." Each morning from his isolation cell Nhu Phong would greet the watchers at the collective cell peephole across the hall with a cheery "Good morning!" From there the news would spread to adjoining cells: "Nhu Phong has said 'Good morning.' " It became a ritual, Nhu Phong's "Good morning." One day, a month or so into the strike, he hadn't appeared at the peep-hole, and the prisoners were dismayed that he might be dead. But the next morning, there he was again.

Colonel Tu Tuan, the prison commander, had come in person with a squad of *bo dois* to force-feed him, but word got around that Nhu Phong had vomited the rice gruel they forced down his throat. Later Tuan tried persuasion, telling Phong that he had no right to commit suicide, that it was his duty to live for his family. Phong had laughed at him; his parents were dead, and from one jail to the next he had never had time to start a family of his own. Aside from his more distant relatives, he was alone.

Like the bonze Thien Hue, Phong had no attachments, and that gave him a strength his enemies could not overcome. There was simply no way to blackmail him, no hostages through whom his will could be assaulted. And because only his own life was at stake, he held out, taking no solid food for fifty days. At the end of that time he agreed to eat a little; he had won his point, proving that his determination was even more powerful than that of the watchdogs. To the rest of the prisoners, Phong's heroism was an inspiration—a symbol of the potential of the human spirit. Those who saw him after-ward said that his eyes still shone behind his huge glasses and that within his spent body his will was as indomitable as ever.

◊   ◊   ◊

Another courageous individual is one of my cellmates in number four, a high school student named Dang Co Ban who is in jail for organizing a clandestine counterrevolutionary group among his friends. They were all arrested, along with three others who had not been members but had the misfor-tune to bear the same name as Ban. During my barbering chores I give haircuts to each of these other three and find that I'm able to put together a composite of what had happened. It is a story that shames me for nursing resentment over the arbi-trariness of my own fate.

In the middle of the night on July 30, 1975, a *can bo* arrived at the police station for Vo Di Nguy, a Saigon neighborhood near the airport. The *can bo* had orders to arrest immediately one Dang Co Ban, sixteen or seventeen years old, a student in the district high school. The station chief was at a loss. It was past midnight, school wasn't in session, there was no father's name to help identify the student, and everything had to be done on the spot, before the criminal had time to escape.

Since the *can bo* had brought along plenty of manpower in the form of a troop of Vanguard Youth, they decided to sweep the neighborhood. Because no one had yet dreamed of the "3/76 Law" and its warrant requirements, the young searchers were instructed to make assurance double sure by arresting any Ban they found who looked to be about the right age. The police would sort them out later.

The hunt began at once. Spreading out through the neighborhood, the Vanguard Youth pounded on doors and questioned families who had awakened to fear. Amid the barking of Vo Di Nguy's dogs, they located and hauled away four different Bans:

1. Tran Dinh Ban, who had been drafted into the southern army just before the fall of the old regime, had spent three days in reeducation (all that was required of the lowest-level soldiers and government functionaries), and was preparing to leave with his parents for one of the New Economic Zones.

2. Nguyen Duc Ban, who in 1974 had succeeded in postponing his military service for a year by bribing an official to provide him with a false birth certificate. A week prior to his arrest, Nguyen Duc Ban's Youth Union had awarded him the much envied title "An Obedient Nephew of Uncle Ho." His father was a tailor who during the war had been sympathetic to the Front and who afterward had been named head of a local *to*.*

* In the general population, as in the prison cell, the *to* is the smallest subdivision. A neighborhood *to* consists of a few dozen families, whose activities are monitored and

3. Nguyen Dan Ban, seventeen years old and a classmate of Dang Co Ban, who was the object of the search.
4. The real criminal, Dang Co Ban, who had organized a group called "Tu Nguyen" (The Volunteers) which was distributing leaflets against, as they put it, "The new tyrannical regime which betrayed the Front."

In his leaflet, the young Dang Co Ban had said nothing more than what many of the Front leaders themselves thought about the course of events. After the victory the Front had been broken, its leaders shunted aside, and its program junked. But Ban had had the naiveté to put it in writing. Now he found himself handcuffed and thrown face down with the three others onto the floor of the bus carrying fifty or so Vanguard Youth still invigorated from their night's work.

In jail, Dang Co Ban admitted the truth immediately and said he hoped his fellow passengers on the bus floor would be freed. But the investigators had other ideas. After all, the three had been arrested, so they must be guilty of something.

And indeed they were. When the investigation was completed the three other Bans were locked away in Le Van Duyet for the same indefinite term as everyone else, because:

1. Tran Dinh Ban had been a puppet soldier and his interrogation revealed that he had not sincerely repented of his crimes;
2. Nguyen Duc Ban had used a falsified birth certificate to become a member of the Youth Union, thereby demonstrating suspicious intentions (yes, it was the same certificate he had bought to escape service in the puppet army);
3. Nguyen Van Ban was in the same high school as Dang Co Ban, and though he was not personally implicated in the

---

controlled by the *to* leader. Above the *to* is the zone (*khu vuc*), which includes twenty to thirty *to* and has its own control personnel. The zones in their turn are units of a neighborhood (*phuong*) and the neighborhoods units of a district (*quan*). Under the new order, Ho Chi Minh City was divided into twenty-one districts. The whole structure, from district to *to*, constitutes a tightly woven interlocking mechanism for maintaining revolutionary vigilance over all the city's inhabitants.

leaflet affair, he was in a position to have known about it and had not reported it. A period of reeducation would instruct him in the need for revolutionary vigilance.

◊   ◊   ◊

My new job not only allows me to learn the stories of many of Le Van Duyet's most interesting cases, I also hear about new prisoners when they come in. And eventually, carrying my stool and clippers to a new cell each day, I get to meet each of them. Some come in from the labor camps, to which they were shipped for thirty days of reeducation back in June of 1975. Others are transferred from Chi Hoa, or other jails, bringing with them their descriptions and comparisons, and their information about the prisoners they have lived with—who they were and how many.

Slowly, I begin to get a wider view of what has happened, of the immense swath that has been cut through southern society in the aftermath of the revolution's triumph. The writers, the artists, the lawyers, the scholars—the entire generation that embodied South Vietnam's culture has been smashed, and the remnants are dying slowly in the revolution's gulag of jails and hard labor camps.

But not all of them are suffering their fate passively. Many of the southern intellectuals are fiercely independent people who have done time in jail before. In the revolution's prisons they find themselves living cheek by jowl with veteran insurgents and militants who have spent the better part of their lives warring against repressive regimes. It is a potent combination. Many of these new-era prisoners are traumatized by what has happened, by the consequences of the victory they and their comrades have fought thirty years to bring about. Some, especially the old Communists, are too shell-shocked to do anything but cling pathetically to the tattered remnants of their faith. But for others, shock gives way to rage.

Because of my position as mobile talker and listener, I become the conduit, not just for news and private exchanges, but for these prisoners' efforts to strike back at their tormentors. Within Vietnam there is no way to do that effectively. The revolution has in fact won decisively and has followed up its victory with a series of brilliant moves that has eliminated any possible center of opposition. But two protracted conflicts, one against the French, one against the Americans, have conditioned Vietnamese to regard war as a political as well as a military phenomenon. And throughout these two struggles, political warfare has been focused, not on Vietnam itself, but overseas. And it is from overseas that the prisoners believe their help might come.

Regardless of Dienbienphu, the French had lost their Vietnam War, not in the field, but in the home arena. After nine years, exhaustion and popular disgust with *la sale guerre* (the dirty war) had moved France to renounce her claims at the bargaining table. It was on the domestic front too that the United States had lost its war. By 1973 the American Congress had practically destroyed the Nixon administration's ability to use its might.

Looking toward the vocal and militant foreign constituencies for help, a movement has started in jail to get the word out, to declare to the outside world that had supported the revolution what has happened in Vietnam and to raise a cry for help. A "testament" of Vietnamese prisoners has been composed that circulates by word of mouth among several jails in the hope that one day it would will find its way out. A number of prisoners (including myself) commit the "testament" to memory. Eventually, I was to make the "testament" public in France in 1978, where it created a few waves in the press, but, of course, brought no substantial results.

The fact is that in jail we are dreaming, still living in an era that ended on April 30, 1975, when the *bo dois* marched into Saigon. Up until that moment the war had been not only Vietnam's, but the West's as well. In the United States and France, the war had excited passions of varying sorts: patriotism, but also militant opposition—opposition from people who came to believe in the justice of Vietnam's revolution, as indeed so many Vietnamese believed in it.

But the shock of the betrayal, though it crashed onto the

Vietnamese people in a cyclone of terror, reached the West only by degrees, like the widening ripples in a pond. A rumor here, a refugee report there, were not much to dispel the conviction among Western activists that the right side had won, or the relief among others that at least it was over. Even the boat people disaster, when it broke, aroused only the West's compassion. It did little to stir a reassessment and moved not a soul to think about how the tragedy might be redressed. Someone with a clear understanding of American psychology and American political realities would perhaps have expected nothing different. But in the sweatboxes at Le Van Duyet in 1977, we think otherwise.

We are living in a fool's paradise, where hopes and dreams feed on illusions. In July of 1977 one of these hopes surfaces, and a wave of excitement washes through the prison. News comes in from recent arrivals that Representative Nguyen Cong Hoan has fled the country. Hoan was the Buddhist student leader who had won an Assembly seat back in 1971 in the election that had nipped the bud from my own political hopes. From 1971 until 1975 Hoan had toiled in the opposition bloc, creating a reputation for himself as a compassionate independent of great moral courage. In the wake of April 30 he went back to his home province of Phu Yen and became a teacher—until the revolution called on him to serve.

In 1976, Hoan was one of a number of nonparty people to be nominated for the first congress of unified Vietnam. The revolution had found it expedient to include a small group of popular southern politicians among the assemblymen, to give the impression that the affair was not completely a Communist creation. Hoan, with his oppositionist and social welfare credentials, was a perfect candidate. Having been chosen, he was duly elected, and in the summer of the year he was in Hanoi representing his native Phu Yen.

Hoan's impression of the first congress apparently was not good, and though he returned for the second, shortly afterward he managed a daring escape to Japan. The prison grapevine said he was incensed about conditions in the country and particularly about the prisons and reeducation camps. Hoan was a man who spoke his mind, and the political prisoners were enthusiastic about the international pressure that was sure to follow from his forceful revelations.

Two years later I was to learn firsthand from Hoan himself about his desperate odyssey. But in prison, after the first rush of talk, we hear no more.

We hear a great deal, however, about another brave attempt to get word out of the closed society, an attempt that preceded Hoan's by several months. In late April of 1977 a small group of prisoners arrived in Le Van Duyet together, but were shunted off to different cells. One of them, the lawyer Tran Danh San, was placed in Zone C's cell number eight, where I came to ply my trade as a barber shortly after his arrival. San was the talk of the cell, and before long the entire prison knew about the act of heroic madness that had brought him and his colleagues into the Le Van Duyet disposal system.

San and his companions were all well-known militants from past years. He himself had been president of "The Progressive Youth Forces" back in 1965 and had paid for that involvement with three years in prison. One of the group, Ton That Duong Ky, was a former Front leader, and the others were professors and lawyers who had played their roles in the opposition.*

On April 18, San had stood in front of the Saigon Cathedral and in a loud, resonant voice had to read a declaration calling on all the workers and intellectuals of the world to demand an accounting from the Vietnamese government for its systematic outrages against human rights. That is, he had tried to read the declaration. In fact, one of his companions told me, San only got through the first few sentences: "We, with what remains of our weakened strength, with what remains of our mutilated spirits, determine to struggle through nonviolent action, demanding respect for human rights in Vietnam. . . . We have

---

* The others were Pham Bieu Tam, vice-president of the Association of Patriotic Intellectuals; Huynh Thanh Vi, president of the Vietnamese Press Association; Nguyen Huu Giao, a lawyer and former vice-president of students at Hue University; Trieu Ba Thiep, another lawyer and president of the Committee of Students for Struggle against the Dictatorship of Ngo Dinh Diem; and my old friend Nguyen Van Thang, the 'southernist.'

chosen the voice of nonviolence, for only thus may we avoid the sacrifices and the shedding of blood of a people martyred without respite for many decades . . ." Then they grabbed him.

The cathedral had been chosen because the group thought they would be able to catch the attention of a Vietnamese Frenchman who was about to leave for France. If this imminent traveler to the West might hear, and if a few dozen other pedestrians would stop to listen, then, they thought, their arrests would be worthwhile. As far as press was concerned, there wasn't a non-Communist reporter in Ho Chi Minh City, nor was there likely to be in any future that they could see.

San's remarkable personality transforms the mood in his cell. Cultivated, articulate, and witty, he creates around him a climate of enthusiastic rebelliousness that infects everybody in the vicinity. "Ah," he jokes as I talk to him about the declaration, "if only we had obtained Mrs. Ngo Ba Thanh's signature, she would be with us now, and we'd be a lot less bored." (Ngo Ba Thanh was a Saigon lawyer famous for her acerbic tongue. Close to the Front, for a number of years she had been the favorite source for Western journalists looking for the most virulent criticism of Thieu and his gang.) In contrast to the hunger striker Nhu Phong and the bonze Thien Hue, San had plenty to lose: a beautiful wife and five children. It made his defiance all the more magnificent.

The Declaration of Human Rights that San and the others composed was an eloquent document in the classical Vietnamese style of a call to arms. It addressed the workers, farmers, and intellectuals of the world and urged on them the business of Vietnam's catastrophe. It called on the United Nations and the governments that constitute it to act on the basis of Articles Thirteen and Sixty-three to intervene, "to stop the savage violations of human rights, the systematic usurpation of liberty, the state policy that dehumanizes man . . . ," and it concluded: "Each day that passes is a day of additional suffering for millions of Vietnamese. These millions await the voice and the acts of humane souls throughout the world."

This I commit to memory as well.

22

Prayers for the Dead

One morning in early August I am shearing heads in Zone A when a *bo doi* walks by me, then turns back briefly, as if inspecting my technique. Without looking at me, he touches my free hand, then slips something into it. As casually as I can, I reach inside my pajama waistband as if to scratch, then slide the object into the elastic of my underpants. It is a small, rectangular piece of stiff paper, glossy on one side, smooth on the other—a photograph.

All day long my excitement grows, and anyone watching would have seen me scratching occasionally at some bothersome irritation on my waist. I touched the photograph a dozen times, reassuring myself that it is there, trying to guess what it holds in store.

By the time I go back to my cell at mealtime, I can't wait any longer. Taking a wild chance, I sit facing the wall and slip out the forbidden object, shielding it as best I can from those around me. There, peeking out at me from the picture in my cupped hand, are Dinh, Binh, and Huy, my three boys. On the back is a message from my sister.

8/4/77
My Lovely Dear Brother,
    This morning the children are going to their grandmother's [Yvonne's mother]. Everyone is saying good-bye to them, and everyone is crying. The house is a lonely, desolate place, a desert without the children's sounds. Our parents are weaker because of sadness and separation after separation. Now our family has only you. You are the only hope we can rely on. Have courage and bear up. We all believe in the justice of the revolution and hope to see you soon.
Your loving sister

    My ears began to thrum with blood. Yvonne has just now been able to get out, so long after I told her to leave. At least she and the boys are safe. But I feel a surge of anxiety for my parents, "weaker because of sadness." My sister never would have written that unless she were desperate. I can't imagine how she managed to get the message in, unless one of my friends was able to arrange it. The business about "believing in the justice of the revolution" was in case the message was discovered—flimsy insurance.
    Over the next weeks my anxiety heightens. I'm convinced that my parents are breaking down under the multiple blows of my brother's flight, my arrest, and now Yvonne's departure. In Vietnam, a family's sons are conditioned to care for their aging parents—not that it always works out that way. But when it doesn't, the psychological effects are felt by both parents and children. When my brother left, our parents' care became my duty. Since Yvonne's visit the previous year they have had no news of me. They aren't even sure if I'm still alive. My sister's letter said nothing about Trung and his family—has there been word from them? Or of them? I can imagine my mother and father passing each day in a welter of fear for both of us. The determination surges up in me: I must get out.

Through September I find it harder and harder to bear the separation. I am preoccupied with thoughts of my parents. I feel strongly that I cannot exist without seeing them and alleviating their anguish. A desperate mood comes over me, far worse than anything I've previously experienced. I don't have the strength to lift the barber shears anymore, or the will to force the black rice down my throat. I begin to feel I can't live like this any longer. Slowly I become aware that I no longer care what happens to me. These bastards might just as well kill me now, I think, and somehow that thought gives me the courage to act.

On October 12, I ask a *bo doi* for permission to write to the prison administration. The request is approved, and I'm given a quarter sheet of paper and the stub of a pencil to write with:

Le Van Duyet
October 12, 1977

The Director
Security Administration
Ho Chi Minh City

Sir:

After spending more than two years in the Tran Hung Dao and Le Van Duyet Prisons, no one has yet explained to me what the charges are against me. I have never been against the new government. But if it can be shown that I have made any mistakes, even small mistakes or mistakes in talking, or if any members of my family have acted in support of the puppet regime, or against the party, I am ready to receive a harsh sentence, even the death sentence.

I have already made several formal requests to learn the charges against me. But they have either not come to your attention, or you have not had time to respond to them. It seems unacceptable to me to arrest a man without any indication of guilt and to keep him in prison without a trial.

If within a hundred days I have not been brought to trial by the government, I will bring myself to trial.

Doan Van Toai

As I write this letter I have a vision of the engineer Lam Truong Thi, who found a way to slit his wrists last year over the shame of having stolen food. I remember his blood collecting in a pool underneath the door of his isolation cell; in the dim light of the hall, we thought it was water and called the water bearer to take care of it. I know I could manage the same thing, even if after reading the letter they take away my barber's scissors. I recognize these macabre thoughts for what they are, but my mind is now set. At least it will remove this unbearable weight that is crushing me into the ground.

A week passes. Then I am summoned to leave the cell "with my things." Someone, I think, actually read the letter; now what are they going to do? But instead of being taken to see a *can bo*, I am led to Zone A, the French-built haven from which I was expelled over a year ago. The difference is remarkable. When I last saw Huynh Cu's cell five, seventy-two inmates were sharing the sleeping bench and floor. Now, wonderous to say, I am shown into a cell housing . . . twenty-five prisoners!

I quickly learn that all the residents here have recently been transferred. And among them I am overjoyed to see the bonze Thien Hue. I am also overjoyed at being able to sleep flat on my back for the first time in over two and a half years. An unimaginable luxury! Another luxury is the running water at the back of the cell, still a trickle, but running—whenever you want it.

Nobody in this cell knows why he's been transferred, and there isn't anybody who's not astounded by the spaciousness of it. One cellmate says, "Such comfort . . . it must be the antechamber of death. They're giving us one last chance to enjoy life before they . . ." "No," says another, subtler in his black humor, "this is the place where one prepares for a new life." No one misses the allusion to reincarnation. Even the bonze Thien Hue smiles.

Obviously we are special cases, but what kind no one can figure out. The bonze was arrested for nothing, but since his arrest he's caused them nothing but trouble. There's a former Front district chief who got on the wrong side of his superiors; there's a former attaché at the Thieu regime's Washington embassy. There's a twenty-year-old kid who bribed a Thieu intelligence official to put his name down as an agent so he could dodge the draft. (His only intelligence duty was to pay off the official once a month.) Of course when the lists were discovered, there he was, one of the "wicked and cruel tyrants." The fact that he looks fifteen obviously meant nothing.

Could they be collecting people for a convoy to one of the jungle slave labor camps? Or could they possibly be preparing us for . . . release . . . our minds won't even acknowledge the thought, lest it curse the prospect. Better to think they're going to ship us north. Then no matter what happens we won't be disappointed.

◊   ◊   ◊

Zone A's grilled cellfronts look out on a walkway, then into the little courtyard on the far side of which stands the kitchen.

One day shortly after my transfer, my cellmates and I watch as the courtyard fills up with a group of prisoners, who look terrible. Many of them have severe beriberi symptoms, and some are covered with scaly skin infections. They loll there in the sun, letting its healing warmth play over them.

One of them, sitting with his knees hunched up less than ten yards away from me, begins staring in my direction, then opens his eyes wide in recognition. It takes me a moment to realize that I am looking at an old and close friend of mine from the student movement days. There is nothing improbable about his presence in Le Van Duyet, but it comes as a surprise anyway. I would have thought he'd be working for the government. (Perhaps he assumed the same about me.) Seeing he has caught my attention, the trace of a smile crinkles his cheeks, and he stretches his eyes wide open, pulling down with his thumbs and up with his index fingers. I understand the gesture immediately; it says clearly: We're wide awake now, aren't we, Toai?

Then he begins mouthing words at me, one phrase over and over, five, six, seven times. But I can't make out what he is saying, and after a minute or two he stops, afraid of being spotted by the guards.

A few hours later, when the kitchen workers bring our pail of rice into the cell, one of them whispers to me: "There's a message from your buddy. He says your mother has died!"

For a moment my mind goes blank. Then the premonitions of the previous months come together in a jumble of emotion. Is that what my sister was telling me: that my mother was dying? In my mind I saw her as she was when I left for the concert more than two years ago. As I walked out the door she said, "Don't come back too late, Toai." What I answered I don't remember, probably the standard "Sure, Mom, I won't." Ritual leave-taking between mother and son. Ritual for the son anyway; for the mother perhaps, a hint of real fear, with the eldest son already gone, and the *bo doi*–infested city an uncertain place.

That was already close to a month after Trung's departure. From the time he left she had been weepy. Her whole life had been one of war and travail and worry, and now, as the days passed with no word of my brother or his family, she began suffering visions of disaster. Then I had disappeared.

In Tran Hung Dao I had been anxious about both her and my wife. But while I habitually went to sleep thinking of them and the children, the nighttime images I summoned up were of happy times. Dwelling on what they were going through was, I knew, a road to madness. By the time I got to Le Van Duyet, I was already wrapped tightly in my cloak of survival, the armor each prisoner forges to shield himself from the full impact of his tragedy.

But now all I can think is that Mother had no son with her when she died. I wasn't there. What did they do at the funeral, where it is the son's place to stay with the coffin, greeting friends and relatives who come to say good-bye? Like all Vietnamese Buddhists, my mother believed that the soul hovers above the body in its coffin, praying for the forgiveness of those whom it offended in life. Next to the body, dressed in mourning white, the son accepts the words of pardon and farewell and expresses the gratitude of the lingering soul.

Although not a believer, I agonize over my failure. I talk for hours with the bonze Thien Hue, relieving my feelings and drawing wisdom from his gentle counsel. I ask him to teach me the prayers for the dead, and each evening I close my eyes and chant them softly, comforted by the familiarity of these formulas I have heard since my youth, and by the thought that I am doing what has to be done.

But I'm also seething, consumed by a cold-blooded determination to protest my imprisonment in the most dramatic way I can. My mother's death has pushed me over the edge. Anger and grief combine to make me indifferent to anything beyond my two goals of either getting out or making a last, vivid demonstration of my hatred. I begin to plot the details of my suicide.

As part of my plan I ask for and receive permission to write another letter to the prison administration, in which I explicitly state that if I'm not brought to trial, I will condemn myself and carry out the sentence.

I suspect that neither of my letters is read, except in a routine way by the Le Van Duyet censors, who then file them with my dossier. Reason tells me that I was transferred to Zone A, not because of my threats, but because "the politburo gods on their thrones" have decreed that Doan Van Toai belongs to that category of southerners whose potential to endanger the revolution has diminished to nothing.

I'm convinced that it is for that reason too, and for none other, that a few days after my second letter, I am summoned to speak with an official. The unfamiliar colonel sitting behind the interrogator's desk introduces himself as Tam Nam, assistant chief of security for Ho Chi Minh City. In his brief and rather formal little speech he makes no allusions to either my letters or to my mother's death. He states simply and clearly that my case has now been fully investigated and that I have been found to be a "patriot." But because my previous activities were outside the party's control, I had brought great suspicion on myself. Now, thanks to the party's goodwill, I will soon be released . . . "on the condition, of course, that you are now prepared to cooperate with the Revolution."

"What kind of cooperation do you mean?" I ask.

"We will talk about that again," says Tam Nam in the same official tone. "Right now, you will not speak a word about your release to any of your fellow-prisoners. Is that understood?"

Is it ever! I come out of the colonel's office flustered with joy, the first feeling in weeks that has intruded on my grim obsessions. Somewhere a doubt gnaws, telling me to beware of a trick. And that business about "cooperation," was that just a standard speech they make to every freed prisoner? Or do they really expect something, something impossible of course?

Back in the cell I mull it over. And the more I think, the more it seems to me that "cooperation" might be a real test. Everything I know about them and everything I've heard from the jail's old Communists tells me that the party never trusts anyone who is once suspected. If that's true, it might be wisest to play the role of the exhausted prisoner (pretense is hardly necessary) incapable of thinking beyond reunifying himself with his family. If they originally put me in jail because I was dangerous, how can I persuade them that I no longer am?

I've just about decided on this course of action when, three days after my interview with the assistant chief, a *bo doi* presents himself at the cell door and shouts, "Doan Van Toai! Get dressed in your street clothes and come out with all your things!" It is almost exactly four. We can hear the kitchen help clanking a rice pail down in the next cell. Realizing that something unusual is happening (the *bo doi* told me to put on my *street clothes*, which I've cared for meticulously since the advent of prison pajamas), my cellmates say their good-byes, and I leave, turning at the door to bow toward Thien Hue.

The *bo doi* leads me directly to the office of Tu Tuan, Le Van Duyet's warden. Tuan greets me courteously and asks me to sit down, motioning toward an armchair at the side of his desk. No sooner have I settled into its luxurious softness when another soldier appears with tea. I think I'm dreaming. Smiling, Colonel Tuan looks at me and says, "I am happy to inform you that from now on you are a free citizen. As representative of the party and of the government, I declare that you are cleared of all accusations."

I feel dizzy as I listen to the rest of his speech, on the theme of helping to reconstruct the nation and "build socialism." Then he says, "I also have two other pieces of news for you: one good, one bad. First, your wife and children have arrived in France and are awaiting you there. The second is that your mother has died. I am sorry to have to tell you this. She was elderly, was she not? But you are a free man. You must look forward to the future, not back to the past. The revolution will need you!"

I felt suddenly light-headed when Tuan announced that I was free. Now I am thoroughly confused. I didn't expect him to tell me anything about my mother, let alone my wife's flight to France. I don't understand how Tuan can suggest that I will be allowed to join my family there, and in the same breath say that "the revolution will need me." I certainly don't understand how this representative of "the party and the government" can refer to my wife's departure from socialist Vietnam to capitalist France as a piece of "good news."

Nevertheless, I retain enough presence of mind to follow my plan. "I'm very tired," I tell Tuan softly. Then, even more quietly, "In what way will the revolution need me? I want most of all just to go home."

"Yes, of course," says Tuan sympathetically. "The revolution will let you know in good time what is expected of you."

With this, he signals to the *bo doi* who brought the tea, and a wrapped parcel appears on the desk. Inside are the things that were confiscated from me that first night in Tran Hung Dao, though somewhat metamorphosed. My expensive Seiko banker's watch has been transformed into a cheap throwaway. (Why did they bother?) My old-regime piasters have become twenty new-regime dong. My driver's license has disappeared. But my identification card is still there—a huge relief, since without an identification card former prisoners must rely on their prison release certificates, which insure that they will henceforth be placed under restrictions by the local police.

With a special show of friendship, Tuan then accompanies me past the guard station, occasioning a display of obseqious politeness from the ordinarily insufferable *bo dois*. Does Tuan's personal interest in me suggest to them that I might have been a clandestine party informer all along? Whatever the case, I treat myself to the pleasure of refusing their proffered hands, though I shake Tu Tuan's firmly. A moment later I am standing on Chi Lang Boulevard. It is five o'clock in the afternoon—November 1, 1977, the fourteenth anniversary of Ngo Dinh Diem's fall from power. I last set foot on a street 863 days ago. As I wonder whether to go left or right, a pedicab wheels by the jail, driven by a young man wearing a hat with holes in it. For an instant I wonder why he is wearing such a hat, but only for an instant. Then, checking the folded dong bills in my pocket, I flag him down and get in.

23

Breaking Free

"Where to, Comrade?" asks the driver, turning his head slightly to glance at me.

"I'll tell you in a bit. Right now just drive around. I need some air."

I'm struck by the unreality of these words, or maybe it's their very reality that sounds so strange: "Where to?" "Just drive around." It's too sudden, this freedom. In my mind I'm still in Zone A marveling at the space, or maybe it's Zone C, gasping for breath at the peephole.

"Sure thing," says the driver, glancing back again. "You're awfully pale. All that office work, huh? I'm lucky; I get to spend the whole day outside, where the air's better. Of course it's even better than it used to be, now there isn't so much traffic. Any special direction you want me to go? Toward town? Away from town?"

This guy's a talker, but I find it soothing. Then I know why; he's living in the normal, everyday world, and who talks more about normal everyday things than cab drivers? The weather, the traffic, food, wives, girlfriends, money—all those things that do not exist inside, but are the stuff of life outside. I couldn't have chosen a better guide to reintroduce me to Saigon, a guide who addresses me formally no less, instead of the "hey you" I'm accustomed to hearing. And that business about the office is delicious.

On the other hand, his remarks about how clean the air is now that there's not much traffic ring false. In the old days the dream of every pedicab driver was to graduate to taxis. They coveted each hack that went by, no matter how broken-down. Maybe he thinks I'm some kind of threadbare *can bo*. I'm wearing the clothes I was arrested in, good enough 863 days ago, but now the pants are ragged in the knees (and seat) where I wore holes in them and then managed to patch them clumsily. I remember that the northerners who arrived on April 30, 1975, didn't look much better than I do know. They weighed about the same, and their clothes had a notable drabness. Another laugh. Not only am I on the street, but I might even be a *can bo*.

Perhaps to confirm the cab driver's impression of me as a serious person, I take out the official papers Tu Tuan gave me and look at them closely:

> The Central Office of the Investigation Section of the Public Security Department orders the release of:
> Doan Van Toai, born in Vinh Long Province in 1946.
> *Reason for Arrest:* [this space left blank]
> *Reason for Release:* [this space left blank]
> Doan Van Toai will report to the local offices of the Public Security to regularize his status.
> Copy to: People's Committee of Ho Chi Minh City.
>
> By authority: Bai Hieu (Tu Tuan)
> Commander, Le Van Duyet Prison

There it is. According to the only official document they have ever given me, I was arrested for nothing and released for the same reason. I reflect that in some ways I'm lucky. Hundreds of thousands are imprisoned even longer for even less. At least I had an active political life and an unfortunate streak of independence to blame. But so many in prison don't even have that, and most of those in the hard labor camps—the soldiers and civil servants—are only pawns who were just trying to survive. Had they lived in Front-controlled areas, they would have made their accommodations with the Front; they would have been the revolution's cannon fodder and petty functionaries. Certainly the bulk of them are less "dangerous" than I. And certainly in the disease-infested jungle camps their fate is even worse.

As the driver pedals I remain quiet, musing. My silence has affected him, and he chooses not to disturb my reverie as we wheel randomly through the streets observing Saigon's new face. Most obvious is the quiet of the town. Though the sidewalks are as jammed as ever, few cars, and far fewer motor scooters with their cowboy drivers, traverse the streets. That internal combustion background noise is almost gone. Also gone are the *ao dai*, the graceful women's tunics with the long flaps that would catch every breeze. The streets used to be speckled with their colors. But only the clumps of loitering *bo dois* stand out now, in dull, mustard-yellow uniforms.

As we pass a restaurant it dawns on me that I might have something to eat, something like a *pho*, for example, Saigon's noodle soup standby, garnished with thin slices of succulent beef and a variety of tasty greens and sprouts. "Hey!" I tell the driver, suddenly finding myself salivating, "Let's stop over there on Hai Ba Truong Street and eat a *pho*. I invite you to join me."

The driver turns again. "What? A *pho*? Sure . . . I wouldn't mind at all. Actually I haven't eaten there in quite a while. Not that one should eat too much meat, understand. You've got to watch your diet, and meat's bad for the digestion. Still, if you're inviting me along, I can't very well refuse."

I've noticed that many of the city's shops are closed and shuttered with metal grills, quite a number with posters announcing Confiscated by the People upon Denunciation. But the Hai Ba Truong *pho* restaurant is open. Right in the center of Saigon, it was an old student hangout, noisy and alive; I used to love it for the raucous atmosphere and the deliciously steaming bowls of soup.

But now, there are only a few customers inside, speaking in low voices. A heavy, ominous atmosphere hangs over the place, as if something sinister is about to happen. At least so it seems to me, as I compare the scene now to what it was the last time I went in.

On the other hand, the driver loves it. The moment the *pho* arrives he begins slurping it happily, smacking his lips and sucking his teeth after each slice of meat, somehow keeping up a steady patter of talk the whole time. "You understand, I can hardly ever go for a *pho* these days, at four dong. Of course all the prices have gone up, but it's part of being free, huh? No Americans around to pay off their lackeys and whores, right? Everybody knows that. So it'll take a few years to get things going again by ourselves, but that's okay, it's the way it should be, am I right?"

He's certainly right about the prices. At four dong a *pho* that works out to more than seven times the old price—for a sparse few slices of meat instead of the brimming bowlful it used to have. Of course even before I went into prison the whole economy was spinning crazily. I do some quick mental arithmetic: if a bowl of *pho* is four dong, that's the equivalent of maybe half a week's pay for a pedicab driver, assuming they still make as much as they used to, which wasn't much. No wonder there aren't many customers.

I know this young driver will tell me anything I want to know (and more) if I handle him right. The only reason he hasn't opened up completely already is that he's unsure who I might be. So I say, "Listen, you know that building where you picked me up? You know what it is?"

His spoon pauses for a second on the way to his mouth: "Oh, sure, I drive by there a lot, near Duyet. There are always a couple of guards out front; it's, you know, some kind of administration building, right?"

"No, it's a prison, Le Van Duyet Prison. I just got out of it."

The spoon lowers to the bowl. "No kidding! I took you for some kind of official. I'll be darned, a prisoner! But listen"—a note of caution enters his voice— "for someone just out of jail you've got an awful lot of money."

I explain that at these prices the twenty dong in my pocket aren't going to go far.

"You can say that again!" says the driver, trying to smother a laugh. "You know what I make these days? Six, sometimes eight dong a month. Some months it's only enough to buy the rice ration and nothing else. You know what meat costs? Twelve dong a kilo—on the black market of course. Everybody's got coupons for a half a kilo a month at the store, but what does that mean? There's never any meat there anyway, so the damn things are worthless!"

I've obviously got him started on his favorite subject. As I sip the *pho* I listen to the tale of Saigon's economic woes as seen through the eyes of the pedicab driver: people selling off their televisions, furniture, and whatever else they own in order to eat, wives of jailed soldiers whoring for the *can bos* when there's no other way to earn money, the unemployed being shipped off to "New Economic Zones," and then sneaking back half-starved months later to live in hiding with relatives, sharing their already marginal rice rations.

While he's talking, I realize I've finished the *pho*. My first meal out of prison, and I've hardly tasted it. But what did I expect Saigon would be like? The depressing restaurant and the driver's description have put me in a more realistic mood than the euphoria that hit me outside the prison. Now I feel I'm ready to go home and face whatever's waiting there.

On the drive to my house on Hong Thap Tu Street, I prepare myself to meet my father and hear the story of my mother's death and funeral. I steel myself for the worst that might have happened to him, to the house, to my sister, while I've been gone. If you expect the very worst, I tell myself, anything different is a pleasant surprise. That was one of my rules of thumb for survival in jail. You can't breathe? Shit's oozing around your feet? Just get a good firm vision of your own death. After that, it's easy to start counting your blessings.

I have the driver stop at the end of the street, in front of 149, just down from 153/1 and 153/2, my brother's house and my father-in-law's. Although I insist on paying him, he forcefully rejects the money, telling me he can't take anything from a prisoner, and besides, the bowl of *pho* has more than covered the fare.

Apparently our little discussion has attracted attention. As the pedicab moves away, the mechanic who uses 149 as a motorcycle repair shop rushes out into the street and shakes both my hands in his. "Toai, you've been released! Welcome back! Welcome back!"

I'm taken aback by the mechanic's show of emotion. I didn't know him well. He was only an acquaintance, a neighbor among a street full of neighbors.

"Toai, I heard you've been at Le Van Duyet. My son's there too, Triet, you remember him don't you? Seventeen years old? They arrested him eight months ago. I don't know why, he was on his way to school. . . . Did you . . . see him by any chance?"

Unfortunately I didn't, or maybe I did. I can't remember very well what he looked like. I have the feeling he was only a child the last time I saw him, and I know I'd never recognize him unless he was pointed out to me. "No, no, I didn't," I tell the mechanic, whose eyes are beginning to tear and whose face is now a mask of unspoken misery.

Other neighbors are also gathering around now. "Toai, you're back, you poor dear." "Toai, you know your mother died, don't you? And that Yvonne left for France?" "Did you hear that your house was confiscated?"

The older people, friends of my mother's, weep and hug me. I sense in their feeling something more than the sympathy one might have for a neighbor struck by misfortune; it's more like the need for togetherness that people feel for each other in the face of a great catastrophe.

A sign catches my attention: Keep Your House Clean! Keep Your Street Clean! It's true, Hong Thap Tu Street has never been so clean. Then I see that the entranceway to my father-in-law's old house is closed off with barbed wire. With two of my mother's friends holding on to my hands, I walk up to the window and peer into the living room, bare without the divan and chairs, the table gone too. Beyond it, the dining room looks equally barren.

"Toai!"

I turn around. Across the street, ten yards away, my father and sister are at the doorstep of 153/1, moving toward me.

"Toai," my father hugs me—I can feel his arms trembling—"Toai, they let you come home for your mother's death."

"No, *Ba* [Father], I'm out for good. I've been released—with all my civil rights." Then again, loud enough for the neighbors to hear, "With all my civil rights!"

My father stammers in French, *"Très bien, très bien,"* his habitual phrase, a phrase belonging to the older generation of educated people. My sister is pressing her palms together: "Oh, Toai," she says, "our mother must have protected you."

Over the next few hours I need all the strength I have just to keep my composure. I hear the details of how, when I was arrested, Yvonne and my mother knocked on every door they could think of to find out what had happened to me. They went to all the prisons and police stations, also to my old friends from the student movement who were now officials. Even Duong Van Day, the young Communist I had helped get out of prison in 1970, couldn't tell them anything, nor could Huynh Tan Mam—who had become almost like another son to my mother after all the time he spent in my house and with everything he and I had been through together.

I hear how the house was taken after Yvonne's parents had left, and how Yvonne and the kids moved in with my parents. How a uniformed official had approached my parents, telling them he could "do something about my case," and how before he finally disappeared they had given him their entire savings, including the little cache of gold *luongs* that every Vietnamese keeps as an ultimate reserve.

Finally, I hear how my mother became ill with some kind of flu that would not leave. Aged, weak from worry and from the constant crying, she worsened quickly. My father and sister were desperate to get her into a hospital, but the political officer at the district health center refused authorization. The state was not about to waste its precious medical resources on a woman with one son in prison and another who had fled the country.

Afterward my sister went to plead with Huynh Tan Mam, who was now an administrator for one of Saigon's districts. Mam did everything he could. His feeling for my mother was as warm as hers for him. But it was five days before even he could get the proper authorization, and by the time he came to the house with it, my mother was dead.

Most painful of all for me to hear is the story of my mother's burial. With the private funeral homes closed down, each step required official authorization, and for a deceased person with such a reprehensible family background, each authorization presented problems. For my sister it was a living nightmare. First at the office that issued death certificates, where the bureaucrat in charge either was "not in at the moment" or would not see her. Then with the death certificate to the administrative section that issued permissions to buy a coffin from the coffin factory, then to the factory. At each place dealing with the same bureaucratic indifference and hostility.

Finally, with all the other arrangements made, she faced the task of extracting a car from the Transportation Office to carry the coffin. This last hurdle proved too much. But in the end my sister was able to borrow a car from a coworker. Buying sufficient gasoline on the black market, they drove my mother's body to Vinh Long Province, to the hamlet of Ba Cang, where her sister lived. They buried her there, in my aunt's garden.

◇   ◇   ◇

On November 2, the day following my release, I present myself to the neighborhood Public Security Office to put my papers in order, as the discharge orders directed me to do. I re-

My mother's funeral. My sister is in the middle at back wearing a white mourning headband. My father is in white to her right.

port at nine o'clock to the handsome five-story building, whose former tenants have either fled to the United States or been evicted. Already there are a dozen people in the hallway waiting for the lieutenant in charge. He arrives at ten, and my turn comes shortly after noon.

"I'm reporting, as they told me. I was released yesterday."

The lieutenant examines my discharge papers, where he reads: "Reason for Arrest: [this space left blank]; Reason for Release: [this space left blank];" Arrested for nothing, in jail two and a half years for nothing, then released for nothing. Really! I can practically hear his skepticism.

"Were you a puppet officer?"

"No."

"A puppet civil servant?"

"No."

"Then why were you arrested? Were you a thief? A looter? Did you try to escape?"

"No. I don't know why I was arrested, and I don't know why I was released. That's just what happened!"

"Listen," says the lieutenant, getting angry now, "you don't think I'm some kind of goddamn fool, do you?" He hits the table with his open hand, hard. I try to stay calm, to control my own temper.

"When he discharged me yesterday, the chief of Le Van Duyet stated that I had been found innocent of any wrong-doing. Colonel Tu Tuan said that."

I purposely use the prison chief's party name, instead of his real name, Bai Hieu. Party members, I knew, always pay attention to this kind of detail, and the one who uses the right code words places himself almost imperceptibly within the circle of the initiated.

"Well, I don't think I can do anything about your case in this office," says the lieutenant. "You'll have to go to the district."

Okay, I expected as much. But before I leave I insist on getting his signature on the papers, as proof that I have followed orders. After arguing halfheartedly about it, finally the lieutenant writes on the back: "Doan Van Toai reported today to the neighborhood Public Security Office, First District, Ho Chi Minh City. Signed: Lieutenant Le Phuoc Sung, chief, Public Security Office, thirteenth *phuong*. Dated: November 2, 1977."

At the First District police headquarters, a captain asks me the same set of questions the lieutenant asked, then gives me a form to fill out: another *so yeu li lich*, my autobiography, demanding the usual details about my parents, grandparents, siblings, wife, children, in-laws, where and when I have lived, studied and worked, whom I have associated with, and what my other activities have been. But there's a new twist. Before, I had always been given blank sheets of paper to fill out; now I've got real forms in front of me, complete with headings and standardized questions. So the inquisition has organized itself better for mass processing of its clients. I can imagine how difficult it has been up to now for the harried collators to get the millions of autobiographies into some kind of usable order.

I'm so used to writing my *so yeu li lich* that I surprise the captain with the speed of my responses. "You've answered all the questions already?" A glance through the forms tells him I have. "You have an identification card?"

After examining the card, he's more at ease. The fact that I have one proves that I've never been in the army or the civil service, and that no matter what it is I might have done, my rehabilitation is complete.

"Where do you live?"

"With my father."

"And your wife, does she live there too?"

"No. *Ve que.*"

Ve que means literally "return to one's village," or "return to one's land." I've been thinking about this for a while, how I will handle questions about my wife and children. Of course the disposition of my case is in the hands of the hierarchy, and they know all about my wife and where she is. Tu Tuan had even implied that I'd be allowed to join her in France. But at the same time, my fate depends on low-ranking officials like this police captain, and their suspicions must on no account be aroused. If this individual and his colleagues in the other bureaus I must go to know that my wife is in France and that I intend to go there myself, they won't even consider making any decisions about me. And any interruption in the chain of signatures and official stamps that I need to leave the country can set me back months, even years.

So *ve que* was the answer. The phrase is in constant use, since the government has been trying everything, including forced deportation, to get people out of the city and back either to their native villages or to the New Economic Zones. If my wife and children are *ve que*, then that's clearly where I should be too.

Reassured by the ease of this particular case (as strange as the discharge papers seem), and anxious to get on with the mountain of files piled on his desk, the captain writes on the back of the papers: "Doan Van Toai is permitted to remain in Ho Chi Minh City for a period not to exceed six months, following which he must *ve que vo* [join his wife in her land]." I try not to let the joy sparkle in my eyes.

"Come back tomorrow," says the captain. "The decision has to be approved by the head of the district."

The next day the precious countersigned document is placed in my hands. I am ready to climb the next step on the ladder to freedom.

◊   ◊   ◊

A little less than three weeks later, on November 20, Hong Thap Tu Street witnesses an event of no little magnificence: the arrival of Colonel Bai Hieu (Tu Tuan) in full panoply— personal car, escort car, armed guards, the works.

"I told you," he says, seated in the chair of honor at the head of the divan, "that I wanted to get to know you a little better. Now that you're free, it's easier."

Understanding the delicacy of the situation, I keep as quiet as possible. I want something from these people—to be allowed out. And without a doubt they are going to want something from me.

Once again Tu Tuan begins discussing the resolution of my case, emphasizing the fact that I have been found to be a "patriot," certainly no enemy of socialism or of the party. "The party," he says, "follows a humanitarian policy. To the extent possible it wishes to resolve the problems of those Vietnamese who have French citizenship, which includes, of course, your wife."

Tuan is a careful speaker, and I know he's chosen every word for a particular purpose. I listen intently. "We know, Toai, that you are eager to see your wife and children again, and eventually you will be able to." I wait silently for the inevitable "but," for the conditions. "Yes, one day you will be allowed to go to France, and when you are in France we hope you will do your best to let people know about the humanitarian policies our government follows, the humanitarian and socialist policies, if I may say so. You were a critic of the puppet regime, were you not? You have contacts in the West, you have been there before. You have the ability to speak correctly about the revolution that is taking place in our country."

I'm dumbfounded. They can put you away for twenty-eight months, they can kill your mother, and then they can ask you to your face to attest to their humanitarian policies? It's unbelievable. Even to someone familiar with their breathtaking arrogance, it's still barely credible.

Trying to test Tuan, I say, "And what if I speak against you after I'm abroad? Then what?"

Tuan smiles at me paternally, "The one who tells about it in advance does not do it. The one who says, 'And what if I betray you,' will not betray you."

"But I don't have any obligation to the party," I say. "None at all."

"Perhaps, but you do have common sense, don't you? And you do know that the party can defend itself very nicely."

Then, as if changing the subject, Tuan says, "I understand that you live in this house"—he pauses to look around—"with your father and sister."

There it is, he's said it. What he doesn't know is that my father and sister have already given me permission to speak out if I ever do get to France. The experience of losing the family's savings and watching the confiscation of the house, not to mention my arrest and a hundred similar tragedies among families they know, have demonstrated thoroughly to them the arbitrariness of life under the party. They could find themselves homeless and destitute tomorrow, and so could anyone else, regardless of what I might or might not do overseas. And my mother's death and funeral have given them a cold hatred that complements their resignation.

Colonel Tu Tuan is not aware of my father's and sister's feelings. But I am not sure exactly what he has in mind either. Could he truly think that after all that's happened I will blithely turn into a flack for the revolution? I know the line between arrogance and preposterousness is thin, but it does exist.

I have also been thinking hard about the lesson the former

Communists have taught me in jail. Once "they" have doubted someone, they will never trust him again. This has been clear to me since the assistant chief told me in Le Van Duyet that I would be expected to "cooperate." I decided then that the safest course would be to plead exhaustion and a broken spirit. If they are going to let me out, it will not be because they think I can help them—they will never trust me enough to seriously expect any help from me. It will be because they are convinced that I am not a danger to them.

This suggests to me that Tu Tuan's request that I become an overseas spokesman should not be taken at face value. They do not need me for that, nor can they really expect it of me. And if Tu Tuan's talk about "doing my best to explain the humanitarian policies of the revolution" is not serious, then it is a ploy—a test of some sort.

I know that any sudden enthusiasm for the revolution on my part will be viewed as a sign of deceitfulness. I also sense that this self-controlled manipulator of men is testing me for signs of political vitality. How did he put it—"a critic of the puppet regime," "contacts in the West," "the ability to speak"? Does he wonder if I am still dangerous? Still capable of political action? of doing active harm? There may indeed be reasons for letting me out; France may well be pressuring Hanoi to "resolve the problems of French citizens." But is Toai reliable? I realize that if I were Tu Tuan, that is precisely what I would be trying to find out.

"Yes, Colonel Tu Tuan," I say, "we live here together. As you know, my mother has recently died. It has been a very hard time for us. My only wish now is to be reunited with my family—to see my boys again and to lead a normal life. Can you understand how I feel?"

"Yes," he says, with a hint of sympathy, "of course I understand. Your family reunification will be taken under advisement."

◊   ◊   ◊

From that point on I know exactly the role I have to play. I swim and play tennis, trying to build my strength back up.

I spend time with friends, but stay aloof from talk of politics. I am, I say, just happy to be alive and to be out, the luckiest man in the world. I am cynical to a fault, disillusioned with every-thing, and interested only in myself and in my own pleasures.

When word gets around that I am out of prison, old col-leagues start to come by, student movement people, remnants of the old "third force," even some who years ago joined the underground. All of them want to "do something." "Toai," they say, "look around, the country is dying under these bas-tards. People are starving to death. Everybody's fed up with it. Let's get something started." But each time I take the coward's way out: "Look, I know how bad it is, I've been in prison for the last twenty-eight months. But I'll tell you, that's enough for me. I'm through with it, I'm planning to go back to Vinh Long."

I begin to develop a reputation as a quitter. It's just what I want. I know that "they" are watching.

Meanwhile I start to sell off the household furniture. Nei-ther my father nor I have ration cards. I am only a temporary resident (prior to *ve que*), and since my brother Trung fled the country, my father has been excluded from those who have the right to buy rice. But there's always the black market, and for-tunately, the house is well stocked with furniture and fixtures.

In 1977 Saigon is swarming with buyers for every kind of household article—mainly northern cadres who have come south to visit or for temporary assignments and are anxious to carry back with them as much as they can to dress up or fix their own homes. The northern economy has not turned out consumer goods for a generation, and the southern economy has been paralyzed since the takeover. With no foreign cur-rency, imports are nonexistent. All this means that the south, particularly Saigon, has become a bazaar of consumer treasures for the northern officials and soldiers, newly awake to their own deprivation.

In this climate, the principle that one man's trash is an-other's treasure carries the day. You can sell anything: old clothes, furniture, sinks, toilets, building material ripped from

My sister and I—about a month after my release

your house. All of it brings a price, and all of it eventually finds its way into northern homes. As I become aware of the pervasiveness of this trade, I realize that even without jobs, my father and I can live for perhaps a year and a half on the house and its contents.

So I begin to sell the furniture, slowly, starting with the dining room chairs. The money that comes in supplements the salary my sister still manages to bring home from her job teaching Vietnamese literature in high school. She has kept this position, in spite of her family connections, through the quiet intervention of Huynh Truong Truc, the head of Ho Chi Minh City's education department. Truc's father (also a teacher) and my father were close friends even before the French war, and Truc himself was my father's student in the Rach Ranh pagoda school.

December passes, then January and February. Each month sees the house a little emptier. One by one I sell all the beds, keeping a cot for my father to sleep on and mattresses for my sister and myself. There is no further word from Tu Tuan, and I have by now gotten practically all the signatures I need for an exit visa. But there is something holding up the last step, some administrative difficulty that frustrates all my attempts to identify it or discover how to deal with it.

With the time on my Ho Chi Minh City residence permit beginning to run short, I decide to ask for help from Duong Van Day, who has recently become the chief of the First District, a position of considerable power. I never knew Day well, but I led the effort that got him out of jail seven years ago, and I feel he owes me some help at least. When I call, he readily agrees to see me.

Day's office, in a luxurious building near the old Intercontinental Hotel, is a spacious suite furnished with beautiful Louis XVI–style pieces that must be from the collection of some particularly wealthy French colonialist. The irony of it makes me smile, but only until I catch myself. Day's secretary brings coffee (an unusual treat), and then Day himself appears, looking thin and overburdened.

"Toai, come on in. What can I do for you?"

For Day's benefit I describe my situation, putting heavy emphasis on my fatigue and on my desire simply to mind my own business—in the company of my wife and children. I ask if there is any way that he might possibly help speed up my visa application.

"Well," he says, "I can try. But that's not such an easy thing to do . . ."

To this I hint, with the greatest subtlety I'm capable of, that however poor I may be, I would somehow show my gratitude to anyone who could help.

Day says he'll see what he can do, and that he'll get back to me one way or the other.

A few days later, the First District deputy comes to see me in my house to say that he thinks he might be able to do something for me. But though my case isn't impossible, he has discovered there are a lot of difficulties involved and that a great deal of effort will be necessary to resolve it. Not to put too fine a point on it, he believes the whole situation can be settled for sixty gold *luongs*. Sixty, I tell him, is impossible. But I think I might be able to raise thirty, then send him thirty more once I get to France.

Day is insistent; there are a lot of people who must be induced to cooperate, and it is, as I know, a rare privilege that I am asking. What he says is no doubt true, but that doesn't mean I can draw water from a stone. It takes a round of haggling before I'm able to get him to agree.

Once I have Day's assurances, I begin to raise money. My father and sister are as determined as I am, though I know that they are sick inside about my leaving. Still, once I get out I can begin sending money back. With parcels from overseas, life could become little easier. We even talk about finding a way out for them by boat. But my father's mind is firmly made up. He's going to stay in Vietnam no matter what. It is his country, and he is going to die in it. "But you, Toai, you must get out!"

Faster now, I sell of most of the remaining furniture. I get a huge price for the glass windows and the garage's metal roofing. My father even sells the small parcel of land he owns in Vinh Long. In the end, I get the money. And then, as promised, I have the exit visa in my hand as well.

On May 11, 1978, my father and sister go with me to the in-town air terminal, from which I will take a bus to the airport for the weekly five o'clock Air France refugee flight to Paris. In the same sports bag that accompanied me on the last plane from Qui Nhon to Saigon three years earlier, I pack underwear, some family picture albums, and a pair of socks. From the side flap my tennis racket sticks out. I also carry a small cylindrical aspirin tube wrapped in plastic and inserted deep into my rectum. Inside is a tightly rolled-up United States hundred-dollar bill that I bought on the black market, and several closely written sheets of paper on which I have recorded lawyer Tran Danh San's declaration of Human Rights.

In the outer terminal we say good-bye. I look at my father for what I know will be the last time. Throughout his life he has been a strict man who always gave off an aura of tensile strength. But now his face has aged immeasurably, and his body no longer has its obstinate stiffness. In the last six months I have seen him cry often at reminders of my mother's death and my brother's family. He is crying now, as is my sister. My eyes, though, are dry as I hold my family to me, my face set against the waves of guilt that wash through me. I know, as I feel his bony chest pressed against mine, that as I have failed my mother, so I will fail him, that he too will die untended by his son.

◊   ◊   ◊

Inside the terminal building I join a long line of people waiting to be processed. With mounting apprehension I see as I draw closer to the front that the guards are inspecting each person and each article of clothing meticulously. They feel along the seams of shirts, searching for items that might be sewn into cuffs or collars. They make people open their mouths so they can check inside. "Anything to declare?" they ask threateningly. "Any lies and you won't leave, now or ever!"

With each person they take five to ten minutes, looking carefully at their papers and asking questions. By the time my turn comes, I have calmed myself enough to put on a show of innocence and nonchalance. I'm not immediately concerned about the aspirin tube; they are obviously not doing routine body searches (they almost never do). But I am shaking inside about what they might find in my papers, all of which are proper except for the Ho Chi Minh City residence permit with its order to *ve que vo.*

When they take my documents away, obviously for a closer look, I almost faint. As far as I've seen, they have not done that to anyone else. But the fright passes when after a time they bring them back and resume the questioning: "Anything to declare? The truth! Dollars? Gold?"

"Absolutely not! Go ahead and search."

They do, but cursorily. And then I'm through.

At Ton San Nhut Airport we wait for hours, repeatedly glancing out the window for signs of the Air France jet that will take us out. Finally, at four in the afternoon, the room fills

My father and I visiting my mother's grave shortly before I left the country

with excitement as the giant plane taxies into sight. A short while later the French pilots walk through the waiting room and are immediately accosted by people asking them about the departure—people who in fact simply can't control their urgent desire to talk to a foreigner, to some personal symbol of life outside. Their enthusiasm, however, is cut off sharply by a guard's curt command: "Hey! You! No talking aloud! Just sit down!" The waiting room is still Vietnamese territory, and no breach of discipline will be tolerated, regardless of the fact that in another hour the passengers will be talking about anything in the world they want to talk about.

This last reminder of the giant prison camp Vietnam has become fades quickly as we board the plane and take our seats. Then the engines build to a rumbling crescendo, and we are racing down the runway, the airport buildings flashing past outside the window. As the jet lifts off the ground, a tumultuous round of applause sweeps through the plane, a spontaneous outburst of relief and joy that we, the fortunate, have broken free at last.

Epilogue

We arrived at Charles de Gaulle Airport in Paris early the following morning. Despite the hour, a crowd of relatives and friends swarmed around the arriving passengers, welcoming them to their new lives. But neither Yvonne nor her parents were among them; I had written nothing to them about my departure. Even after I had received the exit visa and bought the ticket, I knew there was nothing certain.

For the same reason, I did not join the applause when the plane took off, thinking to myself, "Just because we've left Saigon doesn't mean we've landed in Paris." It wasn't until sometime later that I began to feel safe—after the captain's deep voice had come over the public address system, announcing in French: "Ladies and gentlemen, we have now left the airspace of Vietnam. Congratulations on your new freedom!"

From Charles de Gaulle I took a taxi to Yvonne's parents' apartment and climbed the stairs to the fifth-floor address. When my mother-in-law opened the door, she stood there for a moment in shock, as if trying to decide whether to believe her eyes. Then she was hugging me, crying and talking, asking me a thousand questions and telling me everything at once about Yvonne and the children and their lives in Paris.

Nobody else was home: Yvonne was working at an insurance company, the boys were at school, my father-in-law was at his restaurant job. After we talked for a while and she fed me, I went out to find a telephone booth to call the Vietnamese Student Association* to try to set up a meeting for the following day. I had no idea what kind of reception I might get there, but I knew that my days of playing a broken-spirited prison invalid were over for good.

That afternoon I went with my mother-in-law to pick the boys up from school. Only Dinh (at seven, the eldest) recognized me at all. But even he wasn't sure, and he looked me over warily, deciding to wait before making any firm commitments. Binh (five) and Huy (four) hadn't any idea at all who this stranger was that grandmother was making so much of, and Huy objected noisily to my attempts to pick him up and carry him in my arms. As we walked back he held tight to his grandmother's hand, looking up occasionally and catching my eye as I gazed at him.

At night Yvonne walked into the apartment and stopped, speechless, on the threshold of the living room. Neither of us could find words as we embraced for the first time in almost three years, losing ourselves in each other's tears.

That evening, the four adults sat in the living room and talked as the children played loud games on the floor. While we exchanged news and stories, my mother-in-law kept trying to get the boys to come over to me, telling them, "That's your dad, that's *Ba* Toai, say hello to *Ba* Toai." (*Ba* [Dad] is the usual term of address used by Vietnamese children, but *Dad-Toai* violated the norm. My careful parents and parents-in-law had taught the children to use this expression from the time they were able to speak, as insurance in case they ever got sepa-

---

* The Vietnamese Student Association in Paris had been an active political force on the side of the revolution since Ho Chi Minh's visit to France in 1946.

rated from the family. After my arrest, the custom was kept up, in the hope that at least their father's name would stick in the boys' memory.) Eventually they began to get the idea. "Ba-Toai" was familiar, even if the man himself wasn't, and the names helped them feel comfortable with this new addition to the already crowded household.

◇   ◇   ◇

The following days I spent meeting with political leaders and student activists in France's large Vietnamese community. The emigrés had supported the Vietminh against the French and the Vietcong against the Americans. They had provided money and supplies, and had agitated vigorously for an end to both conflicts. Over the period of two wars they played the same role in France that the American antiwar movement played during the latter years of the United States' involvement.

These were people I felt comfortable with, people with whom I shared ideals, and with whom I had also shared a deadly naiveté. They were, I realized, the audience I wanted. It was their passion and commitment, and those of people who believed as they did, that had clarified and focused for the outside world the issues of Vietnam's struggle for independence. And it was their efforts that had been so callously manipulated and betrayed by the revolution.

But for the most part, I was greeted with a confused embarrassment. These people had cheered the revolutionary victory, and now they were doing their best to believe that under the new order the nation was prospering. During the war I had been one of them, but now I brought unpalatable news. Even the few monks and antiwar people who had begun to understand the nature of the new order were dispirited and tired, unable to think about the implications of what had happened.

Finally the Que Me (Homeland) group, previously an antiwar organization, now increasingly concerned with human rights, heard that I was in Paris and worked hard to give me a forum. A press conference was set up for May 30, 1978, to which they invited all the leading French newspapers and a

In Paris with Yvonne and the three boys

group of East European dissidents and human rights activists, including the Czech Illios Yannakakis and the Russians Natalya Gorbanevskaya and Leonid Pliouchtch.

We rented for the conference the same hotel at which Nguyen Thi Binh, the Front's foreign minister* had given her famous press conferences during the Paris negotiations. We publicized it as best we could. And then we worried that no one would show up.

We needn't have been so anxious. That morning the room was crowded, according to the Que Me people, as crowded as it had ever been for Mme. Binh. The entire French press, radio, and television seemed to be there. They listened intently to my

* Technically the foreign minister of the Provisional Revolutionary Government.

long statement and to my recitation of lawyer San's Declaration of Human Rights, then asked question after question.

That night I couldn't sleep, wondering what kind of treatment the conference would receive. Early in the morning, I went down to the street for the papers, and there it was, front-page news in *Le Monde* and many of the other papers, of both the Left and Right, reporting the facts of the gulag Vietnam had become.

Coverage, as always, attracted more coverage. Conferences and interviews followed each other—*The Observer*, the BBC, *L'Express*, even *Newsweek*—and I was invited on a speaking tour by the various Vietnamese organizations in France, Germany, Holland, and Belgium. At first I was surprised by the size and intensity of these audiences, as if their attention had suddenly been riveted by the fate of their homeland. Then I realized the reason for all the agitation: Fate had made me the first articulate messenger from the new order, and one, moreover, who had experienced its workings in his flesh.

The effect was dramatic. For thirty years the motivating passion of the Vietnamese people had been to free themselves from a shameful colonial heritage. Against the French, the issues had been clear and morally certain. Against the Americans and their protégés, they had been less so. But to my generation, at least to those who had not seen life in the post-Geneva "democratic" North, the outlines of the issues had remained the same. We were part of a heroic struggle to assert our Vietnamese identity against the backdrop of a century of Western domination.

But shortly after the complete victory of that struggle, the Vietnamese in Europe began to receive intimations that the promise of a new flourishing of Vietnamese life had been built on lies. People had discounted the stories of those Vietnamese who had fled in 1975 (much as I had discounted the reports of Catholics who had fled south after Geneva). And they tried hard to avoid believing the scattered and incomplete reports from refugees who had begun to escape by boat after the new order had established its apparatus. But now the French newspapers were headlining news about the hard labor camps and prisons, and about rule by starvation and blackmail, and the Vietnamese in France found it impossible any longer to avert their eyes.

The understanding hit them that what they had believed was a heroic struggle for independence, on the same order as the historic struggles against the Chinese, had been manipulated from the start by the architects of an insidious inhumanity, far worse than that of the foreign oppressors on whom they had poured their hatred. At each of these meetings I shared my perception that we—those of us who had supported the cause—had been damned to contribute to the tragedy. And now we were condemned to recognize and bear witness to the nation's fate. We (and by this I meant the Vietnamese people) had fought magnificently against our outside enemies, but we had been powerless to protect ourselves from the enemy within.

◊   ◊   ◊

From the *Newsweek* interview and other reports, the story of the Vietnamese gulag made its way to the United States. I exchanged letters with my old friend Jerry Tinker, for whom I had worked as a student interviewer back in 1966 and 1967. He wrote that he was now an assistant to Senator Edward Kennedy. He had read one of the articles and was happy to learn that I had gotten out. From the United States too came invitations to speak at meetings sponsored by various Vietnamese refugee associations and by American colleges and universities, Harvard University Law School among them.

In the late fall of 1978, I left France for America. I spent two months in Canada talking about Vietnamese human rights issues, then I traveled to the United States. Everywhere I went, the story was covered in newspaper articles and interviews. Following the Harvard speech, I was invited to address the National Press Club in Washington. There, sharing the dais with me was the Buddhist philosopher and translator, Nguyen Huu Hieu, whom I had first met in Zone C after Dr.

Quang agreed to treat his abscess. Hieu too had been released, and had escaped Vietnam by boat at about the same time I left.

After an emotional reunion and an enthusiastic reception from the Press Club audience we flew together from Washington to California, where the University of California at Berkeley had again invited me to speak, though this time my lecture was sponsored by the Institute for East Asian Studies, rather than an antiwar group.

At San Francisco airport I walked through the gate to find a welcoming group from Berkeley and from the local Vietnamese community. Standing in the middle of the small crowd, beaming with happiness, was my brother Trung, his wife Mai, and their youngest daughter. In the confusion of the moment we embraced and joked briefly, struggling in this public place to deflect the emotion and relief we felt at being together again.

Later, at the home of a friend where I was staying, Trung brought me up to date. He and his family had gone by fishing boat all the way to Singapore. From there an American ship had taken them to Guam, and from Guam they had flown to a refugee camp in Pennsylvania. After several months he had moved the family to California, where a friend had arranged to sponsor them. There Trung and his wife had first opened a restaurant, counting on Mai's cooking skills to draw the customers and his business acumen to make a success of it. Their confidence in Mai, he laughed, had been well placed.

When it became clear that the restaurant would not support them and the seven children, Trung had rented a small parcel of farmland and had begun to grow oriental vegetables. He and Mai worked the land with help from the children who were old enough, and now it looked as if the work was beginning to pay off.

I marveled at my brother. An educated man, he had been a manager and business consultant in Vietnam and had owned his own plantations there. He had arrived in the United States without a nickel, and now he and his wife were doing the backbreaking labor necessary to put a roof over their heads and food on the table. When the South fell, he lost everything except his resilience, his humor, and his philosophical cast of mind. The things he needed most and that most endeared him to me—those he had retained in great measure.

In San Francisco I also met Nguyen Cong Hoan, the Buddhist opposition assemblyman under Thieu who had been chosen as a representative to the 1976 Unified Assembly in Hanoi. His escape from Vietnam in 1977 had sparked hope among the prisoners, who thought Hoan's message to the West would focus international opprobrium on Vietnam and force improved conditions in the prisons and labor camps. That hope had died quickly when after a month or two nothing further had been heard of Hoan or his quest.

Hoan and I had known each other slightly during the student movement days, when the Buddhist student groups had often cooperated closely with the student union in organizing demonstrations, marches, and sit-ins. Now we felt something like a sense of shared destiny. He told me he had been disgusted by the rubber-stamp conformity demanded of representatives in Hanoi. In the Saigon Assembly, he said, at least you could speak your mind and represent your people—if you were willing to stand up to the intimidation and abuse. But in Hanoi you were simply an automaton whose presence and vote were required to stage the show of unanimity ordered by the party.

Unable to stomach the hypocrisy, and sickened by his insider's knowledge of the party's policies of revenge and brutal social reorganization, he had fled in a fishing boat from his coastal province of Phu Yen. Making his way to Japan, he gave a press conference that attracted international coverage, then was invited to Washington to testify before a House committee investigating human rights in Vietnam. For that testimony the Hanoi authorities had sentenced him to death in absentia.

Like the prisoners, he had believed that the West must be told about the monumental deception carried out by the Communist regime. Specifically, the Western antiwar movement with all its energy and commitment to the cause of Vietnamese freedom must be educated to what was really taking place. Once they knew, he thought, they would turn their attention to the task of pressuring Vietnam's leaders back inside the pale of human conduct. Hoan smiled wanly as he told me this; "Toai," he said, "you're excited by this trip and by your successes, but believe me, you will get nowhere substantial with these people. Vietnam to them was a fad, or something they did out of anger at their own government. Now they don't care, I doubt if they ever did. It's not their fight."*

As if to reinforce Hoan's remarks, my reception at Berkeley, while not unfriendly, was a good deal cooler than it had been in 1970, when I was shouting about self-determination and getting the United States out of the war. Nevertheless, at Berkeley I had one of those chance encounters that have important consequences. In the audience was a representative of Amnesty International who was a friend of Joan Baez, who had been a leading antiwar figure. Through this woman a luncheon meeting was arranged for Hieu, myself, and Baez. We discussed the prison and camp conditions in Vietnam, and Hieu and I described the system of oppression that had settled onto the nation's people. As we parted, I told her, "If your cause was the suffering of the Vietnamese people, then that is still your cause."

I did not yet know whether Hoan's perception of the antiwar movement was generally accurate, but I found Baez to be intelligent, compassionate, and openminded. After our talk she thought deeply about what had happened in Vietnam, and about the principles that had brought her into the antiwar movement in the first place. As a consequence of our discussion, she began to investigate the Vietnamese human rights record more thoroughly, an issue most Americans were happy to ignore.

---

* Nguyen Cong Hoan's personal crusade was not entirely unsuccessful. Shortly after I met him he was invited to Holland to address the Dutch parliament. Subsequent to his speech, Holland withdrew its aid to Vietnam over the regime's violations of basic human rights.

With Joan Baez and Nguyen Huu Hieu

Finally, Baez wrote an open letter to the *New York Times* (May 30, 1979) addressed to the Socialist Republic of Vietnam and signed by seventy-eight other prominent individuals, including Cesar Chavez, Daniel Berrigan, I. F. Stone, Jerome Weisner, and Nat Hentoff. It read in part:

> We appeal to you to end the imprisonment and torture—to allow an international team of neutral observers to inspect your prisons and reeducation centers.
> We urge you to follow the tenets of the Universal Declaration of Human Rights and the International Covenant for Civil and Political Rights which, as a member of the United Nations, your country is pledged to uphold.

We urge you to reaffirm your stated commitment to the principles of freedom and human dignity . . . to establish real peace in Vietnam.

For her efforts, Baez was attacked by Jane Fonda in a letter circulated among a large number of former antiwar movement people and excoriated in an open letter entitled "The Truth About Vietnam" (New York Times, June 24, 1979) and signed by another group of antiwar people who "recognize and acknowledge the remarkable spirit of moderation, restraint and clemency with which the reeducation program was conducted." This letter continued:

> Vietnam now enjoys human rights as it has never known in history as described in the International Covenant on Human Rights: the right to a job and safe, healthy working conditions, the right to join trade unions, the right to be free from hunger, from colonialism and racism. Moreover, they receive—without cost— education, medicine and health care, human rights we in the United States have yet to achieve.

The signers of his letter included Harry Bridges, Joshua Kunitz, Corliss Lamont, and Karen Ackerman.

When I saw this letter some months later, I was especially taken by the absolute conviction of the writers, although to my knowledge none of them had ever seen the inside of a Vietnamese reeducation camp or prison, and none had ever experienced the "free health care" or the "right to be free from hunger" guaranteed by the Socialist republic.

Even more striking in the letter was the burning hatred they evinced for their own government. And it was this emotion, still red-hot six years after the 1973 pullout of American troops from Vietnam, that inspired my thinking about the psychological consequences of Vietnam for future "nationalistic" conflicts (a subject to which I would in the future devote a great deal of attention.) The letter combined an utterly simplistic understanding of Vietnamese issues with a deep antagonism toward American motives—obviously a potent mixture. I won-

dered how pervasive that orientation was in American public
opinion and whether it would permanently debilitate United
States policy toward Vietnam.

But these thoughts were still a bit in the future as Hieu and
I left Berkeley for more speaking dates in Los Angeles. When
we arrived, Hieu informed me that he would now undertake a
plan he had been incubating for a while, but had not told me
about. Although primarily known for his translations of classic
Western philosophers, my traveling companion had also ren-
dered several French, German, and American poets and novel-
ists into Vietnamese. His work on the novels of Henry Miller
was especially notable; I had in fact greatly enjoyed Hieu's
translations of Miller myself. "Did you know," said the former
monk, "that Miller lives right here in Los Angeles?"

I didn't.

"Yes, in Beverly Hills," he said, taking an address book out
of his pocket.

Before I knew it, we had ducked into a little florist shop to
buy a flower and were in a taxi on our way to Beverly Hills.
While the taxi waited we deposited the flower on Miller's
doorstep with a brief letter under it, introducing ourselves, asking to meet the author, and leaving the phone number of the
apartment where we would be staying.

The next day, Henry Miller's secretary called with an invitation.

Miller I knew as an analyst of human behavior who had also
been a strong critic of American society. But though Hieu
might have had some idea of what to expect from the author, I
was surprised by the ancient, bony vision in a red plaid bath-
robe who greeted us from his wheelchair. Miller was eighty-
eight years old at the time, and though his eyes were not clear
and his voice was rough with age, there was no question that
the juices of life were still flowing freely. He was mentally
sharp and vastly curious, a wonderful listener and raconteur.

In two days of talking with him it struck us that he was still
rather surprised by his own fame and angry at the same time
that he wasn't even more famous. I mentioned that since he

was one of my favorite writers I occasionally mentioned him in my discussions with American college students. "Sometimes," I told him, "they haven't heard of you."

"Yeh? Really?" came the gravelly reply, and after a moment of silence, "Well, they're idiots, then!"

He told us that it wasn't until he was more than sixty that he felt he had succeeded. Now his books sold in the most surprising places. "The strange thing is, you know where I'm beginning to be famous, selling like hotcakes? The state of Mississippi—Mississippi! Kosciusko, Mississippi! I've got a friend, a bookseller down there, he talks to them, tells them 'come in, sit down.' They buy the books."

He had a lively interest in Vietnam as well. He hadn't known his books were favorites there, but he had thought a great deal about the war, and he was concerned by the outpouring of boat refugees that had already begun. "Oh, yeah," he growled, "I've thought about that, I think it's just as bad as the Nazis."

◇   ◇   ◇

I came back to France overflowing with images of the United States. My chief impression was of the country's vitality and intellectual excitement. I had spent months talking with specialists on Vietnam, former antiwar people, and thousands of students who wanted to know what had happened, and what was happening now. (Vietnam was front-page news again with its invasion of Cambodia.) I found that the experiences I had had on the tour had pushed my own thinking in new directions.

From the time I was arrested, certainly from the time I was transferred from Tran Hung Dao to Le Van Duyet, I had been consumed by the desire to record the story of Vietnam's prisons, and to tell it. It was a desire spurred by my personal outrage over what I and hundreds of thousands of others were living through. The natural audience for this history I saw as the Vietnamese community abroad who had supported the revolution, and the foreign antiwar movements that had done so much to bring it about. They would be moved, I thought; they must be moved by the suffering to which they (like I) had unknowingly contributed.

But in the United States I had begun to see things differently. It was not that my personal shock at the revolution's betrayal of ideals had worn off; it never would. But I began to understand that the plain fact of the betrayal was less important than the method of the betrayal, which had been the single most potent weapon in the arsenal of the Vietnamese Communist party.* My trip to the United States had helped me to distance myself from the personal dimension of the tragedy. And it helped me toward an understanding of the more global significance of what had happened.

I knew that my anger was in part due to the cold-blooded way in which the revolution had victimized my ideals. Motivated by my hatred of the dictators and by my view of myself as a Vietnamese nationalist, I had played a role in weakening the American-backed regime and isolating it from domestic and international support. Now I understood it was not that my motives had been wrong, but that my understanding had been woefully incomplete. The passion of my ideals, combined with a belief in my own political intelligence, had led me down a trail at whose unforseen end lay terror and destitution for the nation. And I had walked that trail in company with millions of other passionate idealists, Vietnamese, French, and American.

Together we had been caught in a "people's war," a concept of fighting that gave precedence to the techniques of psychological warfare. As the American military had belatedly recognized, the battlefield of this "people's war" was the mind and heart of the Vietnamese peasant. But, as no one sufficiently realized, the battlefield was also the minds and hearts of those who created public opinion in Vietnam and in the West. And the way to those minds and hearts, the party saw, was through

---

* During the war years the official name of the party was the *Dong Lao Dong*, the Workers' party.

the ideals they shared: a hatred for colonialism, an abhorrence of violence, a love of social welfare and of liberal democracy.

That was why, from the beginning, the Vietnamese Communist party had built its strategy, not on the forthright social promises of Marxism (the rock upon which the Russian and Chinese parties had built their revolutions), but on the Vietnamese people's fierce desire for national independence. That was why in two wars the Vietnamese Communist party had hidden itself in the background and created in its place two "fronts," the Vietminh and the Vietcong, whose appeal was to the grass roots longings of the Vietnamese—and to the ingrained ideals of the very Western nations that were the party's bitterest enemies. (In 1945 Ho Chi Minh had proclaimed the independence of the Vietnamese people in the following words: "We hold the truths that all men are created equal, that they are endowed by their creator with certain inalienable rights, among which are Life, Liberty, and the Pursuit of Happiness.")

The results I could judge from my own experience. The venal habits, political suppression, and common brutality of the Saigon regime I saw firsthand, along with the war's human carnage and the grotesque social impact of the American army. But the heart of the other side remained hidden.

I was familiar enough with the effects of newspaper and television coverage to know that the Americans' images of the war were of course far less comprehensive than were my own. What they saw, through the eyes of their reporters and cameramen, was the dramatic and vivid account of South Vietnam's civil disarray and her tragic human suffering. What their reporters could not convey to them was the secret strategy that made the American people themselves the chief target of this "people's war." And what they could not see at all were the iron social theories and the alien disregard for human decency that animated those whose target they were.

I knew too that Vietnam was not an isolated incident on the stage of world affairs, that the "people's war" techniques that had been developed there were applicable to every Third

World conflict in which the West had an interest. But just as Vietnam was a casebook for revolutionary strategy—a casebook to be studied with the greatest care by the world's democracies and by the world's emerging nations, for whom the Communist road to national liberation is in fact a road to national desolation.

◊　　　　　◊　　　　　◊

In the fall of 1979 I returned to the United States for another lecture tour. During this stay arrangements were made for me to come to the Fletcher School of Law and Diplomacy at Tufts University as a special student in international relations. The following spring I took up residence in Boston, Massachusetts, where I was joined several months later by my family.

I've been living in the United States ever since. I have found it a blessed land, a place where one can work freely and give one's children a decent life, a place where one can be oneself and go about the business of life unafraid and unintimidated. I have also found that Americans are largely unimpressed by the peculiar beauties of their culture—the rights they enjoy. Perhaps it is the immigrants' function from generation to generation to remind them of what a treasure it is they own.

But regardless of my love for this country, I share with every other Vietnamese a longing to return. It will not, I fear, be fulfilled. And even if it were possible, our children are now American. They have their language here and their lives here. To live in a land that will always be half alien, with our children who belong to this land as much as they belong to us, that is the burden of our failure. Yet with all the longing for an impossible return, we know that we are the fortunate, that we, at least, are free.

Doan Van Toai
Berkeley, California
June 1985

Appendix

Yvonne Vo Duc (Doan Van Toai's wife) worked in the personnel department of a large bank in Boston when she first came to the United States. After the family moved to California in 1982 she became a farmer, working with her brother-in-law. For the past two years she has been a social worker.

Doan Minh Trung (Doan Van Toai's brother) became an American citizen in 1980. He and his wife Mai are now successful farmers in California's Central Valley. Of their seven children, one is a computer engineer, four are in college, and the remaining two are still in school.

Doan Trang (Doan Van Toai's sister) fled Vietnam as a boat refugee in 1980. After spending some time in an Indonesian refugee camp, she was sponsored by her brother and came to the United States. Living in California, she worked as a teacher's aide and studied computer science. She is currently a computer technician in San Francisco.

349

Doan Minh Chau (Doan Van Toai's father) gave his daughter permission to escape in 1980. Subsequently he left Saigon and went back to his home town of Cai Von in the Mekong Delta to live with his brother. In 1983 at the age of seventy-five he died of complications stemming from a viral infection. For him, as for his wife before him, no medical treatment was available.

Nguyen Cong Hoan (opposition assemblyman) escaped from Vietnam by boat in 1977 and came to the United States in 1978. At first he worked for an electronics company, then opened a printing business specializing in Vietnamese Buddhist literature. In 1979 he addressed the Dutch parliament on Vietnamese human rights issues. Subsequently he was invited to testify before the U.S. House of Representatives. After his escape from Vietnam he was tried and sentenced to death in absentia. His wife and four children were evicted from their home and the children expelled from school. In 1979 they too became boat refugees, eventually joining him in California.

Tran Van Tuyen (the "dean" of opposition assemblymen) was sent to the Long Thanh reeducation camp in June of 1975. In 1976 he was transferred to a camp in the North, where he died of a "cerebral hemorrhage."

Venerable Thich Tri Quang (leader of South Vietnam's wartime Buddhist opposition) is presently under house arrest in Saigon's Anh Quang pagoda. After the war the independent Unified Buddhist Church was suppressed and its place taken by the government-sponsored Patriotic Unified Church. Tri Quang was one of the many religious leaders who refused to cooperate.

Venerable Thich Thien Minh (chief strategist of the wartime Buddhist opposition movement) was permitted to exercise his religious functions until 1978. At that point he was arrested for allegedly giving a sermon calling on worshippers to oppose socialism. Imprisoned in the Ham Tan Prison, after several months the government announced that he had died of a "cerebral hemorrhage." Buddhist spokesmen continue to insist that he was tortured to death.

Venerable Thich Thien Hue (imprisoned with Toai in Le Van Duyet) was released in the fall of 1977 after spending a year and a half in prison. As far as is known, he still lives in the Saigon pagoda that took him in following his release.

Nguyen Huu Hieu (former monk who addressed National Press Club with Toai in 1978) currently lives in Washington, D.C. He has lectured widely on Vietnamese issues and writes on cultural concerns for several Vietnamese-language magazines in the United States. He served as editor of *Thoi Tap* (*The Times*), and now devotes himself chiefly to research on Buddhist subjects, translating, and painting.

Nhu Phong (the hunger striker) was transferred to Chi Hoa Prison in 1982, then to the notorious Phu Khanh camp in Phu Yen Province. As far as is known, he is still alive in Phu Khanh.

Dang Giao (writer who was arrested under the "3/76 Law" with his wife and newborn son) was released in 1980. He supports himself by making lacquerware while awaiting an emigration permit.

Tran Danh San (lawyer who led the Declaration of Human Rights group) was transferred from Le Van Duyet Prison to a hard labor camp in central Vietnam. As far as is known, he is still alive.

Nguyen Van Thang (the "southernist") was imprisoned in Le Van Duyet until 1982. He now works as a carpenter.

Huynh Tan Mam (president of student union) became an assemblyman in the first Unified Congress, then an official in the Saigon city administration. He is presently working for an obscure group called the Committee for Socialist Study.